Copyright © 1978 Pentagram Design Partnership

Published 1978 in Great Britain by Lund Humphries
Publishers Ltd 26 Litchfield Street, London WC2
ISBN 0 85331 396 2

Published 1978 in the United States by Whitney Library of
Design; an imprint of Watson-Guptill Publications,
a division of Billboard Publications Inc 1515 Broadway,
New York, NY 10036
Library of Congress Catalog Card No. 77-95220
ISBN 0-8230-7355-6

Designed by Pentagram
Printed in England by Westerham Press
Typeset by Inline Graphics

Living by design

The partners
of Pentagram

Theo Crosby
Alan Fletcher
Colin Forbes
Kenneth Grange
Ron Herron
Mervyn Kurlansky
John McConnell

Editor Peter Gorb

Lund Humphries, London.
Whitney Library of Design, New York.

Preface

The partners of *Pentagram,* the authors and designers of this book, make their living by design and spend their time living by design. Design for them means the efficient achievement of planned purposes and the artefacts which are the end results. There is not much in the book about *Pentagram* and the partners; but a lot about their work and their belief that design can fulfill both a social and an economic purpose.

The book is not aimed at the experienced designer who knows about these purposes, and perhaps agrees with and contributes towards their fulfillment. It is mainly for those who have a sympathy and interest in the subject and would like to know more about the scope of design, the ideas behind its practice, and the ways in which it is put to work.

The introductory essay attempts a definition of design, and establishes the structure of the book, which is divided into sixteen sections under four main headings: *Identity design, Environmental design and Product design.* Each section is prefaced by an essay which is loosely related to the ensuing text and pictures. The fifth and final part of the book is devoted to *Pentagram* and the people who work there. It has two essays which describe how the partnership operates. Thus the essays deal with the theory of design and the pictorial sections illustrate its practice. This framework is set out in the contents list opposite.

The reason for acquiring design knowledge will vary from the reader who intends to practise design to the reader who intends to use it. Hopefully it will include a goodly number of people who are as obsessed and enchanted by the subject as are the authors and their many helpers and contributors, to whom acknowledgement is made at the end of the book.

Contents

Using design

dėsï'gn[1] (-zī'n) *n.* **1.** Mental plan; scheme of attack (**have ∼s on,** plan to harm or appropriate). **2.** Purpose (**by ∼,** on purpose; *whether by accident or design*); end in view; adaptation of means to ends (**argument from ∼,** deducing existence of a God from evidence of such adaptation in the universe). **3.** Preliminary sketch for picture, plan of building, machine, etc.; delineation, pattern; art of making these. **4.** Established form of a product; general idea, construction from parts. [f. obs. F *desseing* (*desseigner* f. L *designare* DESIGNATE[2])]

dėsï'gn[2] (-zī'n) *v.* **1.** *v.t.* Set (thing) apart *for* person; destine (person, thing) *for* a service. **2.** Contrive, plan; purpose, intend, (*designs an attack, to* do, do*ing, that; design* thing or person *to* be or do something). **3.** Make preliminary sketch of (picture); draw plan of (future building etc.). **4.** *v.i.* Be a designer. [f. F *désigner* appoint & f. L *designare* DESIGNATE[2]]

Concise Oxford Dictionary

6

The purpose of this introduction is to identify and classify the uses of design, and to do so in a context which gives priority to the needs and views of the user of design rather than to those of the designer. However, before we can identify and classify we need to define what we mean by design.

Definition

A careful reading of the dictionary will clarify the most common mis-use of the word *design;* the transfer of meaning from the process of designing something to the thing itself. For example we comment on a "beautifully-designed chair" when what we mean is that the chair is beautiful. The design is what made it so.

This confusion between intent and product is less probable when the product is unlikely to be judged aesthetically. We are clear about what we mean when we talk about a well-designed national electricity grid, but when the end product is primarily designed to please the eye (or other senses) the confusion is almost impossible to sort out. We talk about a wallpaper design or a textile design, and in these cases design means what we see. A similar confusion has arisen around the word *pattern;* originally a model from which repeats were made, but now used to describe the end product of repetition, over a carpet or a teacup or whatever.

Design or pattern; the words get even more careful when "aesthetics" creep in. The design field is full of phraseology like "fitness for purpose", "form and function", "beauty and utility" and words like "integrity", "truth" and "discipline"; all of them attempting to relate the measurable purpose of one use of the word to the unmeasurable effect of the other use. So on the way to our definition we can make two negative statements:

A design is not to be confused with its end purpose. The end purpose of design is not necessarily aesthetically pleasing; it can be so, it often is so, but it need not be so.

However there is yet another confusion to deal with; the proposition that design is creative. Creativity bulks large in the designer's concept of self. High creativity is certainly an aspiration of all designers. It is also true that many designers are recruited from educational streams which are traditionally thought of as seedbeds of creativity. Yet these self evaluations, aspirations and breeding grounds are neither exclusive to designers, nor indeed to anyone else.

All one can say is that for design, like many other professional and specialist activities, a spectrum from high creativity to low creativity exists, against which to measure the people who work in the field. Because of the nature of their work, the opportunity to operate at the creative end of the continuum is relatively high for designers. Higher than say for quantity surveyors. But all designers will also spend a lot of their working lives on productive, useful and rewarding design work which is not creative. Having cleared some ground, we can venture our definition.

A design is a plan to make something.

Let us exclude philosophical systems, organisation structures, legal procedures and so forth. They are important activities, but this book is not concerned with them. "A design is a plan to make something: something we can see or hold or walk into; something that is two dimensional or three dimensional, and sometimes in the time dimension. It is always something seen and sometimes something touched, and now and then by association, something heard. It is often a single item and just as often a mass-produced product".

With this definition we can get somewhere. If the plan works, then the product (not the design, but the *product*) is appropriate, or truthful, or functional or whatever. If the plan demands aesthetic standards, and it works, then the product is beautiful or elegant or whatever. If the purpose of the plan is to make something which was not there before, and it works, then the designer who is concerned with that process is creative. If the plan needs techniques and skills to succeed, and it succeeds, then the designer can also be complimented as a professional.

The professional designer

In classifying the uses of design it is important to look at the ways in which designers classify themselves; to avoid pitfalls of creativity and to concentrate on techniques and specialisations. After all, these things are quantifiable, more easily measured and sorted and assessed than qualitative concepts like beauty and creativity and aesthetics. However, a first look at the designers' description of their profession is nearly as confusing as the definition of the word.

Designers possess a multiplicity of ways of describing themselves, and sometimes have three or four ways of describing a person doing one thing. Is the man who helps to plan the products in a motor car factory an industrial designer, or a product designer, or a design engineer? These overlapping descriptions, true for nearly every design field, tend nevertheless to settle in two sets: those which are characterised by the world in which the designer works, and those which are characterised by the training the designer has received.

The designer classified by his world is fairly easy to recognise. The work of a theatrical designer is clearly understood, so is that of a fashion designer or textile designer. We would know what to expect in the studio of a ceramic designer or a book designer; we would recognise the worlds of the landscape architect and the interior designer. "Industrial designer" is too broad a definition. We might expect to say "what industry?" and when the designer legitimately replies "it doesn't matter – I can design for them all" we begin to see that this kind of classification is not perhaps as useful as we first thought.

Firstly, there are too many sub-divisions: indeed as many as there are human occupations. We need broader and simpler classifications. Secondly the classifications are uneven. Some are very specialist, like the design of dentistry tools and some are very general, covering widely ranging skills, like designing an operatic production. Variety of this kind is the life blood of design. It is culturally enriching for both the designer and the design user, but for classification purposes it is confusing. Certainly the designers themselves prefer the second set of classifications we have described; those which are characterised by the training most designers receive. We are not concerned at this point with the specialist activities such as theatre design, nor with the vitally

7

important development process which enlarges the designer's individual perceptions and capacity for original thought. All we are seeking is a formal classification of basic design training. The great advantage of this kind of classification is that it falls into three main groupings which are capable of easy recognition and description.

Product design, which is generally three dimensional and is often described as *Industrial design* because the thing designed is often the end product of an industrial or manufacturing process;

Environment design, which is nearly always three dimensional and covers the design element of the work of architects, interior designers and town planners;

Graphic design, which is almost always two dimensional and covers those things which are drawn, painted, written or printed, and is traditionally related to printing, illustrating, advertising, promotion, packaging and so on.

Described in this way, the design profession is easy to identify, and in using design, the first step is to identify. After all, if the user of design is proposing for example to build a factory, his clear choice of design expertise is in the environmental field for an architect. Or is it? He will need a graphic designer for the signs in the building and the advertisements for staff. He will need a whole range of product designs to fill his building with the things needed to justify its existence. These multiple needs blur the frontiers of our classification. And the blurring would be acceptable if it were not possible to describe nearly every kind of artefact in terms of at least two of our three groupings.

Take the design of a book, which is at first sight obviously the work of a graphic designer. Yet in the printing works in which it is produced, the constraints and opportunities placed on its production needs the work of an industrial or product designer. Finally the user is surrounded by books and probably cannot work without them. They are part of his environment and need to be designed as such.

It is particularly easy to think of the environment design as the big stuff. Yet to the writer, his pens and papers and reference books are part of his environment, however little space they occupy. Nor does technology help us to separate these two. The space capsule, to its

manufacturers, is a product; to the astronauts it is an environment. Clearly, classification shifts according to where we stand, and becomes less useful the more we try to use it. Moreover we certainly need to clarify the distinction between *Product* and *Environment design.*

Design and purpose

If a design is a plan to make something, then whether an individual or a group of people is concerned with the design activity, a purpose is implied. The achievement of that purpose is a product and the design activity is *Product design.* This proposition is seen most clearly in a manufacturing industry, where a group of people gather together with the common purpose of contributing to the manufacture of a product. But the same idea holds good for any corporated group; a revolutionary party, a dance group, a football team, even if their *product* is remote.

For all these groups there are a range of influences which are designed to help or perhaps hinder the achievement of product. These are the tools, the work places, the transport systems, the living places, the leisure places and landscapes which constitute their environments. They may be consciously selected, or acquired by accident, the result of history or mistaken policy. So if *Product design* is the planned expression of individual or organisation purposes, then *Environment design* is the planned expression of the frameworks supporting them.

Design and communication

We have now achieved a classification which separates *Product design* from *Environment design* and allows us to understand how a chair can be both a *product* and an *environment.* There is however a third area with which the designer, and particularly the graphic designer, is intimately concerned; the process of communicating about products and environments. Communication is a buzz word which is much used and abused. It can mean anything from a telephone system to a group dynamics activity. For our purposes it is useful to divide the fields covered by communication into two, and discuss the designer's role in conveying *information* and in signalling *identity.*

The designer's concern with information is to present it efficiently; to simplify the complex, to suggest the subtleties behind the obvious, to enlarge the "micro" and

8

reduce the "macro". Furthermore, the work stretches along a spectrum which at one end may be concerned with objective descriptions of the technology of products and environments and at the other with the highly emotive and persuasive, the advertising and sales promotion of these products and environments.

The most complex in all design activity is the design of identities, which applied to groups of people is called *Corporate identity design*. The actual design work may appear simple, yet in signalling an identity by a simple symbol or logotype, a designer needs to take regard of the interaction of the other aspects of the design process described above, and indeed of the complex social and economic systems which govern their organisational behaviour.

Using design

We have now argued that a "user classification" of design needs to include the terms *Product design* and *Environment design*, redefined in terms of product purpose rather than in terms of the designer's specialisation. It also needs to include the two aspects of the designer's work in the field of communication; *Information design* and *Identity design*. Our fourway classification is therefore as follows:

Product design, which is directly concerned with the plan to make something and is the end purpose of an individual, but also and more often of a corporate body;

Environment design, which surrounds and contributes to the organisational purpose of a corporate body, and provides the individual with a framework for both living and working in organisations;

Information design, which is concerned with communicating facts and feelings about the products and environments of corporate bodies, and the work and lives of individuals;

Identity design, which is concerned with signalling and identifying either the individual or the corporate activity, and, for the latter, is a complex activity much concerned with organisational behaviour and policy.

This fourway classification is the one we use in this book. It is not entirely perfect. But for the user of design and the student of design, it is likely to prove a practical one. However, in the book we have reversed the order we have used here. For whether one is concerned with an individual or a corporate body, it is its identity of which we are first aware. As our contact deepens we are the recipients of information about it, leading to a familiarisation with the environments in which it operates, and finally a knowledge of its products.

Peter Gorb

9

Identity design

Man's urge to identify himself is built into his earliest consciousness. Almost certainly it arose from the need to distinguish efficiently between the hunting packs into which primitive man had grouped himself. At the earliest stages of language, the naming of individuals was based on visual distinguishing characteristics. Language grew by the gradual sophistication of these symbols, as both individual activities and group activities grew more specialised and more complex.

The symbolic identification of the groups themselves, and the interaction of group and individual identification, is now the basic material of the behavioural sciences; and the designer, whose main task it is to deal with the outward and visible symbols, cannot avoid at least a nodding acquaintance with the work of the sociologists and the psychologists.

However, the work still divides itself into that which is concerned with corporate groups and that which is concerned with individuals.

Corporate design can be undertaken for very large or for very small organisations. The examples which follow show work done for organisations ranging from international companies to a small partnership of three photographers. The work itself can cover every aspect of the way a group expresses itself, and requires extensive exploration into the organisational purposes of the company before the design can be effective.

Whatever the nature of corporate design, it requires from the designer not only an understanding of the policy and purposes of a corporate body, as well as the organisational procedures which it uses to achieve the policies and purposes, but also a high level of skills in the full range of design disciplines. For corporate identity

10

design can touch on every aspect of the company and its activities; its products, its buildings, its letterheading, its symbols, its advertising, its systems and its procedures. Hopefully this multi-disciplinary activity is demonstrated in the following pages.

Design for individuals requires a wholly different stance from the designer. To help a person to express and demonstrate his personality and to seek a mechanism for so doing requires a high order of sensitivity. Most people of course attempt much of this process for themselves. They do so by selecting from the range of personal consumer products available to them, first those close by, clothing, cosmetics, jewellery; and then by extension to motor cars, living places, offices and so forth. Not all of them succeed in avoiding uniformity, and it is questionable whether the designer can or indeed should be concerned too deeply with personality expression for other people. The designer as *Svengali* is an unattractive concept. So too is the designer as butterfly, flitting from personality to personality, identifying with each. Luckily most of us possess neither the inclination nor the resources to misuse the designer in this way.

In the field of *Identity design*, most design work is concerned with programmes for large corporate bodies, and of the three sections under *Identity design* in this book, the one which we have called *Corporate programmes* is much the biggest. We have introduced it with a small section on *Trademarks* – usually our first visual image of a corporate body. The final section, called *Personal signals*, deals with design for individuals.

A syntax of symbols

As the world grows steadily smaller through the rapid development of technologies, the need for easier communication becomes increasingly acute, and paradoxically man has apparently now come full circle – from prehistoric symbols to sophisticated verbal communication, and now back to symbols.

The earliest known inscriptions date from the fourth millenium before *Christ* and developed from the mnemonic mark to the pictograph, the ideogram and hieroglyph, and finally to the abstract linear symbols we use as letters. The fundamentally visual language which *Ezra Pound* esteemed in the ideography of early peoples was based on common human experiences which could be widely understood, while the sophisticated formulae of written language and specialist knowledge codes is confined to those who know the forms. Today there are some 5,000 languages and dialects in use, and although only a hundred are of more than parochial importance, intercommunication between them ranges from difficult to impossible. It becomes increasingly apparent that we need an adjunct to speech and the written word, and require to work towards an understandable symbology.

Three hundred years ago *Leibnitz* dreamed of a universal system of pictorial signs that could be read in all languages like $1 + 2 = 3$. This is a subject which has occupied many minds but has probably been methodically pioneered furthest by the American *Charles Bliss,* who coined the term "semantography". Semantography is a lexicon of a hundred basic signs which can be combined for any meaning needed in communication, commerce, industry and science, and could easily be reproduced by an *IBM* typewriting ball or computerised typesetter. In a return to the iconography of the pictogram his symbols are semi-abstract, although reminiscent of actual objects and actions.

The Austrian social scientist and teacher, *Otto Neurath,* conceived a similar technique for translating complex figures and activities into symbolic forms which would be accurate and meaningful to a broad audience. This he called the *International System of Typographic Picture Education,* or *ISOTYPE* for short. His design images are more illustrative than those of *Bliss,* and seem well tuned to illustrate statistics, working activities or situations. The configurations have added potential for imparting further meanings and associations by the use of colour and textures. The *International Organisation for Standardisation,* not as sinister as it sounds, is at present conducting research and development of *Neurath's* system in countries around the world, in an effort to achieve a common acceptance of this pictorial grammar for general use.

The late *Henry Dreyfuss,* a designer of international repute, dedicated much of his life to semiotics, a scholarly term he coined for the science of signs indicating ideas or symbols. He enthusiastically collected and classified graphic devices, and created a Data Bank which contains over 20,000 symbols many of which he reproduced in his comprehensive publication *Symbol Sourcebook*. Similar compilations are being made by many organisations, the most notable being *ICOGRADA,* an international association of national design societies, and *Glyphs Inc.* which is under the direction of the anthropologist *Margaret Mead* and *Rudolf Modley*.

Probably the most familiar manifestation of the early utterances of a newly created and universal visual language are the traffic guidance signs adopted by the *United Nations,* and now seen around the world. As design solutions they smack of committee compromise, camels rather than horses, and, often being abstract, require to be learnt to be understood. Nevertheless they are now part of our global environment. When design aesthetics are considered in conjunction with design purpose, the results can be happier. For example, the identification system created by *Otl Aicher* for the *Munich Olympic Games* was effective and conceptually elegant, in that it incorporated the modular advantages of the alphabet with the pictorial associations of the hieroglyph.

In addition to cultural and institutional symbols which inform and regulate human activities there are also commercial and trading devices. As a specialised area of identification, trademarks provide an intriguing study; and their history is often a fascinating observation of social mores and personal foibles. The Sumerians, who invented writing around 3,000 BC, also invented the personal seal. Worn around the neck, the seal bore a unique engraved pictorial image, proprietary to an individual and non-transferable to another. Legal and trade transactions were inscribed on wet clay and the impressed seal provided the stamp of agreement, in much the same way as the penned signature we use today.

The company emblem might be specially designed to reflect the business or occupation, it is also often developed from heraldic sources, or haphazardly evolved from inauspicious and humble beginnings. *Bibendum,* the eighty year old trademark of the *Michelin Rubber and Cartographic Company,* was conjured up from a heap of old tyres by the *Michelin* brothers, who created the image and made a world famous figure. The unlikely name of *Shell,* so the story goes, began in the days when shells were used as ballast by ships returning from trading in the east; until oil took their place – and the company adopted the name and the design. Sometimes marks and meanings even become a part of our spoken symbology. The term "private eye" is said to be derived from the emblem of the famous *Pinkerton National Detective Agency,* their trademark was an eye embellished with the slogan "we never sleep".

Emblems and insignia used for commercial marks can be labelled according to form, purpose and function. The designer's terminology, although not altogether precise, generally defines symbols as pictorial or abstract devices, logotypes as signatures, and monograms as intertwined or connected letters. Specialised occupations also have their special terms, and publishers for example

refer to their imprints as colophons, while clubs have badges and the aristocracy coats-of-arms. However the term "trademark" is generally used to describe all of those marks concerned with commerce.

Research, which on this and other occasions confirms common sense, has shown that public recognition and recall of corporate marks is greater with logotypes than initials, and that the least memorable are symbols. Pronounceable words like *Kodak* or *Esso* (*S.O.* from *Standard Oil*) are more memorable than initials, and devices using letters like the *Volkswagen* monogram are more universally recognisable than a total abstraction like the *Chrysler* pentastar.

The value and importance of trademarks in the commercial world has created a need for copyright protection equal to that of patents. The Trademarks Office of the *Department of Trade* says that the registration of a trademark "confers a statutory monopoly in use of the mark for which it is registered" and defines a trademark as either a "word mark" or a "device mark".

An anecdote concerning *Coca Cola* underlines the importance of trademark registration. Unable to maintain the exclusivity of the word "Cola", the *Coca Cola Company* undertook a world wide programme to shorten their name to the colloquial "Coke". Instructions were given to register this name and a company director in South America, who was a little slow off the mark, arrived at the appropriate registration office only to find an unscrupulous employee had got there first. They had to pay him à half a million pounds to buy back the name! Presumably they also fired him!

Alan Fletcher

13

Identity design: Trademarks

The design of a mark of identity requires a distillation of an idea into a simple visual configuration. This arbitrary collection of design solutions is categorised loosely into columns: single letters, monograms, symbols, logotypes, abstract and pictorial motifs.

A monogram for a sign company called *Wilson Walton*. The interlocking initial letters, which usually appear in red and blue, provide a natural and regular play of angles.

Mr Purser was a joiner who put up the shelves in our first studio and didn't understand what we did – so we designed him a trademark.

The British *Design and Art Directors Association* was founded in 1962. This ragbag of letters is the symbol, and is reminiscent of our early days and the graphics of that era.

This figure with curious three dimensional properties expresses not only the initial letter, but also the businesses represented by the *Zinc Development Association.*

The initials represent a holding company *First Finance Options*. The method of joining the letters in a stripe formation unified the elements and created a pattern. The stripes also allowed for a simple application of different housecolour combinations.

Liverpool Metallising is a company specialising in metallic plating on plastic materials. The mark graphically applies the same process to the initial, which incidentally was also printed in gold foil.

Gebrüder Heinemann, or Heinemann brothers, are a German company who retail duty free goods. The brief was for a monogram based on GH, in which the letter H needed to be dominant. This was achieved by a use of typographic licence and figureground – the G is only seen if the H is background.

Identity design: Trademarks

This set of dimensional letters stack to create an architectural environment for the initials; the motif of the journal of the *Royal Institute of British Architects*.

This is a refurbishment of an old and established logotype for a large chain of menswear shops. The redrawing of the letterforms and definition of the details invested the traditional style with a modern touch.

A symbol with contrasting dimensions, designed for the *Zinc Development Association* to identify an international conference on die casting held in 1966.

The brand namestyle for *Michèle*, a range of cosmetics produced for *Marks and Spencer*. A simple idea of cutting the bar of the letter created the necessary accent without loss of legibility.

MICHĒLE

Yes is the name of a successful pop group, and the speak balloon device graphically related the name to the spoken word.

Derived from an anarchist broadsheet, this logotype was designed for a nightclub. When the stationery was delivered the local plumber blowtorched the top of the letterheads to obtain a realistic charred edge. Unfortunately this final touch took place in our photostudio, and it took a week to get the ashes out of the equipment.

REVOLUTION

15

An obscure typographic design to the layman, but a meaningful mark to industry for events and publicity about lead (Pb) electric (+ −) battery powered vehicles, sponsored by the *Lead Development Association*.

Sometimes a name can be subtly distinguished by an existing typographic nicety. Here the ligature, between the S and T, invests the logotype of this jewellery company with an element of tradition.

prestige

Identity design: Trademarks

This symbol was part of a corporate graphic programme developed for the *Conference of Islamic Solidarity* in Saudi Arabia. Alternate white and green crescents represented six Islamic countries, the device as a whole is similar to the cord on the burnous, the traditional Arab headress.

An ambiguous visual configuration was designed as the mark for a new advertising agency, *Manton Woodyer Ketley and Partners*. The device is used graphically for print as well as in reality in the reception where it also undergoes a daily floral change.

Buro Happold, a group of trendy civil engineers well into lattice structures, were delighted to be represented by an optical illusion.

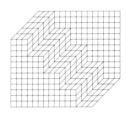

In a three sided competition we submitted a design for the new British *National Theatre.* The predictable masks for drama and comedy were unpredictably profiled, and the result we thought seemed an appropriate image. The client obviously didn't since he chose one of the others.

16

This device for *Rowe Rudd,* a London stockbroking firm, was derived from a Victorian cheque mark. The mark is capable of infinite extension, or contraction, depending on the number of loops.

The mark for this private club was suggested by its name, *Speakeasy.* The familiar eye inspecting the thirsty customer through a slot in the door provided the visual interpretation.

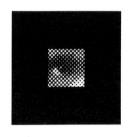

Pharma Information, represents *Ciba-Geigy, Roche* and *Sandoz,* three pharmaceutical companies. The solution is based on a true story about *August Kekulé's* discovery of the Benzene ring. *Kekulé* knew the elements but was unable to relate them together, until he had a dream of a winding snake biting its tail. This vision led him to the hexagonal structure.

Designed in the early sixties, prior to the fashion for graphic Union Jacks, this symbol was produced for *British Trade Weeks,* a government promotional scheme held in continental cities. The device adapts to three dimensions for shop window displays.

Identity design: Trademarks

This happy animated polar bear drawn by *Anna Pugh* was the *BP* presenter for a range of anti-freeze products, and enlivened promotional and packaging material.

An articulated symbol. He was designed to represent the *Pirelli* tyre in much the same way as *Michelin's Bibendum*. The central idea was to issue maquettes to the *Pirelli* agencies around the world. This gave them a freedom of choice of movement but retained a control of the poses.

Oliver Williams drew us five basic portrait figures of two photographers, *Bob Brooks* and *Len Fulford,* enabling them to appear in a number of different juxtapositions on their various stationery items.

Goods & Chattels was the name of the company, and the graphic device provided the visual interpretation. Drawings were changed according to the items being promoted when reordering stationery.

Do you sincerely want to be recognised?

A few years ago, by Act of Parliament, the status of the British *Post Office* was changed from a government department to a public corporation, which was then sub-divided into two businesses, post and telecommunications. Similarly, a company which called itself *British Ropes* changed its name to *Bridon* – a reflection of the fact that its activities were no longer confined to rope-making, nor were they exclusively British. The visual expression of both these changes, which are chosen as illustrations rather than as models, is called *corporate identity design*.

The origins of such visual systems pre-date not only industrial corporations, but indeed civilisation itself. The markings of tribal and hunting groups emerged as visual manifestations of organised behaviour during man's very early history; and primitive kingdoms, priesthoods and armies reached quite high levels of corporate design. Indeed, modern manifestations, for example the *Klu Klux Klan* or a football team, are perhaps less striking than their counterparts 2,000 years ago.

Through the whole of history, the military has of course consistently maintained the highest level of sophistication in corporate identity, with its system of expressing a complex hierarchy by means of simple, recognisable imagery, which has seldom been improved upon. Corporate identity manuals would have held few surprises for even the earliest armies.

Nor should they surprise the modern man. We have lived through the days of *Shell, IBM, General Motors, ICI* and *ITT*. Each of them has for us a clearly expressed corporate identity and now we are not sure that we like it. Monopolistic trading, price-fixing, the corruption of governments; these associations with the big corporations are hardly ones with which they themselves can be happy. Yet the corporate identity programme, usually with a brief to the designer to demonstrate the unity, size and pervasiveness of this business' enterprises, still seems to get itself sold. Local authorities, departments of governments, charitable institutions and educational establishments are joining the ranks of the "corporately expressed". Clearly there must be a good reason, even in a decade where small is beautiful and big is bad.

It is, surprisingly, a moral one; the need to tell the truth. *Polonius's* aphorism holds in any large enterprise: truth to oneself is a necessary pre-requisite of corporate behaviour if the organisation is to function effectively. It is the prime role of a corporate identity programme to arrive at and guard such truths.

Managers, being not much given as a breed to introspection, need a framework in which to pause, re-examine, and re-define their activities. A corporate identity programme, with its uncompromising and neon-lit statements, provides a highly disciplined route towards re-thinking, and often re-organising, the enterprise.

Yet even today, those who are responsible for initiating and commissioning corporate identity programmes are often motivated by little more than a desire to "tidy up" what they may see as an out of date or ill-defined corporate image. The designer must relate the old imagery to the company's history in order to gain a thorough understanding of what it was intended to represent. He must also attempt to construct a model of the entire organisation, understanding how and why it has evolved in one way rather than another.

In the process of designing and implementing a corporate identity, there are many areas of possible contention. How, for example, do you explain to the Managing Director of a highly successful division of a large corporation, that he should accept changes that are designed to bring his division into line with other less successful divisions? From his point of view, he can only lose, and his arguments will inevitably have a lot of force. Wedged between conflicting forces of this kind, the designer needs thorough familiarity with the objectives of the company. This means spending time not only with the managers, who will be living with and responsible for implementing the proposals, but also with the decision

18

makers, who have to resolve the conflicts which corporate identity design throws up.

Like the system evolved by the military, the corporate identity programme has as much to do with making important distinctions clear as with presenting a unifying appearance. It is in the resolution of the contradictions inherent in these twin requirements, that a major part of the creative input comes into play.

In complex programmes, separate hierarchical identities may be required within a corporation. This might be for the parent company, the major divisions, established brands and finally individual products. Yet this same corporate group may be active in a variety of markets – the food market, medical market and motor car market; all of which will have widely differing traditions of design which can never be entirely discounted.

This calls for design in the broad sense, as the dictionary defines it – a plan or strategy. Decisions about colour, and the design of a symbol or alphabet, and all the other narrower concepts of design, will often evolve out of the broad strategy, and the options for creative decision making will be severely restricted by the complexity of the requirements that must be met.

It is also important to realise that a strategy is quite different from a definitive, once and for all design solution. Once established, the guardianship of a corporate identity is a massively effective monitoring mechanism on both the effectiveness and efficiency of the enterprise; for inconsistencies cannot be implemented without blazoning their presence. Changes are signalled on the sides of vans, and changes of place and purpose are printed and distributed.

None of the above is about clearer sales messages, or pretty artwork, or saving money on cost-effective stationery systems. These things come a long way behind the real benefits. Any design consultant who sells corporate identity on standardisation and elegant alphabets is only doing a "paint job".

An example of this was seen with *British Rail,* whose corporate identity only assumed real validity when new and faster trains were introduced on the *Inter-City* services, and the capital investment became available to give substance to the outward appearance.

A designer undertaking a corporate identity programme must make a long-term commitment to a project if he is to successfully solve his client's problem. The length of time will vary according to the size of the company, and the degree of involvement may decrease over the period, so it is reasonable to expect that the commitment will be for years rather than months.

Although it is frequently thought of as the glamorous, big league end of the design industry, corporate identity is also a long way from the instant satisfactions of producing the spontaneous design for say a poster or book jacket; and the designer who makes a contract to hold himself accountable for five years has got to make sure that he produces solutions that work.

There are many corporations whose purposes are not standard, whose products are not beautiful, whose faces to their markets are necessarily differentiated, and whose best interests are met by keeping them this way. The designer serves these interests best by designing this way. His work may not be noticed alongside the oil companies or the airlines. It is, however, just as valid.

For design consultancies, the rigours of undertaking corporate identity work and the multidisciplinary design requirements have meant changes in their own organisations. The traditional breakdown of their work into graphic design, environmental design, product design and so forth, is not practical. They, too, are beginning to recognise a truth about themselves – that whatever their training, however high their technical skills, their most valuable asset is the ability to apply creative effort across the full range of visual artefacts by which a corporate body is identified.

Colin Forbes

Lucas

Lucas Industries is a group of companies manufacturing automotive, aerospace and industrial components, a world leader in its field.

In accordance with the traditional company policy of not wanting to be seen as too large, each subsidiary company had a separate identity and trademark. When viewed together, *(see left)* they gave no indication of belonging to one organisation, or even a common activity.

The rapid growth of the group, both at home and abroad, and increasing competition, indicated that a group corporate image could be advantageous.

Lucas appointed *Pentagram* as design consultants with a brief to present recommendations after surveying *Lucas* manufacturing centres, interviewing personnel, dealers, agents and advertising agencies. This exercise confirmed the desirability of a group image.

Three fundamental decisions formed the basis of the new programme. To identify the specialised operations within the *Lucas* group, such as aerospace, defence systems, industrial marine and a new service company for the automotive after-market. To retain the valuable brand names, for example *CAV* and *Girling*, as well as product names. To link these with a new group identity comprising a symbol, alphabet and colours.

The *Lucas Diagonal* is the new group symbol. Green is the group colour, and there is a *Lucas* corporate alphabet.

Agreeing a corporate design policy with senior management is one thing, making it happen within a large international company is another.

To implement the programme a corporate design committee was formed, representing production, marketing and administration, and sub-committees represented stationery, transport, packaging and signs.

These sub-committees ensure that design standards are practical and the interests of subsidiary companies are safeguarded. They also act as local specialists who interpret detailed design problems.

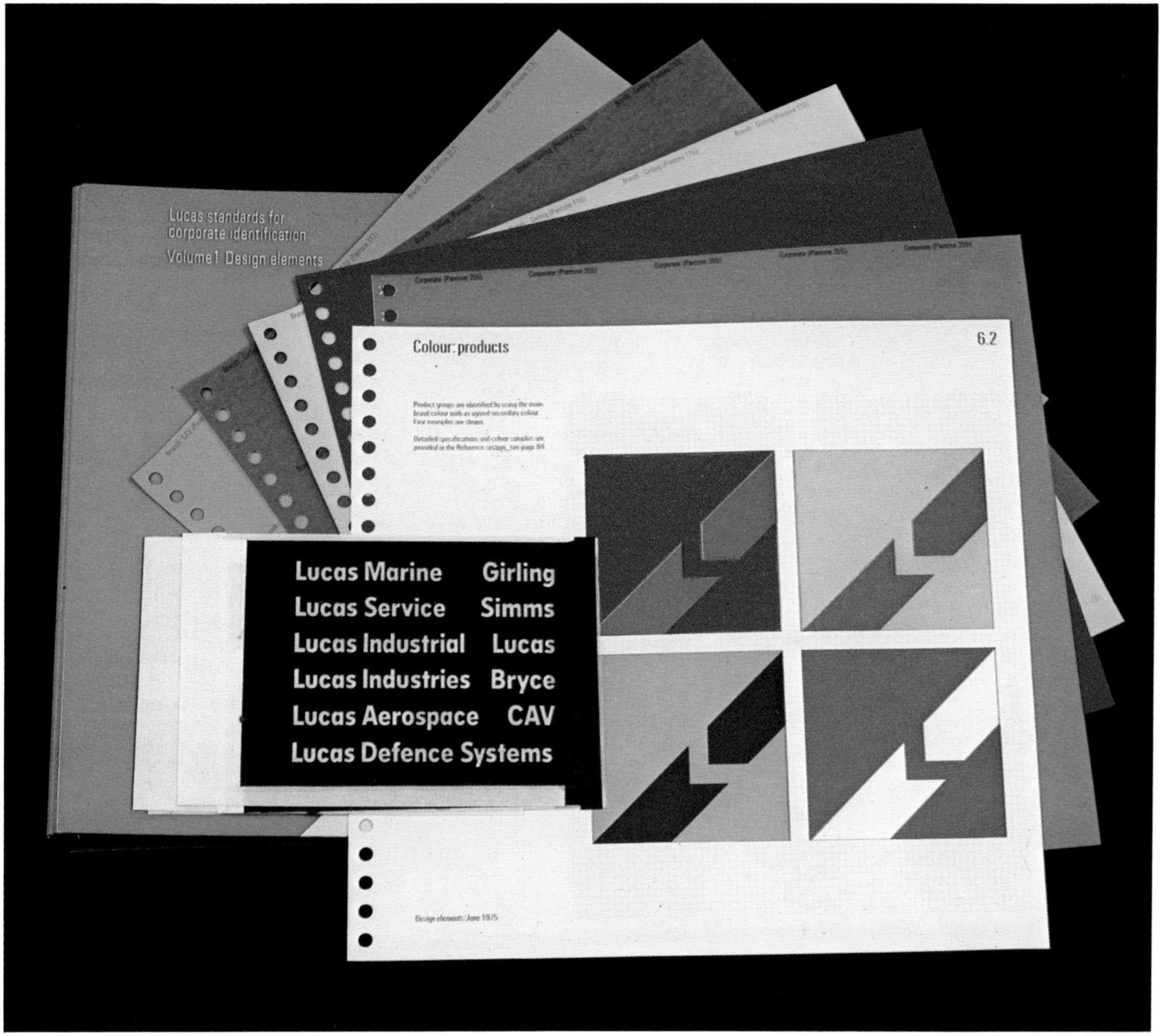
Lucas standards for
corporate identification
Volume 1 Design elements
Colour: products
6.2
Lucas Marine
Girling
Lucas Service
Simms
Lucas Industrial
Lucas
Lucas Industries
Bryce
Lucas Aerospace
CAV
Lucas Defence Systems

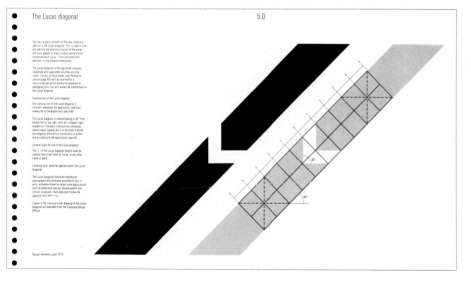

Alphabet   3.0

A new Lucas alphabet has been designed for use
as specified, throughout the group. It is a sans
serif face which includes the numerals, accents
and punctuation necessary for use in all Western
European languages. Bold and light weights of the
alphabet have been provided to allow for degrees
of emphasis.

Acting as a signature the corporate market
sector or brand name must appear once in the
Lucas bold alphabet on every item to be
identified as belonging to Lucas. For example
printed material, vehicles, products, etc.

Negatives and Letraset sheets for the new Lucas
names and the complete alphabet are available
from the Corporate Design Officer.

ABCDEFGHIJKLMNOPQRSTUVWXYZ&
abcdefghijklmnopqrstuvwxyzßÆŒØ!?
œøœäåçéèğñõôš1234567890(-).,:;'`/

ABCDEFGHIJKLMNOPQRSTUVWXYZ&
abcdefghijklmnopqrstuvwxyzßÆŒØ!?
œøœäåçéèğñõôš1234567890(-).,:;'`/

Design elements June 1975

The Lucas diagonal   5.0

Design elements June 1975

Complex corporate identity
programmes need rules, to
preserve visual discipline,
cohesion, continuity and
standards.

The *Lucas* design manuals
provide such guide-lines for
each major identification
sector. They include written
specifications, visual detail
sheets, colour swatches, film
negatives and other relevant
information.

The design of the *Lucas
Diagonal* originated in the
need for a flexible device. The
special characteristics of the
stripe are that it is capable of
infinite length, can carry or
reverse out of colour, is able
to wrap around dimensional
objects.

The configuration was
evolved by cutting a right-
angled figure L (for *Lucas*) in
a stripe and moving the two
pieces apart. This converted
a plain geometric form into a
personalised heraldic motif.
Three versions with different
terminations cater for varying
applications.

The corporate alphabet,
drawn in association with type
designer *Matthew Carter*, has
two weights with accents and
punctuation for western
European languages. Bold is
used for group, market, brand
and product names, and light
primarily for agents' names
and signs. A spacing system
ensures consistency in word
constructions.

23

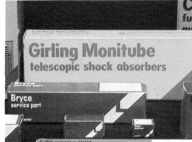

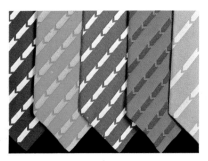

The *Lucas* programme was implemented in manageable categories so that the vast range of applications could be organised and monitored.

The amount of stationery and documentation used by an organisation totalling some 80,000 employees is a major exercise.

The sign system for dealers and distributors was sub-divided into identification, brand and information signs. This was not only a typographic exercise but also involved experiment into materials and structural methods.

As an international organisation serving the automotive industry, *Lucas* have over fifty makes of vehicles in the UK alone. Each needed different specification drawings for application of transfers.

Apart from the major areas of identification there were peripheral items which needed care and attention. For example fabrics, company ties, key rings, executive gifts, house magazines and sports posters.

A corporate identity programme can graft a visual personality, but in the end it becomes a reflection of the organisation it represents. The trademark is a symbol of a corporation. It is not a sign of quality, it is a sign of *the* quality.

The wide ranging requirements of a large company can impose difficult and stringent demands on a designer or design group. They are employed, not only to provide a service, but also creative concepts and imaginative thinking.

The first part of the assignment was to conduct an analysis of the existing company alphabets, and make recommendations on how these could be rationalised.

Other programmes briefly described in this section are outline studies on the *BP* mark *BP* self-service stations and *BP* self-service equipment.

The recommendations were produced as audio-visual slide presentations, and the illustrations shown on the following pages are just a few of the many visuals which were produced to demonstrate the points.

The bulk of the design

programmes were carried out by *Crosby/Fletcher/Forbes*, before the name was changed to *Pentagram*, and since one is constantly learning from experience, it was a salutary lesson in understanding how corporations tick, and how the administration of design can be as important as the creation of concepts.

The page opposite has extracts of the salient points taken from the lengthy detailed *AlphaBP* study.

26

British Petroleum is one of the world's major oil companies, represented in over eighty countries by subsidiary companies, and with more than 100,000 service stations. In the fifties, *Raymond Loewy*, Paris, had been commissioned by *BP* to examine their visual image. They noted that the shield shape symbol of *BP*, maintained for many years commanded a high visual equity testified by a 96% recognition by Europeans.

To reinforce *BP's* image, we were assigned to examine the elements of the corporate identity, the shield, colours and alphabets, design self-service stations, stationery and documentation, signage, packaging styles, and the day to day graphics for print, publications and promotion.

The AlphaBP study

"The *BP* corporate identity and its relation to market sector service and product names can be established by a special alphabet. The names can only be related by letters in the same style, and identified by a consistent use with the trademark. The existing situation does not conform to these criteria." *See figure one.*

"Well over a thousand typefaces have been designed since 1900, and although the necessity for yet another may appear extraordinary, the vast majority are not suitable for corporate identification uses."

"The alphabet specification should fulfill the following: be related to the *BP* trademark, be legible, not subject to change in fashion, be adaptable to languages, have a light and bold version, be suitable for reproduction in any size and application."

"To fulfill the first condition, the obvious choice is to develop an alphabet based on the letters "BP" used in the shield. The result however is patently old-fashioned, additionally the serif and capitals makes for long words and less legibility." *See figure two.*

"One of the existing *BP* standard typefaces is Helvetica. This fulfills most of the conditions but it is currently used by a large number of governmental and commercial organisations." *See figure three.*

"*Herbert Bayer's* alphabet designed at the Bauhaus in 1928, was a break with traditional forms. It eliminated serifs and followed geometric rules using the square, the triangle and the circle." *See figure four.*

"The *BP* letters in the current trademark, a serif face, also conform to geometric proportions." *See figure five.*

"The preliminary designs for a new sans serif *BP* alphabet observe this precise geometry, and produce a distinctive character." *See figure six.*

"A judgement has to be made as to the degree one accepts distortions of letterforms to achieve distinction. It is considered that letters should be more traditional, as the alphabet is needed for a variety of names, often in different languages. This precludes unfamiliar letters, and developments have been along more conventional lines." *See figure seven.*

"It is necessary to have a bold and a medium alphabet. The bold for names used to promote market sectors and products, and the medium for signs on service stations." *See figure eight.*

"The recommended design of the new alphabet has been produced in collaboration with type designer *Adrian Frutiger*, who has an international reputation. It is suggested that the alphabets are named *AlphaBP*." *See figure nine.*

"The design of a letterform is within restricted limits, but the sum of the details has a significant effect on the total aesthetic appearance."

ENERGOL
BP·ZOOM
visco-static
ANTI-GEL
S T A T I O N
TELEPHONE
①

BP SUPER
②

British Rail
Evening News
Sainsburys
③

abcdefg
hijklmn
opqrstu
vwxyz
④

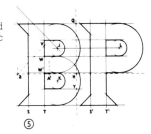
⑤

air BP
super
vanellus
⑥

ABCDEFG
abcdefgh
12345678
⑦

BP regular
BP super
24 hours
Pay here
⑧

Alpha BP
Alpha BP
⑨

27

BP trademark study

One of the major design assignments was a study of the *BP* mark because for years opinions had been expressed, within the company, that the mark was old fashioned compared with competitors. In addition it was claimed that the recognition factor was poor on service station signs.

All the changes made to the trademark since 1922 were reviewed to determine whether they had been for the better, or whether some of the character had been removed *en route.* Before this particular study and over a period as long as five years, numerous new radical alternatives had been proposed but very few found any measure of support. Researched internationally to assess progressiveness, modernity, and so on, tests proved very little one way or the other.

There was no evidence that could possibly justify the multi-million pound expense that a radical change would cost. It was therefore proposed to ascertain whether the existing shield and letters could be improved.

The design study was separated into basic areas, four of which were to test the legibility of the letters, the shape of the shield, combinations of both elements, and the degree of comparable recognition between the existing design and the amended designs.

Two tachistoscope tests were devised – an optical recognition procedure. The first was to evaluate legibility of six different letter forms: the current *BP* letters, the previous standard letters, the new alphabet devised by *Pentagram,* initially for use in company and brand marks; and Helvetica, Rockwell and Bodoni. The incidence of error in distinguishing between the similar but different letters, BP, BR, PR and EP was tested by exposing in random order. The results showed that there was little difference in recognition with the exception of *Bodoni* which had the worst. *Helvetica* and the new *BP* alphabet had the best scores.

The second test, similarly conducted, was to gauge the most recognisable shield. Four variations of shield were tested against a barrel, an apple and a heart. The straight-sided version of the shield was apparently more recognisable than the others.

28

Identity design: Corporate programmes

Finally, the various combinations of shield and letters were tested. The figures beside the different shields below indicate percentages of recognition. The straight-sided shield with the 1946/58 lettering achieved the best results followed by the current trademark.

The test revealed that people tend to verbalise images They remember that the form is a shield, but not necessarily its precise shape. In test conditions they are inclined to assume that the particular shield shape with which they are most familiar, is the one which they recognise.

It was proposed that to reinforce identity the new sans serif corporate alphabet should be used in the straight-sided shield, and introduced over a transitional period.

The management decided, however, that even this change would involve too much expense for a marginal improvement in performance. The whole exercise, of which only a part is described, took two years.

1922-1929

1922-1931

1931-1946

1946-1958

1958

1963

Identity design: Corporate programmes

Self-service study

The *BP* self-service study was
a text book project. It involved
a team of *BP* marketing staff,
operational services and the
designers. The study included
an international survey, an
appraisal analysis, operational
methods, architecture,
equipment and graphics.

The final report was made as
an audio-visual presentation,
some of the diagrams being
shown here. The argument
was made along these
lines . . .

Theory of the facility

"All oil companies have
gradually come to feel the
pressure of rising costs,
shortage of staff, government
price control, and intense
competition. This has made an
increase of diversification
imperative, and has taken the
form of expanding the 'shop'
element of the station."

"The customer is used to the
comfort of his vehicle and if he
is to serve himself he is
entitled to equivalent
protection, convenience, and
to sophisticated equipment.
Each element of the station
must therefore be
reconsidered in terms of
customer handling,
cleanliness and convenience."

"As the payment and visual
control system is a key
element on the site, the way in
which vehicles are moved and
placed is critical. One way
systems give the best layouts,
as vehicles can be made to
present themselves
consistently to the pumps, and
thus to the cashier."

30

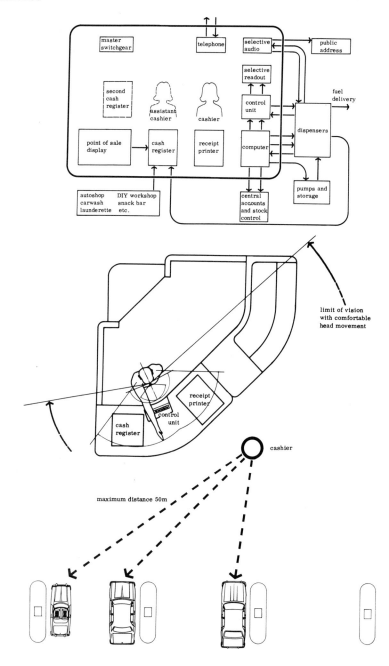

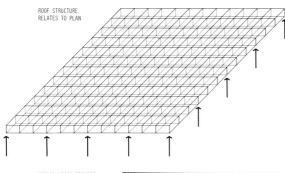

MODULAR GRID ALLOWS
FOR FLEXIBILITY IN
SITE PLANNING

ROOF STRUCTURE
RELATES TO PLAN

GROUND AREAS PROVIDE
INFINATE WORKING
OPTIONS

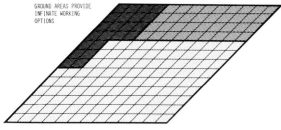

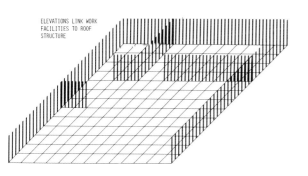

ELEVATIONS LINK WORK
FACILITIES TO ROOF
STRUCTURE

Modular construction

"To provide a good environment for the self-service customer, free from wind and rain, maximum coverage and a certain degree of enclosure is necessary. The way in which this is done will establish the quality and image of the station and the company."

"A large roof structure is primary to the site, and therefore of major importance. The system should be modular, flexible, practical, and capable of adaptation to a variety of configurations."

Service station signs

"On approaching a self-service station the motorist should understand that it is *BP*, a self-service station, and that it offers a marketing incentive."

"Signs are important, not only from the approach but also on the station. Directions are marked on the ground using motorway arrows to simplify traffic flow. The dispenser unit should signalise its number to both cashier and customer. The equipment requires readily understandable operating instructions."

"All the services offered should be clearly seen from the dispenser: the cash desk, toilets, the service unit, car wash, restaurant and so on."

"The overall design must add to the general corporate image and that of *BP* automotive marketing in particular. Continuity of the corporate and product identification is essential."

31

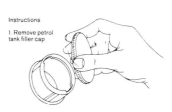

Instructions

1. Remove petrol tank filler cap

2. Select grade on other side of pump

Identity design: Corporate programmes

Self-service equipment

BP self-service station equipment was an important element of the study.

Recommendations were presented showing diagrams, shots of models and prototypes. The six slides (right) show the illustrative techniques used.

Existing equipment was designed for garage staff. In the long run the self-service customer will demand the same sophisticated switch and push button technology that he is accustomed to on his dashboard.

Recent technological developments make it possible to separate the physical components of the "pump" – that is to say the pumping and metering units, the blend selector, the computer, the read-out facility and the hose.

The design objective was to present the dispenser to the customer in as simple a form as possible. Customer considerations included avoiding pipes on the ground, separating dispenser from pump, relating push button selection to prices and gallonage. The "pump" can therefore be regarded as a selection and recording device.

It is possible to use one electronic computer to do all the work formerly carried out by individual mechanical computers in each pump. This can also inform the cashier as to the situation at any position.

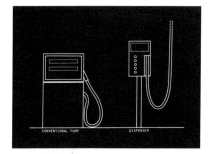

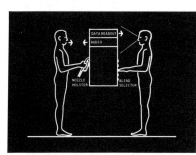

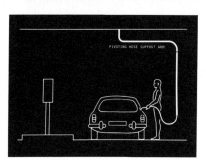

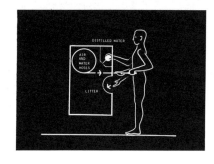

Identity design: Corporate programmes

Developing recommendations

The *BP* studies were mainly concerned with theories and propositions. Developing the recommendations into practical terms followed another sequence of stages.

The development process included assembling data on the available components, studying patterns of self-service, and checking service stations regulations.

The second stage involved drawings and converting these to full size models in elementary combinations of wood and card. This enabled simple ergonomic studies and modifications to be made. From these, prototypes were designed using sheet metal forming, castings and glass fibre mouldings. Finally general arrangement drawings and precise units were developed.

Services by fuelling positions were combined into an amenity unit (far right) containing air and water dispensers, paper towels and a litter bin. The fuelling unit (right) contained metering and blend read-outs, pump number and hose.

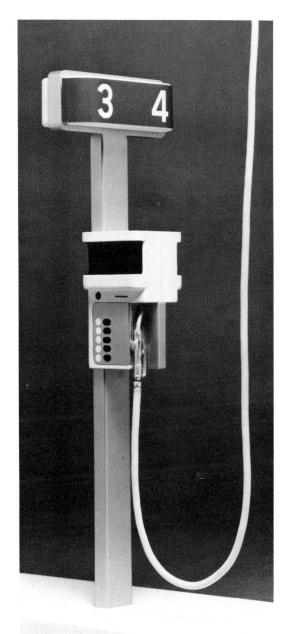

Reuters, the international news agency, is a client who first came to *Pentagram* for one skill and then commissioned another.

The first commissions were architectural, the interior scheme for the Fleet Street headquarters, and a small radio receiving station in Hertfordshire. The design work subsequently developed to include the corporate identity programme, publications, promotion and products.

The idea for the *Reuters* logotype was born out of watching the punched tape used in company transmissions for conveying information at great speed. The punched system is based on a regular modular pattern, and to conform so is the logotype.

Graphically the dots lend themselves to reproduction in a number of ways – here it is punched out for the logotype on the Managing Director's letterhead.

Gerald Long Managing Director

Reuters Limited 85 Fleet Street London EC4P 4AJ Telephone 01-353 6060 Telex 23222 Registered office

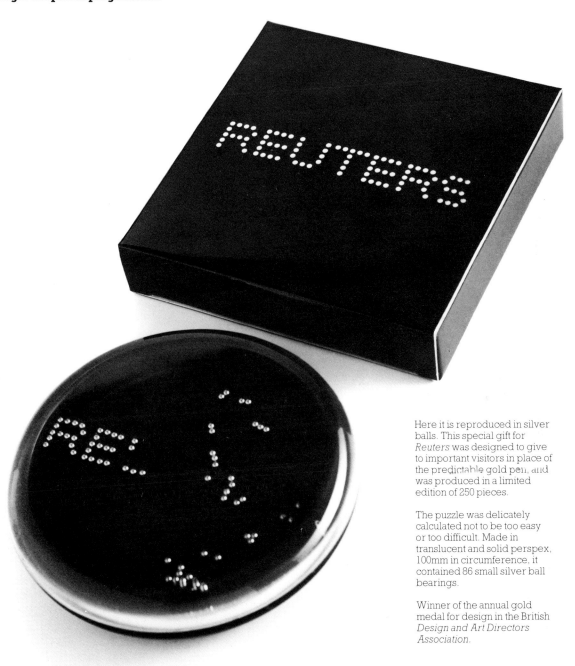

Here it is reproduced in silver balls. This special gift for *Reuters* was designed to give to important visitors in place of the predictable gold pen, and was produced in a limited edition of 250 pieces.

The puzzle was delicately calculated not to be too easy or too difficult. Made in translucent and solid perspex, 100mm in circumference, it contained 86 small silver ball bearings.

Winner of the annual gold medal for design in the British *Design and Art Directors Association*.

The *Reuters* logotype was designed to fulfill the practical requirements of a corporate identification device. That is to say it is able to be used in any scale, virtually be reproduced in any material, able to maintain recognition when reproduced in different techniques.

The *Reuters* logotype is printed on stationery, in nuts and bolts on the gate of the radio receiving station, stamped in the *Reuters Monitor*, punched out of invitation cards, even woven in ties. It appears on everything from doorplates to documents, vehicles to menu holders.

The major area requiring identification is stationery documentation. The vast quantity of printed information required an economical solution, and all items are printed in one colour in a standard typeface. Coding is achieved by coloured papers to distinguish one type of news service and category of information from another, and the items are produced by an internal printing department.

The stationery won a *British Stationery Council* award.

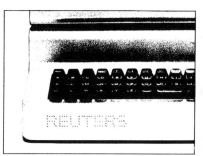

Identity design: Corporate programmes

Although the logotype provides the visual signal to identify the company, a more fundamental expression of personality is reflected in the corporate attitude to all aspects of its visible activities.

This was one of a series of *Reuters* charts, designed for overhead projection, used to explain the organisation to the staff.

Differences of linear treatment and colour coding differentiate between the various departments and clarify the relationships between the Managing Director, departments, and overseas offices.

Diagrams don't just happen, they need to be as carefully considered as any other aspect of design. Since the diagram is essentially a method of expressing a complex situation or process, by definition it needs to be readily comprehended.

Normally considered by the viewer as intrinsically boring it is desirable to try new approaches to communicating clearly with interest.

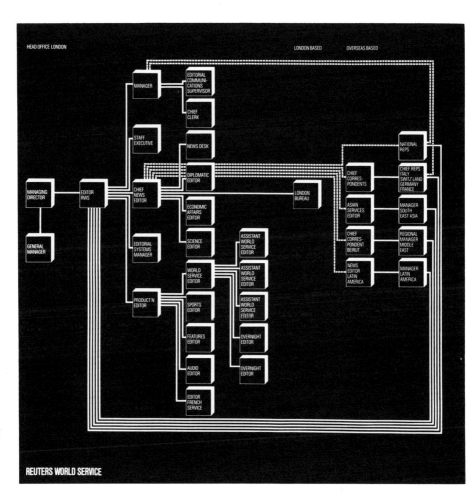

Identity design: Corporate programmes

This small building was the first design commission from *Reuters*. The structure, a radio station, concentrates the monitoring equipment in a single convenient unit. The site is in the grounds of an old manor house, the wartime headquarters of the radio monitoring system. A simple solution, the building is timber framed and clad in cedar boarding, the echelon plan allows for maximum views from the working rooms to a superb landscape.

The drawing is a recent study for a large communications complex and headquarters currently being designed for *Reuters* on the south bank of the Thames. *Seagrams, Chrysler* and *Pirelli* have all stupendously announced their identities in concrete.

Perhaps more dramatically, and certainly more permanently, than by symbol or colour.

The Managing Director's office contains original panelling by *Sir Edwin Lutyens* which it was clearly vital to preserve. The problem was one of refurbishment to bring the room back to its original intention and maintain the panelling.

The desk, conference table, coffee table, stools, television casing and light fittings were specially designed. The angled wall lamp gave a controlled down light for work, and bounced illumination off the ceiling.

Furniture by *Laverne, Eames* and *Bertoia* was chosen to fit the quality of the room. A bright orange Greek rug softens the general austerity.

39

The design of a special alphabet for *Reuters* information display equipment was undertaken for two reasons: to provide the company with a unique set of characters based on matrices, and to achieve greater legibility than is obtained with available and similar computer based character sets.

We are all used to reading typefaces which basically are constructed on calligraphic principles, but reading text formed and reproduced by electronic matrices poses problems of unfamiliarity with new letter forms.

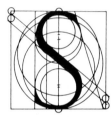

The development of the alphabet was aimed at achieving a computer based letterform comparable with traditional letterforms in both shape and legibility.

The first character set was developed with a very sophisticated matrix in that it enabled both bold and medium characters to be produced from the same dot matrix.

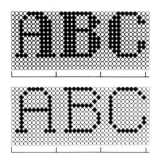

Although two weights of letter proved an asset in distinguishing information in display, the necessary grid was technically too complex. A simpler grid indicated a single weight alphabet, so the design format had to be re-structured.

A box grid formed the basis of the second alphabet, the letters being made up of a number of blocks written in the matrix by a method known as "interlacing". This method optically softens the characters by using quarter units of the grid, and in consequence heightens legibility by a visual reference to traditional forms.

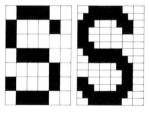

With advice from an *Institute of Ophthalmology* consultant, this character set was objectively tested for character legibility.

In these tests comparisons were made with the Times New Roman typeface, which is considered to have high legibility, and this acted as a yardstick in the assessment.

Testing indicated that the "interlacing" method tended to produce flicker, so an alternative "half dot shift" method was developed with a new matrix, which provided a smoother means of rounding corners and building letter shapes.

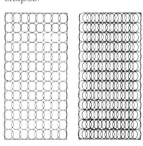

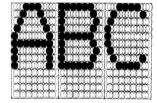

New technologies bring new and unfamiliar problems, and whereas part of the designer's expertise is to try and solve these, another equally important function is to reconcile new communication forms with old.

Reuters have always transmitted information by the fastest technique; pigeon, telegraph, teleprinter, telephone and now computer.

The speed with which information can be found is the key to success. The *Reuters Monitor*, with a constantly updated information store, can be interrogated at will and has become essential desk equipment for the dealer.

This machine is specifically designed for its function and environment, the keyboard is separable from the display for ease of use, and servicing is achieved by easily removable covers and open routes to internal assemblies.

The monitor stands as a physical representation of *Reuters*. In developing it, a deliberate decision was made to present it as modern equipment of higher quality than the normal office standard. The unit can be made more cheaply but the gain in prestige for *Reuters* is well worth the techniques employed. The case is formed from heavy gauge silver aluminium sheet.

41

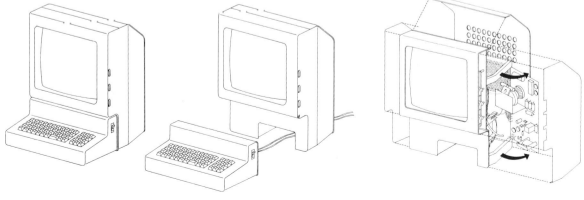

Identity design: Corporate programmes

On 14 October 1851 *Paul Julius Reuter* signed a lease for two rooms in No. 1 Royal Exchange Buildings in the City of London. On the eve of this date 125 years later a statue of *Paul Julius Reuter* was unveiled in the pedestrian square near the site of his first office.

The design of the statue was based on the existing marble bust of *Baron Reuter,* and the size of the figure was calculated in relation to the siting, and the surrounding buildings.

The statue was sculptured by *Michael Black* in Cornish granite from the De Lank quarry on Bodmin Moor, Cornwall, and took three months hard work. The thirteen foot monument weighs five tons.

The lettering was carved by *William Brown* who carefully copied and interpreted a layout supplied by *Pentagram.* The nature of the material and the length of the text precluded using a typeface, so the letters were drawn freehand to enable each character to be individually designed, the length of lines to be equal, and the spaces between lines to be minimised.

The lettering was intended to be both informative and decorative, the bevelling provided a visual textural effect – the natural light forming and casting shadows thereby enriching the surface.

42

A booklet was designed to commemorate the unveiling. The Baron's head had first been carved in marble, then over a hundred years later in granite, and therefore for the book cover a graphic three dimensional embossing seemed to be the logical choice for continuing the portrayal of the gentleman.

This marble bust of *Baron Reuter* was the model for the granite statue. It is mounted on a chrome column which was designed to match other fittings in the Managing Director's office which are shown on *page 39*.

LORD BARNETSON, CHA
REUTERS, OPENED THE CE
WITH THIS SPEECH

Your excellency, my lords, lad gentlemen. If you had stood hundred and twenty-five years as we do now, among the brokers bankers, the merchants, and the linge on-lookers, you might have observed energetic, hirsute, bird-like little m making his way into the Royal Exchang Building. The date was the 14th of October 1851. And the man in question was Paul Julius Reuter, just arrived from the Continent. He had come to take over the tenancy of two small rooms on the first floor; and in this modest establishment he was joined by his wife, Ida Maria, and a twelve-year-old office boy. Thus was the team and these were the circumstances that saw the birth of the vast organisation which today bears his name in practically ever corner of the world.

He had come, as he put it, to 'follow the cable'. He was just in time; for only four weeks later, after many tribulations, the electric telegraph was successfully inaugurated between Britain and France. But he had not only followed the cable: he had brought his own link, as it were; right to the hub and focus of its greatest potential – to the brokers, the traders, and the financial community who represented then, as they do now, such a vital ingredient in the Reuter operation.

One of his very earliest customers was the great banking house of Rothschild. Of course it would be immodest of me to claim that their robust survival since those days should be attributed, even in a small measure, to the Reuter service. But the fact remains that they're still taking it! Their Chairman

Lord B   nschild, your ex   lords, ladies and gentle   . Samuel Johnson said that in lapidary inscriptions a man is not upon oath. That indulgence has been a comfort to many, but it could not apply when the sixth Chief Executive of Reuters, which I am, put chisel to Cornish granite (through the intermediary of several persons) to pay tribute to the first and greatest, the founder, Paul Julius Reuter. I tried therefore, following his example which is always before us, to be

... a place whose
            ...shed, by the spread of cables round the world, a place where information was an instrument of work and a source of profit: the City of London.

For seven years after his arrival Reuter sold no news to the medium, then singular in the strictly numerical sense, the newspapers would not buy his news. But the traders would and did.

In Paris and Aachen and in those seven years here in the City, Reuter gave to Reuters its essential character. For more than a decade the management of Reuters has carefully studied that character, and the aims and methods of Paul

never
       n the
       Reuter
        ocu-
      ong
      at
     ly

... innovator in the ... of news services. We have ...ed, and still live, on the ideas he brought to this place 125 years ago.

I would like to quote this description, taken from the eleventh edition of the Encyclopaedia Britannica: 'By the employment of carrier-pigeons and of fast-sailing boats of his own for the transmission of news he was able to utilize to the best advantage his special sources of information.' The man described is not Reuter, but Nathan Mayer Rothschild, who was born 40 years before Paul Julius. That illustrious name appears among the earliest recorded clients of Reuter.

I now invite Mr Edmund de Rothschild, President of N M Rothschild & Sons Limited, to address us and to unveil this statue. I would like him to know what pleasure and satisfaction it gives to us in Reuters, that it is he who will unveil this

statue and thus lead us in paying tribute to a great and good man, Paul Julius Reuter.

MR EDMUND DE ROTHSCHILD SAID

Lord Barnetson, Mr Long, you have indeed honoured me by inviting me ...to unveil this statue to Baron Paul ...s Reuter. His first major client in the ...t of London was my great grandfather ...al J. Rothschild. As some of ... ...ay be aware, there were other ...ort of communication used by my ...or to Reuters: there is the famous ...geon-post, and also the first news brought back to Britain of the great victory of Waterloo, which came to my ancestor, Nathan Mayer, via his own courier from across the Channel. You and your loyal staff are worthy successors to Baron Reuter and his handful of couriers.

We have many letters in our archives on our relationship with Reuters, and one of them is perhaps to me a little worrying, in that on the 3rd March, 1865, Baron Reuter wrote, and I quote:

"Gentlemen: Since two years I have furnished you with the most important political and commercial news from America, India, China, etc., without having received any remuneration. Allow me therefore to ask you whether you wish me to continue this service or not. In the former case I must charge you £500 per annum. Awaiting your reply, I remain, Gentlemen, your most obedient servant, Julius Reuter."

I very much hope that this bill is not still an outstanding charge, as there is no

record of payment in our archives.

Joking apart, our association remains as cordial today as it was in those far off times. The City of London has indeed honoured Baron Reuter by allowing this statue to be placed here outside the Royal Exchange, a most appropriate site in the heart of the Square Mile. I take great pleasure in unveiling it.

LORD BARNETSON BROUGHT THE CEREMONY TO A CLOSE WITH THIS REPLY:

Being a man of generous and tolerant disposition, I really hadn't intended to raise with Rothschilds the little matter of the unpaid account for the year 1865. After all, the remittance may be held up in the post. And even if it isn't, I suppose that the wind has to be tempered, now and then, to the shorn lamb. But if Mr de Rothschild does feel a bit guilty about it, then I feel sure that we can come to an amicable arrangement.

But seriously, ladies and gentlemen, it would be ungracious to bring this little ceremony to an end without a few words of sincere thanks to those who have made it possible.

To Mr Edmund de Rothschild for unveiling what I hope will be regarded as a most acceptable City landmark; to the Corporation of London for their kind permission to use the site in this way; to Theo Crosby, the designer, Michael Black, the sculptor, and their fellow craftsmen; to the Master and Wardens of the Drapers Company for allowing us to meet in their Livery Halls; and finally to you, ladies and gentlemen, for being good enough to join us on this happy and evocative occasion.

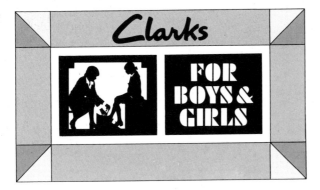

Clarks have been making children's shoes for more than 150 years. During that time they have established a reputation for responsibility to their young customers that is unrivalled in the shoe trade. The tradition stretches back over several generations and has a unique value to *Clarks* and their retailers.

Two factors persuaded *Clarks* that it was necessary to examine their public image. Firstly the danger that the company might be seen as old-fashioned. Secondly the need to visually control and sign the area allotted to *Clarks* in retail shops. *Clarks* do not own their outlets, but sell through a variety of shoe shop chains.

As a result of a study submitted by *Pentagram*, *Clarks* commissioned, and have begun to implement, a new design policy for the identity and presentation of their children's shoes.

The new design scheme was required to look modern, yet provide tangible links to the traditional consumer perception of *Clarks*. It also had to be relevant to children.

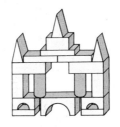

The concept was based on simple decorative geometric shapes in bright colours derived from a set of children's coloured blocks. This idea was modified when second thoughts indicated that children rapidly outgrow such

toys. The final forms were limited to three basic shapes.

The alphabet follows the same style reflecting the elements of the pattern as well as typographically tying the scheme together.

SHOE

The company colour has always been a green, and this was adjusted to a very much brighter shade.

Without surrendering any of the familiarity that has been established over many years, the *Clarks* logotype was given a thicker line, and shown in

bright yellow on a green background for all applications. The intention was to improve impact and legibility within the limitations of retaining the signature.

The essential problem lay in establishing, maintaining and controlling an identity in different sales environments of varying quality.

This need to support the product in the retail outlets required the design of hardware, including shoe display units, footstools, mirrors, pictorial panels for information, amusement and decoration, a do-up-your-own shoelaces device, in fact almost everything except the boundary of the space.

As the design programme is extended and developed, the colourful geometric decorative elements used both in graphics and display units, allow for new items to be absorbed easily into the overall scheme.

44

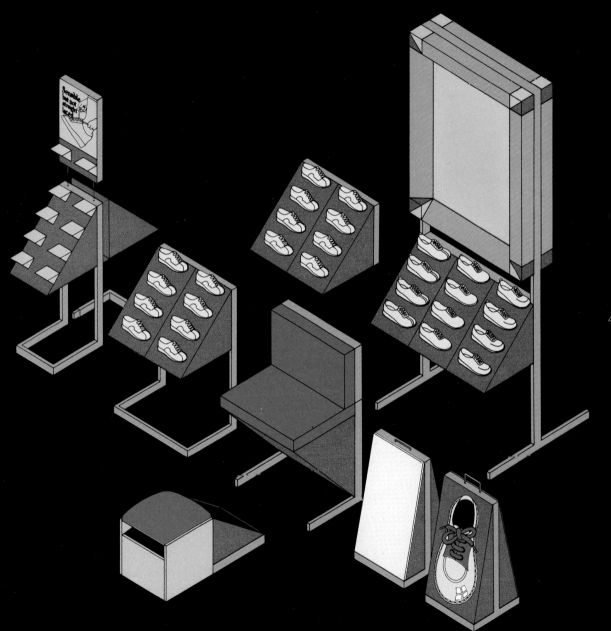

Retailers prefer to keep shoe boxes on display in the shop as contact with the customer is maintained throughout a sale. The box is therefore, in a sense, the keystone of the company identity.

Practically speaking, the box needs to be thought of as a basic unit, whereas the labels carry various permutations of information. For both retrieval and replacement, the end of the box needs to identify clearly and code the size, the fit, and the style of shoe.

Working within these limitations, the intention is that the shoe boxes will have the additional purpose of creating a brightly coloured wall in the shop, not only promoting the shoes but also enlivening what was previously one of the least attractive aspects of most shoe shops or departments.

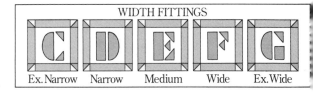

46

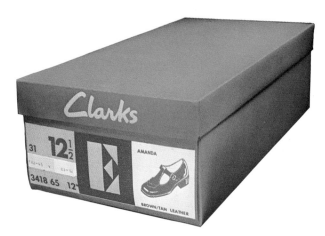

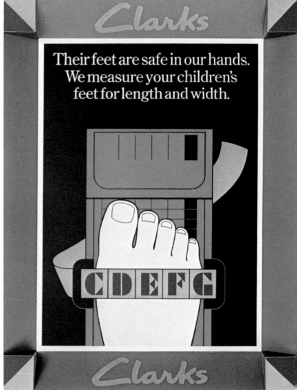

Identity design: Corporate programmes

Clarks' retailers always carefully measure children's feet to be certain of providing the correct size of shoe. Assistants are encouraged to undergo a course to learn to fit shoes correctly, and the graduates of this scheme wear a special lapel badge to denote their expertise.

This concern with fitting is an important aspect of the design programme, and includes furniture specially designed as part of the identity scheme, display panels, an illuminated sign for shop interiors, a kit for window displays and even a carrier bag. All are devoted to promoting the "fitting story."

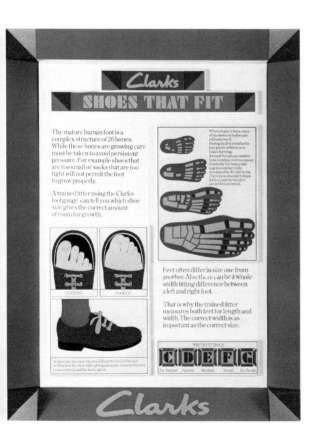

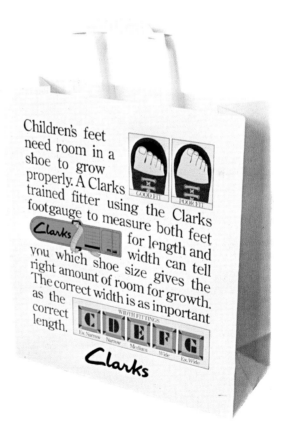

Identity design: Corporate programmes

In the past, *Clarks* have supplied shoe shops with decorative panels designed to amuse children, rather than to promote shoes.

A series of new colourful display panels, moulded in styrene and held in bevelled enamelled metal frames, have been introduced to enliven the retail area. The simple frame enables panels to be changed and circulated around the shoe shops, to provide constant change and to preserve interest.

Subtle promotion of shoes is achieved by pictorial puzzles, varying in content to amuse each age group of boys and girls. When the subject matter suggested a particular illustrative style these were commissioned; for example *'Find the shoes'* was drawn by Graham Percy.

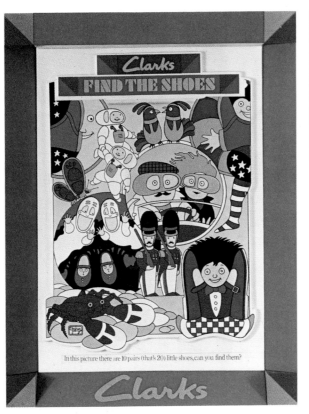

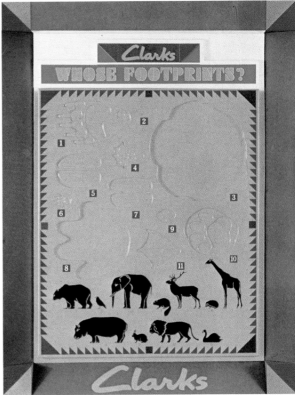

Identity design: Corporate programmes

In addition to decorative and informative display within the shops, *Clarks* also provide promotional items for the retailer to give away.

A series of miniature books, matching the panel themes, contain comprehensive information, fun and games. The do-it-yourself, tie-up-your-own-shoelaces game is made of card threaded with real laces. The make-your-own kite, if not exactly promoting footwear, is an entertaining present.

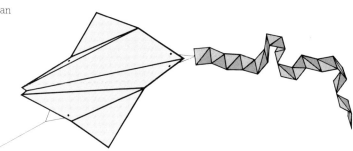

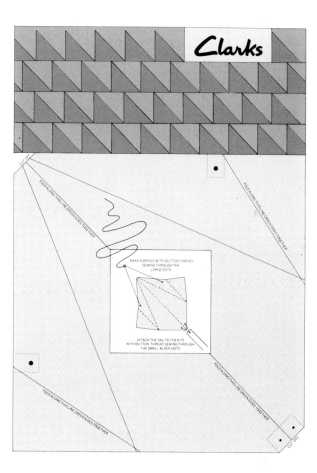

MAKE A BRIDLE WITH BUTTON THREAD SEWING THROUGH THE LARGE DOTS.

ATTACH THE TAIL TO THE KITE WITH BUTTON THREAD SEWING THROUGH THE SMALL BLACK DOTS

FOLD ALONG THIS LINE GREEN SIDES TOGETHER

CUNARD
CUNARD

Pentagram was asked to design the overall identity for the *Cunard Steamship Company,* and the new *QE2* liner. The latter included the graphic programme, the sign system, and the interior of the *Lookout Bar* in the front of the ship.

The client required that the new logotype should be related to the existing version, that it should be visible from a distance of twenty miles at sea, that it should have an alternative outline version for cases where the solid letters might be considered too obtrusive!

In addition to the design of the identity, it was necessary to structure the implementation. Visual analysis and rationalisation is one function of design, and so is saving money. For example it was possible to meet all the requirements of the 35 existing labels, by three new designs.

Most of the graphic work however was concerned with creating an image appropriate to the elegant lifestyle associated with a luxury liner.

50

Identity design: Corporate programmes

The *Cunard* sales brochure for the maiden voyage of the *QE2* had to be designed well before the launching of the liner for promotional and advertising reasons. This needed a conceptual approach and graphic skill as the actual ship was at that time still under construction and no more than an empty shell in the dockyard. The solution dictated by circumstances was to create a realism and ambience by montage, invention and imagination. As the old adage goes, "seeing is believing". The ship shown on the contents page was a large-scale model; this was floated and photographed in a large water tank, and the sunrise simulated by lighting effects.

The party, illustrating the first class trans-atlantic timetable, was readily conjured up by asking a few friends and a photographer around to the studio for drinks, and the images of the interiors of cabins, restaurants and public rooms, were obtained from prototypes and models.

Identity design: Corporate programmes

The *Cunard* logotype was applied in a variety of techniques and sizes. The main booking office fascia was polished steel, the stationery die stamped, the soap embossed, the towels embroidered.

By using the logotype as a pattern the signal of identity can also fulfil a decorative function. This scheme was used for wrapping papers, carrier bags and even this book of matches.

One of the most vital pieces of corporate print was the timetable: a complex exercise not only in logistics but also in layout and typography.

The cover was a photograph of the ship taken from a helicopter over Southampton water, a decision based more on the enthusiasm of a partner to fly than a brilliant idea.

The justification was to use the same photograph switched to sail down on the back page, inferring schedules for both outward and homeward bound voyages. With two solutions for the price of one he certainly didn't feel guilty about the trip, but the client didn't go with the idea.

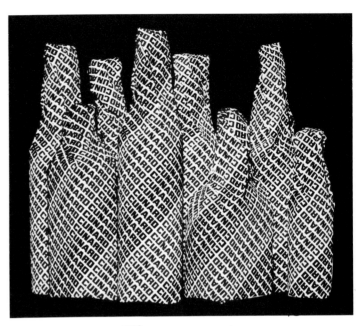

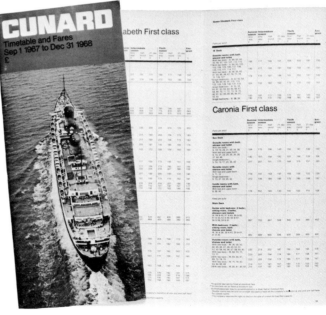

Identity design: Corporate programmes

Different menu designs were required for each day to help offset the boredom implicit in always dining in the same restaurant. In former times the company had bought old colour printing plates from chocolate box manufacturers, and required some persuasion to abandon this practice.

A set of designs, based on rare English silver tableware photographed from the collection of the *Worshipful Company of Goldsmiths,* was thought appropriate for the first class dining room menus.

The objects were printed in silver on a black ground and captioned to help the diner pass the time between orders. National holidays and events were opportunities for special menu designs.

Part of the service provided by *Cunard* for passengers on trans-atlantic voyages and luxury cruises is the daily programme of events. Since they not only vary from day to day, but cruise to cruise, the cover designs needed to be non-specific. The solution adopted was to provide nautical information rather than decorative cheerfulness.

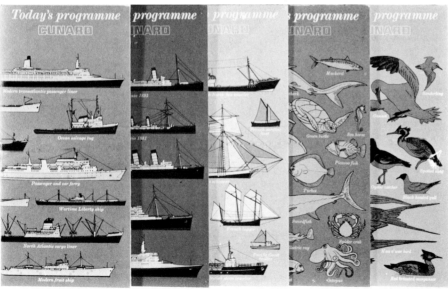

Identity design: Corporate programmes

This description of the *QE2 Lookout Bar,* is taken from an issue of *Design Magazine.*

"The *Lookout* on the Upper Deck offers a view over the bows. Detailing is impressive, and handling of the narrow shape is one of the triumphs of the ship. The problem was to compress the width but provide depth."

"One solution was to line the rear wall with a vast irregular screen of mirrors, steel and bronze, in a free-form linenfold pattern. The design was by *Gillian Wise.*"

"A vermilion piano providing music for dancing, enlivens the club-like atmosphere."

"Seating was profiled on the traditional Chesterfield, and two different units allow for flexible layout."

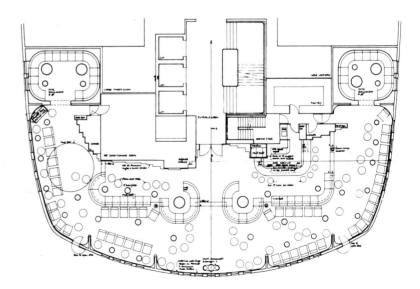

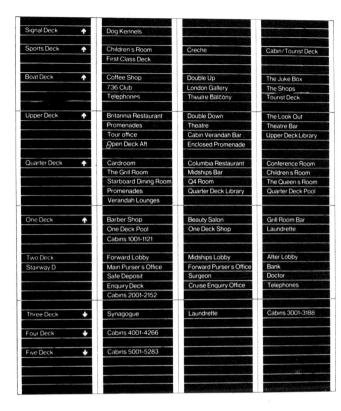

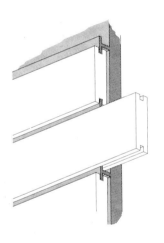

The design of the *QE2* sign system on this floating resort, equivalent in size to six London *Hilton Hotels,* was a complex design programme in its own right. On previous liners, signs had little aesthetic or functional merit, *see left.*

Although the ship was traditionally divided into separate classes, this was now determined more by proportional bookings than

social differences. The first class facilities might therefore alter on each voyage. Accordingly the sign system had to be as equally flexible.

A modular method based on a single panel enabled individual panels to be changed, and banked in different permutations so as to be easily assembled and demounted according to needs.

Panels were made of matt black perspex, white engraved typography, and notched to provide a secret fixing device. Aluminium angled runners were fixed to a backboard, and so removal and replacement was a simple operation.

55

Biba was one of the success stories of the London sixties. Over a span of ten years after starting as a small boutique, it became a department store with a worldwide reputation.

The housestyle and image, designed by *John McConnell*, now a partner of *Pentagram*, was part of the attitude and outlook of *Biba*, a lifestyle rather than an applied programme. For example, the symbol started life as a decoration on a mail order pack. A *Biba* alphabet was eventually designed to be compatible with the motif and to give exclusivity to the namestyle.

The name was used beneath or above the motif and was usually printed in gold on black. As a mark of

identification it appeared on everything from garment labels to posters and was even used as decoration on wallpapers and fabrics, and woven into lace.

When the cosmetics were first launched, production runs were so low that standard containers and jars manufactured for the pharmaceutical industry were used. The original versions even had glass stoppers. They were made in black, with the *Biba* symbol surprinted in gold, and indeed became so popular that specially designed containers were never considered. The only change made was to introduce screw tops to prevent leakage.

57

Identity design: Corporate programmes

Mail order catalogues were produced for each season, and in terms of traditional mail order catalogues they broke every rule in the book. They were too big, too thin, not in full colour but in duotone, and the pictures showed style not detail.

To add interest and bulk, the publications contained fold-outs and inserts. The pictures were taken by photographers of the calibre of *Harry Peccinotti, Don Siverstein, Sarah Moon* and *Helmut Newton.*

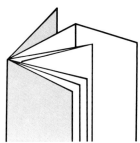

A special booklet was
prepared as a press handout
when *Biba* moved from the
small shop in Church Street
and opened their first store in
Kensington High Street. By this
time *Biba* was growing and
becoming a more sophisticated
concern, enlarging and
carrying a wider variety of
different merchandise, such
as materials for interior
decorating and men's clothes.

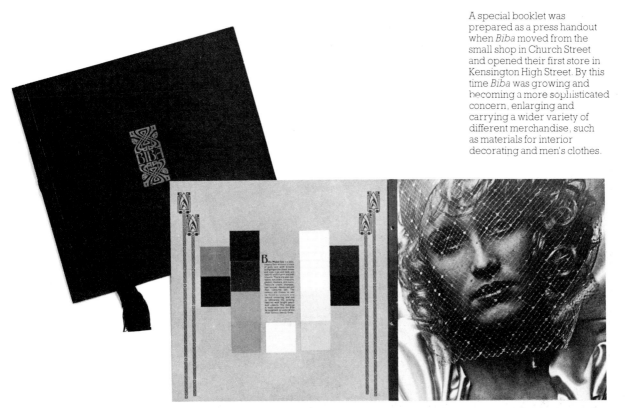

59

Each spread of the booklet
dealt with a different section of
the new shop, and contained
samples of materials and
colours of cosmetics, all of
which were laboriously stuck
on the pages by hand.

As a piece of useless
information, it may be of
interest to know that most of
this work is done out of season
by old ladies in seaside resorts
In this case Bournemouth!

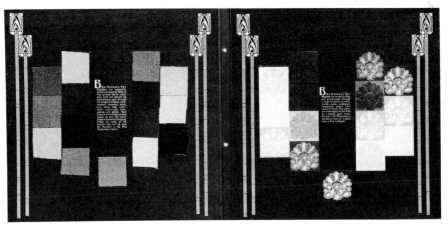

The trademark for *Face Photosetting* is comprised of faces. In addition to the halftone rendering there is a linear version, mainly for use in small sizes or for printing on newsprint paper.

Such variations are customary. They enable maximum quality, or at least suitability, when used in extremes of size, or when technical limitations are encountered with reproduction techniques and materials.

As a company, *Face* believe print promotion is the most direct method of reaching their clients. The business is competitive and in addition to type sheets and catalogues, an important criteria is to make the wall of the advertising agency or designer's studio. The graphics therefore need to be appealing as well as informative.

The name of the company provides the graphic image, and the face is freely interpreted, often by talented designers and illustrators.

60

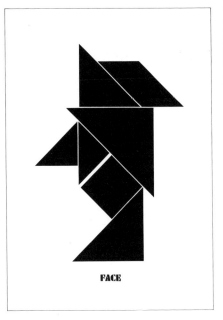

FACE

FACE

FACE

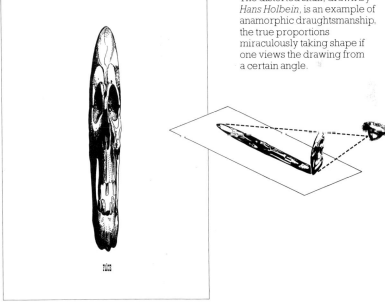

FACE

The portraits used on these black and white promotional posters were selected or specially drawn to promote a range of typefaces.

The name of the game was to visually relate the characteristics of a letterform, with an equivalent expression in the facial image. For example, the ancient Chinese geometrical puzzle game of *Tangram*, a set of seven pieces enabling one to construct an infinite number of pictorial compositions, provided the profile on the far left to match the stencil letters.

The modular portrait of *Mickey Mouse* was unearthed from an instruction manual for "needle point". The Victorian pastime of hand shadows renders yet another form of face.

The distorted skull, drawn by *Hans Holbein,* is an example of anamorphic draughtsmanship, the true proportions miraculously taking shape if one views the drawing from a certain angle.

Identity design: Corporate programmes

It is a policy of *Pentagram* to encourage clients to use the best available talents for specialist abilities. *Face Photosetting,* understanding that roles can be reversed, are imaginative enough to commission the very best illustrators. Of course it's a two way process, the illustrators are equally happy to have *Face Photosetting* mail their samples all over town! These

four calendar illustrations were in several colours and styles. The different personalities produced four quite different interpretations. They were *John Gorham, Graham Percy* and *Bentley, Farrell & Burnett.*

Although a sophisticated client, *Face* nevertheless has a very modest budget, which prompted an inexpensive

solution for this tear-off calendar. The paper was bought from a bankruptcy stock of recycled paper, and the 365 images were found from such miscellaneous sources as classified advertisements, catalogues, and an old telephone directory.

By taking an essentially low quality image out of context,

and viewing it in isolation, one is able to heighten the vigour and energy of a design, unabashed by preconceptions, taste or artistic skill.

The idea of recycling existing artwork on recycled paper had, we thought, considerable merit for a year of economic crisis.

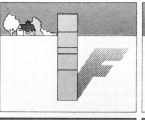
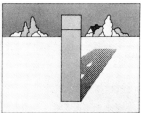

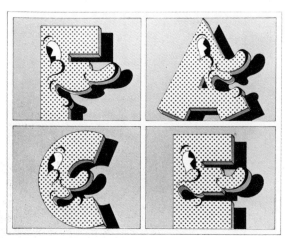

r⊙tring

The logotype for *Rotring* was designed in Germany a number of years ago. The problem was to create a new identity around this mark for *Hartley Reece,* the British agents, as increasing competition highlighted the need to reinforce the *Rotring* image.

The underlying concept of the new identity was to associate the company and its products with the professional user, that is to say the designer, architect and draughtsman.

This was done in several ways; by commissioning well known illustrators and designers, by using *Rotring* instruments to create images, and when these two options were impractical, by showing the products in as graphic a manner as possible.

Within the latter category is this full colour poster which was treated as a photographic catalogue of the products, and the stationery, overleaf, which concentrated on promoting the *Rotring* pen.

The identity of the company was therefore not solely dependent on the signal of logotype, housecolour or layout style.

64

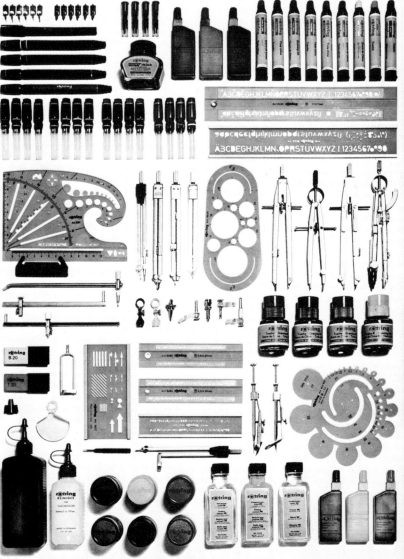

rotring is more than a great pen, it's a great system

r⊙tring

By commissioning well known
professionals, such as
American designer *Milton
Glaser* and British architect
Peter Cook, the company and
the product were able to be
closely associated with
graphic quality. For example
Philip Castle illustrated these
products with *Rotring* inks for
an advertising campaign in
the design and architectural
magazines.

65

Information and instructions were conveyed through the graphic techniques obtainable by the instruments. These technical illustrations by *Wolf Spoerl* were actually drawn with *Rotring* pens.

The maintenance folder pictorially showed the procedure of cleaning the equipment, and the double spread illustrating *Rotring* Primus pens and accessories was specially produced for the student market.

On the stationery, the company name was linked to both the logotype and the product, thus effectively promoting all three at the same time.

The scheme also included cabinets for the display of *Rotring* products. These were designed to be highly functional, clearly presenting the full range to view, and attractive in the sense that the products were offered as quality instruments.

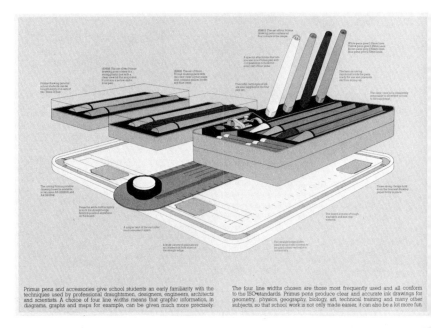

Primus pens and accessories give school students an early familiarity with the techniques used by professional draughtsmen, designers, engineers, architects and scientists. A choice of four line widths means that graphic information, in diagrams, graphs and maps for example, can be given much more precisely.

The four line widths chosen are those most frequently used and all conform to the ISO standards. Primus pens produce clear and accurate ink drawings for geometry, physics, geography, biology, art, technical training and many other subjects, so that school work is not only made easier, it can also be a lot more fun.

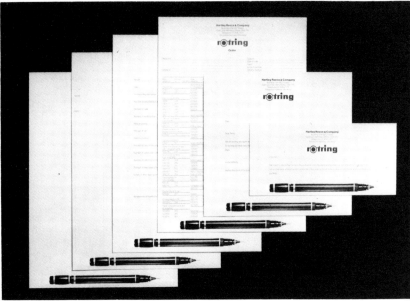

THE CARE AND MAINTENANCE OF ROTRING PENS

Hartley Reece and Company
Building One GEC Estate
Wembley Middx HA9 7PY

rotring

If your drawing instrument fails to work perfectly at any time, the following table should help you to find the fault quickly. If all else fails, replacement parts are available for every component of rotring tubular drawing pens.

Fault	Drawing instrument stops writing when in use.	Variations in line thickness.	Drops of ink appear at the drawing tip when the drawing instrument is being used. Widening at beginning and end of ink lines.	Drawing instrument will not write although ink reservoir is full.	Ink seepage between the front part of the drawing instrument and the drawing cone.
Cause	Drop-weight and cleaning wire blocked by dry ink. Ventilation duct dirty. Drawing tube and cleaning wire bent.	Drawing tip dirty. Drawing surface dirty.	Ink reservoir almost empty. The relatively large amount of air in the reservoir expands on twisting. The volume of ink forced out of the reservoir exceeds the equilization capacity of the ventilation duct. Ink reservoir should never be allowed to be more than a third empty.	Drawing tube blocked.	The cap was not removed before replacing the ink reservoir. The excess pressure thus enclosed forces ink through the ventilation duct when the cap is opened. Also due to excess horizontal shaking.
Remedy	Unscrew drawing cone with cone key. Clean drawing cone and front part of instrument. Renew drawing cone.	Clean drawing tip with cotton or linen rag. Clean drawing surface with plastic eraser.	Rinse front part of drawing instrument with drawing cone under running water and dry out. Fill ink reservoir up to chrome ring, or, in the case of the foilograph series, up to the correct level.	Shake the drawing instrument along its axis horizontally until the drop weight can be heard to rattle distinctly.	Hold the drawing instrument with the drawing tip pointing upwards. Remove excessive ink with blotting paper if ink has dried, unscrew drawing cone and clean together with front part of instrument.

Diagnosing faults

The instructions in this book apply to the five tubular drawing pens shown here. Separate instructions are available for the rapidograph which has a different filling mechanism.
The variant is for drawing to DIN standards 15 series, 2.
The varioscript is for stencilling to DIN 1451, and should always be held at 90° to the drawing surface.
The micronorm m can be used for both drawing and stencilling to DIN 15, 16 and 17 series 1 and for stencilling in accordance with ISO 3098/1. It is the correct pen for work that is to be microfilmed.

The variant   The varioscript   The micronorm m

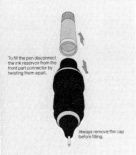

The front part connector and the ink reservoir are connected by a push-fit, not a screw thread. To separate them give a slight twist and a pull. The air vent in the thread of the drawing cone is designed to maintain a balance between air pressure and ink pressure, giving an even flow through the nib. However when the reservoir is about two thirds empty this balance is upset and an excess of air from the reservoir may force blobs of ink through the nib. So always refill the pen when the reservoir is two thirds empty.

To fill the pen disconnect the ink reservoir from the front part connector by twisting them apart.

Always remove the cap before filling.

Filling the pen   1

Never mix two different inks in the same pen.
Never fill the reservoir above the level of the chrome band as the excess of ink will be forced through the air vent when you reconnect the reservoir to the pen. This will make a mess and prevent the ink from flowing freely through the tube.

Fill the reservoir with the correct ink (see rotring catalogue).

Fill to just below the level of the chromium band.

2

Do not reconnect the front part connector and reservoir with the cap in place, as this will prevent air escaping through the nib. The excess of pressure that results could then force ink into the air vent.

Keeping the reservoir upright, reconnect the front part connector by twisting, then tilt slowly and screw the holder into position.

3

It is not necessary to shake the pen violently, just sufficiently to hear the drop weight moving inside. The wire in the tube will protrude and pierce the meniscus of the ink allowing it to flow freely. If after shaking the pen for a while the ink still does not flow, there is probably a serious blockage, and the pen should be thoroughly cleaned.

Before using the pen hold it in a horizontal position and shake it gently.

The ink should now flow through the pen. If it does not, repeat the shaking.

Using the pen   1

Each cap is placed in a hole opposite its pen in the rapidomat and tells you the nib size at a glance. Humid air is circulated around the nibs to prevent ink drying and a colour coded hygrometer tells you when the sponge in the rapidomat needs moistening. For further details of the rapidomat, see the rotring catalogue.

When pens are being used very frequently the rotring rapidomat (rr) (rr) is a convenient alternative to continually removing and replacing the cap.

4

Before the pen is reassembled make sure it is absolutely dry, as drops of moisture left inside the pen will interfere with its proper functioning.

Run the water through from both ends.

Every time the pen is refilled the drawing cone and front part connector should be cleaned by holding it under running water.

Cleaning the pen   1

Never use hot water to clean the pen as this could expand the plastic and damage it.

After washing shake away excess moisture and dry off with blotting paper or tissue.

2

Always use the cone key, which comes with every pen, to remove or replace the drawing cone. If it is done by hand there is a risk that the nib will be damaged.

When more thorough cleaning is required, it is necessary to remove the drawing cone from the front part connector using the cone key.

3

بسم الله الرحمن الرحيم

مؤتمر التضامن الاسلامى
The Conference for Islamic Solidarity
کانفرنس همبستگی أسلامی
La Conférence de la Solidarité Islamique
اسلامی استحکام کی کانفرنس
Mu'Tamar Setiakawan Islam
Islam Tesanud Konferansı

The *Conference for Islamic Solidarity* was a cultural event sponsored by *Saudi Arabia,* to be held in Mecca.

The project included the design of a temporary building to act as a conference centre for 800 delegates, and a graphic identity scheme.

The theme of the graphic image was required to conform with the precepts of the Islamic culture, for example, to a Moslem the representation of the human figure is not acceptable, and birds and animals should only be portrayed in certain circumstances.

Whereas in western societies geometric designs are readily labelled as "abstract" and therefore merely decorative, to the Moslem they have emotional meanings and significances. For the *Kelim* carpet weaver, his design is not just a pleasant composition of colours and shapes, it is a story expressed through figurative patterns.

The symbol was constructed with seven crescents, to represent the seven Islamic cultures, the resultant circular configuration additionally can be associated with the burnous. The colours chosen were black and green, as green not surprisingly, is venerated by the Arab world as a special colour.

The typographic problem of dealing with Arabic, English, Farsi, French, Urdu, Malay and Turkish, some of which read left to right while others right to left, was resolved by a symmetric layout.

The conference was publicised extensively across the Islamic world from Casablanca to Jakarta, and to ensure a consistency in application, a design guide was based on pictorial reference rather than verbal instruction.

The programme was fraught with unexpected hurdles. It is often necessary for a designer to be able to foresee and deal with unlikely complications in order to realise the successful implementation of his designs.

. . . the only manufacturer able to engrave the symbol on the glassware in time to meet the deadline, proved to be of a conflicting faith and unacceptable to the client.

. . . the only readily available Arabic calligrapher was considered lacking in the aesthetic quality associated with that art.

. . . the four metre sculpture based on the symbol and erected outside the conference building was never seen by the designer, as non-believers are not allowed in Mecca.

. . . building supervision was undertaken by mail as the same travel restrictions applied. Fuzzy deckle edged photographs were checked with specification drawings, and returned with further instructions.

. . . the conference building was prefabricated in Belgium and transported, with much difficulty to Mecca. The steelwork having been damaged in unloading at Jeddah, a further 35 tons of steel was airfreighted to make good the losses.

The *Conference Centre* structure consisted of a hall, with wings at either end enclosing courtyards with fountains. The courts were largely roofed, and the auditorium was enlivened behind the dais by a woven hanging designed by *Sheila Hicks,* the other walls being covered with slatted timber panels to break the sun.

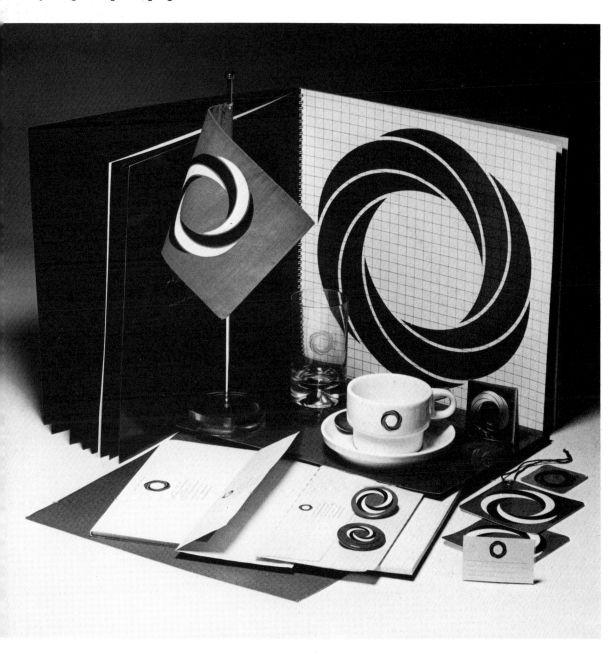

Identity design: Corporate programmes

A small design programme for a commercial and documentary film company, two of whom were still-life photographers with individual reputations.

The idea came whilst discussing the problem with the clients, *Brooks Baker Fulford,* in their darkly lit studio one winter evening. As the ideas were heatedly discussed and the bottles of wine consumed, the blurring of vision merged the white formica conference table into the whiter than white shirts.

Some ideas arrive like the proverbial bolt from the blue, others are the sum of hard work – occasionally they pleasantly slide into focus.

We got them to take a full colour group portrait of themselves, composing the shot so that the white shirts could become the letterpaper. By dividing the image one obtains personal calling cards, this one is for *Bob Brooks.*

Brooks Baker & Fulford

Brooks Baker & Fulford Limited, 3 Princes Street, London W1. 01-629 7916. J. Baker (Managing), R. Brooks (USA), L. Fulford, J. McKeand

The scheme was applied to
film cans, rubber stamps,
filing boxes, matchboxes and
their small van.

Brooks Baker & Fulford
3 Princes Street, London W1
Telephone 01-629 7916

Brooks Baker & Fulford, 3 Princes Street, London W1. Telephone 01-629 7916

71

Madam I'm Adam

This three word palindrome not only identifies a status and a name, but declares two genders, and by reading both ways could be said to contain eight identities.

Adam and Eve personify the origins of our identity as men and women. Like similar legends, this early story is rich in objects which have special, often multiple, identities. For early semitic society, innocent of science, it answered the burning questions of who we are and where we come from, by superimposing symbolic meanings on the familiar phenomena of the natural world. Thus in the story of *Genesis*, abstract qualities are identified with our familiar surroundings, the garden of paradise, the tree of knowledge and life, the tempting apple and the evil serpent.

The habit has died hard. Just about everything that man observes, he endows with some special significance. Indeed a man's whole outlook on life can be deduced from the special identities and values which he attaches to the objects around him – often unknown to himself. Thus while a middle-aged and middle-class father may recognise and condemn the rebellious image which his son creates by cultivating long hair, he can remain totally blind to the image which he himself sustains by living in a mock Tudor house and wearing a club tie. Fantasy, pride, illusion, all play a part in the individual's search for identity among the visual codes which he himself has projected upon the phenomena around him.

The proliferation of such codes has complicated the process of identification however, and it is thanks largely to *Freud* that we have had to abandon many of our cold confident classifications; to recognise that the objects and phenomena around us carry accretions of real and possible meanings of which we were never aware, many of them with deep emotional significance.

Of these emotional connotations, colour evokes perhaps the most powerful associations. Thus would-be revolutionaries are called "red" (because blood will flow?) while those who wish to preserve the *status quo* adopt blue, perhaps because they feel it identifies them with the "blue blood" of an old-established aristocracy. Maybe it is the same association which prompts mothers to dress baby boys in blue – it is through the male line that intelligence and properties descend in most societies. We describe a coward as yellow, and turn white with fear, purple with rage and green with envy. The Buddhist priest wears holy yellow and the Arab, not surprisingly, venerates green. In the west, white means purity (hence white weddings) while black represents death (hence the colour of mourning). In the east, the associations are reversed. So closely related are black and white to life and death, that there is an apocryphal story that the trademark of *Rolls Royce* was changed from red to black in 1933 on the death of *Sir William Royce*.

Among the earliest examples of visual coding are the daubing, branding and scarring which man has practised upon himself. Such marks may simply be decorative, or identify a person as a member of a tribe, family or rank. The indelibility of scarring gives it a special place among methods used to express identity and communicate ideas. When a tribal initiate receives his ritual marking he is committed forever to membership of the tribe, with all which this implies in privileges and obligations. The same applied to the elitism of the German duelling scar. The man was, of course, educated, brave and above all a gentleman.

The visual folklore of the tatooist is rich in colourful and evocative pictorial images and mottoes used to stress the individuality of the tattooed. When a sailor has his girl-friend's name indelibly inscribed on his biceps, he declares not just love but everlasting love. Man's constancy is rarely equal to his occasional enthusiasms. An ironic case was that of *Bernadotte,* the soldier of fortune from *Napoleon's* army who was awarded the throne of Sweden, and was unable to make people forget the revolutionary motto of his youth, "Death to the Kings", tattooed on his arm! A paradoxical contrast to this form of identification was the system utilised by the Nazis to identify prisoners in concentration camps. Here the numbers on the prisoners' forearms acted as a means of totally eliminating individual identities.

Man's belief in the mystical significance of the body print is shown in the notion that the markings behind a mackerel's head are the thumb-print of the Lord, and in the idea that the stigmata of certain saints truly duplicate the marks made in *Christ's* body by nails and a spear. For forty years *Padro Pio,* who died in September 1969, had borne on his body the stigmata, the marks of the five wounds of *Christ*. More fancifully such faith in the power of the body print was exploited dramatically with *J.M. Barrie's Peter Pan*, who depended for his very existence upon his shadow.

In some cases even hair styles can assume more than ordinary significance. The monk's tonsure identifies him for what he is, and the judge's wig has become a symbol of authority. The tradition of short hair for men dates from the days when wigs were worn in an attempt, perhaps, to imitate *Samson* by identifying long hair with virility and strength. More sentimentally, a curl of hair treasured in a locket can assume a special significance as a momento of a loved one, the remnants of an identity.

The most formal expression of visual coding is heraldry; a complex grammar of visual symbols and patterns arranged in defined relationships, each identifying an individual or family. The need for this form of identification was vital for its early user, the herald, an officer whose duty it was to act as a courier between kings. When arms became hereditary the bearing of them was a sign of continuity and a worthy pedigree. An heraldic coat-of-arms represents a knight and his individual attributes. The shield represents his body, the helmet his head and the flourish his mantle. The motto is his chosen moral pretension and the supporters are the pages, designated by heraldic beasts.

Commercial examples of visual coding are to be found in early trade marks which were simple abstract devices with which craftsmen identified their handiwork. Thus stonemasons, potters, printers and goldsmiths all produced distinctive devices. Indeed their symbolic representations are often so strong that they have outlasted the people or the activities for which they were designed, and have been developed and adopted by others; for example the insignia of freemasonry or even the three gold balls of the pawnbroker's sign, originally representing that crafty banking family, the *Medicis*.

Memorials and graves are physical symbols which evoke and reinforce memories of past identities. These are sometimes made on a vast scale to aggrandize those commemorated, occasionally as in the case of the *Albert Memorial,* to the point where the original intention is obscured by the immensity of the statement and the cultural conventions for which it stands.

The creation of a truly unique visual identity is often just a chimaera, for even a distinctive appearance may only be seemingly so. Make-up may distinguish a clown from his audience, but it scarcely enhances his individuality, instead, it produces a conventional identity, though one which satisfies a deep social need to give "face" to a condition or activity.

This conflicting drive towards uniformity declares itself in what is often a depressing sameness among the superficially different. The individuality of an advertised product, political ideology, religious dogma, like that of a man, becomes buried by the sheer weight of numbers of others of its kind. Yet human nature drives us to continue to try and express our uniqueness, even in the face of suffocating cultural conventions, and design is the expressive element of a society which fulfills this need.

Alan Fletcher

73

Identity design: Personal signals

Pentagram is partly a development of an original partnership of graphic designers formed in the early sixties by *Alan Fletcher, Colin Forbes* and *Bob Gill.* The booklet announcing the partnership was based on the children's game of heads, bodies and legs, and was intended to convey that three identities had merged to become one . . . or perhaps through permutations, 27!

George Hoy is a typographer whose initials, by luck, are consecutive letters in the alphabet. For designers, the perceptive eye is as important as the creative idea, and a square cut out of a printer's specimen type sheet provided an appropriate emblem for a typographer.

74

COLIN FORBES is Consultant Art Director to Pirelli Limited. Among his other clients are Penguin Books, and Imperial Chemical Industries. At the moment he is designing a series of directional signs for the new passenger building at London Airport for Frederic Gibberd, Architects.
At one time was head of the Graphic Design department of the LCC Central School of Arts and Crafts.

Identity design: Personal signals

These days letterheads are the prime signal of personal identity.

Min Hogg is a lady who represented illustrators and photographers. Bereft of a fitting idea, and her name being of little help, we traced and had her distinctive profile die-cut on stationery and cards, and arranged the typography so she could vocally state her business as well as her address.

*Min Hogg represents
photographers, cartoonists, illustrators
and designers from
24 Rupert Street, London W1V 7FN
Telephone 01-437 5062*

Tony Evans always gives personalised Christmas presents, this one was a toy aeroplane for which he needed a pack. As he is a professional photographer we perversely did him as a drawing, and as he's a little fellow we put him in his plane.

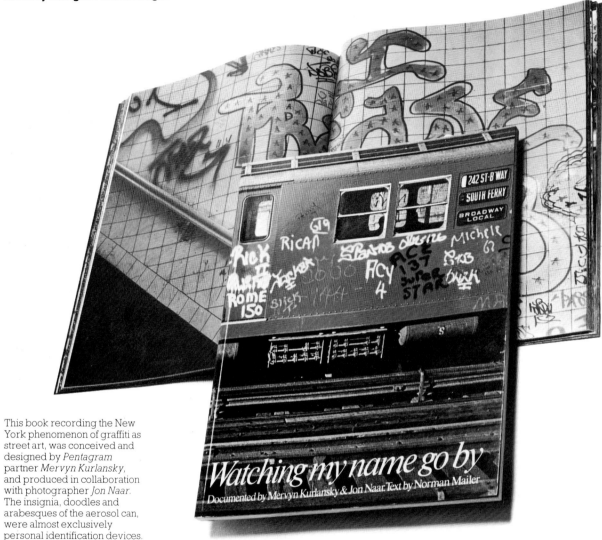

This book recording the New York phenomenon of graffiti as street art, was conceived and designed by *Pentagram* partner *Mervyn Kurlansky,* and produced in collaboration with photographer *Jon Naar.* The insignia, doodles and arabesques of the aerosol can, were almost exclusively personal identification devices.

The forms ranged from the iconographic signs of the artist's initials, to the formalised signatures of *Hondo, Wildcat, Sabu* or *Lollipop.* A cross, so to speak, between action painting and *"Kilroy was here!"*

Identity design: Personal signals

The rhebus is one form of visual pun which is still going strong after several centuries. This design was constructed for a lady called *Lucia*, it needs a bit of working out but then a rhebus is a puzzle.

Ideas are often obtained by a juggling of visual associations and sometimes a designer has to know not only where, but when to look. *Elizabeth* who worked at *Pentagram* and left us to do other things, was pleased when we revived an Elizabethan royal signature – and gave it to her as a personal parting logotype.

A Georgian name deserved the calligraphic obsession with proportions, elegant techniques and the penmanship of that period. The designer's mother, *Georgette Robert*, thought it very pretty.

Medieval illuminated scripts are distinguished for the art of the decorated initial. These prompted the idea to assemble five letters from five different decorative alphabets, to provide a floral namestyle for a boutique owned by an exotic lady called *Flora*.

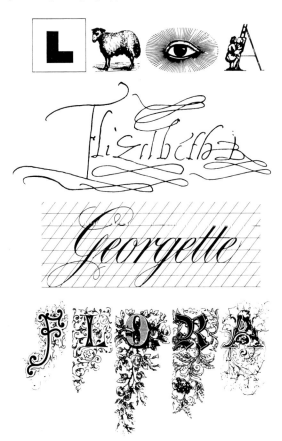

Personalities can become identified with products. This life size articulated figure was specially made by *Ralph Selby* in mahogany. It was produced to represent a range of *Herman Miller* ergonomic chairs. Smaller figures were given as gifts to clients as a reminder.

78

The initial of this lady photographer, *Doris Quarella,* provided the clue for the design, and in consequence the shape for her stationery.

Advertising is a tough business and these two attractive business-like ladies represented a group of illustrators. They asked us to design their stationery and very sportingly accepted our graphic proposals. The photograph, by the way, is from a collection of Victorian pornographic postcards.

Beato Staehelin
Stapferstrasse 43, 8006 Zürich
(01) 60 03 40

Georg Staehelin designed this
letterpaper within the
letterpaper for his wife, a lady
of few words who detests
writing letters.

One of the *Pentagram*
partners moved home and so
we asked *Donna Brown*, who
draws, to go and do the house
for his new letterhead. He
likes it despite the cost of the
four colour printing . . . so his
letters are rare and valuable.

01-794 2129

E R

&

Lila *(everything you've always wanted to know about London and didn't know who to ask)* **Burkeman**

Information design

We have seen how the skills of the designer can be used to identify both the individual and the corporate body. The designer's skills as a communicator, which are used for these purposes, are also used in the design of information. Some individuals and most corporate bodies need to communicate about themselves, and the corporate bodies do so in a bewildering multiplicity of ways.

Not only does the format of the information process vary, but so does the content and so do the groups of people at whom it is aimed. Any large company may use printed or audio visual systems of communication, it may also use meetings and exhibitions, or books or broadsheets. Its messages may vary from the complex and technical to the simple and emotional. They may be intended for customers, or employees or for shareholders, as advertising or company newspapers or Annual Reports. Their impact may be short or long, the information may be restricted or widely circulated. It may induce feedback or be boldly persuasive. The designer works in all these fields and as the illustrations show, has been doing so for many years and in many places. In order to make this mass of work activity intelligible, we have divided this part of the book into six sections.

The first of these we have called *Systems*. The main task of the designer in this field is to take complex and often technical, financial or scientific information, and by using histographic and visual skills, and often aided by computers and computer systems, to present it in a way which is immediately intelligible and usable. A second is *Posters*, where the designer uses his sense of style and his wit to intensify the essence of the message. These two areas are at opposite ends of an intellectual/emotional spectrum. They are followed by two sections, which describe the designer's work in a different context.

One of these, *Promotion,* covers a spectrum of design work from the carefully considered decisions behind an advertising campaign to one off jobs, complete in themselves, needing speed, sensitivity and little reference to the client once the job is specified. The other, *Packaging,* where the designer's work has a dual role. As an information conveyor of the product inside the package, and as the last stage in the design of the product.

The fifth and final area of *Information design* is *Exhibitions*. In this field the graphic skills of the designer are linked to audio-visual and environmental skills to offer information through time and space. Indeed the frontiers between this field of design and the next main division of the book *Environment design* are blurred, but then for design as for other creative activities, divisions are intended to indicate trends rather than create barriers.

Design programmes or programmed designers?

The designer's role in analysing and cohering a range of times that have been probably designed without reference to each other, is one of the most important he has to play. There are many examples, in identity programmes, stationery systems and publications, and product design, where a complex mass of unrelated items can be made more understandable or easier to produce, and given a much stronger identity.

The designer is often faced with projects in which the number of tasks that have to be performed is so large that it is not possible for an individual to undertake them, and systems and procedures have to be evolved in order to achieve implementation. This has a profound effect on the design solution which is inevitably constrained by the need to be capable of explanation to, and interpretation by, other designers. It cannot be an intuitive solution or even one that requires a continuously high degree of intuitive input, even though it may have been based on an intuitive idea. It is in fact not a design but a design programme; and its prime purpose is to programme other designers.

Designers and others deplore the rationalisation and reduction of choice, which is an inevitable part of this process. Balanced against this are the great material gains available from simplified and mass produced products and services. For example, the reduction, this decade, in the numbers of different marques of automobile is indeed a restriction in choice. However it can be argued that it rightly relegates the car from its symbolic importance to a practical piece of equipment and frees the designer's creative endeavour for products that are new and important to society.

It is in the large design projects that most is at stake, both financially and environmentally. The work requires a

84

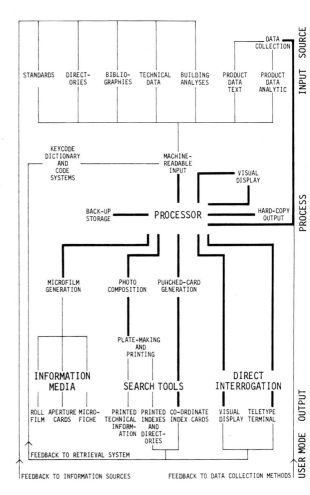

specific set of skills, for which many designers are not trained. They combine intuition and random thinking, with logic and numeracy.

Furthermore, the process is in itself a serial one. For design work on systems, leads on to the examination of systems themselves, and how they are best designed and communicated. Design systems or programmes can be applied to nearly everything. Here we are only concerned with graphic communication systems, which themselves can vary in form, from motorway signs to telephone directories.

It is important to realise that for work of this kind, the programme or information bank is always more important than the way it is made manifest. *Geoffrey Hutton* (of *Hutton & Rostron,* who are primarily involved in such systems) has prepared the diagram shown here which demonstrates how information can be held in electronic form and can be produced either on a visual display unit, as microfilm or as a printed page. Thus the designer's work has been not with the end reproduction but with the process itself.

This idea, when first mooted, was a shock to many typographic designers who pride themselves on a fundamental and logical approach, but whose involvement has only been with the end results in the printed form. It requires the designer to make an imaginative leap back towards an understanding of the information itself, and the systems by which it is coded and classified. A parallel emphasis is apparent in many manufacturing processes where the emphasis on process control is a major determinant in the nature of the product.

As the rate of technical progress increases and economics require further standardisation and rationalisation, "design system" decisions become increasingly important. What *Marshall McLuhan* calls "the information explosion" means that there is now, and will increasingly be, so much information that new ways will be needed to process it, and new low unit cost techniques developed for disseminating it. "Word processing" is the current jargon for tape controlled equipment that can record and store original "keyed in" information and permit subsequent amendment and correction. These systems can be linked through computers to photosetting machines programmed with alternative designs; typefaces, typesizes, margins and line lengths. The name

for these programmes is "firmware", between software and hardware. They mean that at the source of the information, a series of prepared designs can be tried and discarded, and the eventual design implemented, all under the control of the editor. The design therefore is not for one particular report or document but is a mechanical system or process, repeatable for new information, with built in control and feedback devices.

Herein, of course, lies a danger, for all process control has the incestuous quality which lies at the heart of much obsessional activity. Most of the computer jokes of the last decade were an expression of a very real fear of the results of this kind of obsession. In the last resort, a product which is determined by process control is both inappropriate and immoral. The end after all never justifies the means. Products, whether automobiles or information manuals should have as their prime design criteria, the needs of the user.

Perhaps the involvement of the creative designer newly arrived in the systems field will provide the guardianship of the end product, which is, after all, the declared objective of the manufacturing process. It is the designer who is best capable of making the intuitive response to consumer need, and can provide the necessary feedback into the system. Design programmes are with us for the foreseeable future, but let us therefore guard against too much programming of the designer.

Colin Forbes

85

The "pointing index finger" was designed both as a symbol for *Barbour Index* and as a means of identifying cross-referenced sections within the *Compendium*. The *Rockwell* alphabet was re-drawn and prepared specifically for the *Linotron* phototypesetting machine, including refinement such as fractions and foreign accents.

Aa
Aa

E8 02 Q224 (521)n6
CEMB•ISBO•ISSO•MUNO•PITH

Pipekor

TUBES AND PIPES

The sewer and drain system for below ground installation complies with SABS 791·1970☐. It provides a full range of fittings for installation underground in sewers and drains and is made from unplasticised polyvinyl chloride (upvc). The pipes are unaffected by normal climatic variations and have a life expectancy of 50 years. Aldehydes, ketones, ethers, esters and aromatic and chlorinated hydrocarbons are harmful to the pipes and should be avoided. In the event of a blockage, normal cleaning methods should be used.

Size and weight

110mm outer diameter

	External diameter (mm)	internal diameter (mm)	thickness of wall (mm)
Class 51	110	105.4	2.3
Class 34	110	103	3.5

160mm outer diameter

	external diameter (mm)	internal diameter (mm)	thickness of wall (mm)
Class 51	160	153.2	3.4
Class 34	160	150.6	4.7

Piping to SABS 791☐ also available in 200mm, 250mm, 315mm and 400mm

Weight

	110mm	160mm
Class 51	2.28kg	2.52kg
Class 34	1.576kg	3536kg

Appearance
Internal and external finishes very smooth. Pipes available in white only

Temperature range
Product may be used in temperatures from 0°C to 60°C

Sitework
Pipe sections joined by solvent weld or expansion joint of rubber seal

Price
?

CA/SMA/CH/

E8 9 Q224 (51)
BUTA•FERM•FUBR•PITH

Pipekor: Terraflo

TUBES AND PIPES

This pitch fibre piping for sewers and drains, land drainage, or electric conduit application, conforms to SABS 921·1968☐ Bends, junctions, inspection eyes and other fittings necessary for the installation of a complete system are available. The pipes may be damaged by contact with aromatic hydrocarbon (petrol). Prolonged exposure to the sun is also to be avoided as it will cause discoloration and weakening of the pipes. However, pipes and fittings are unaffected by normal climatic variations and the system is expected to last indefinitely.

Size
The standard pipe length is 3m, with inner diameter of 100mm or 150mm

Information design: Systems

The *Barbour Compendium* is the first UK annual directory of building products. It lists some 4,500 manufacturers and 17,000 trade names, with 500 pages of categorised products, and performance and dimensional information, to allow specifiers to make preliminary selections. *Barbour Index* publish a two-language South African edition, called *Specifile*

Compendium and a Canadian edition called *Southam Compendium.*

These product data pages are occupied by "sponsored" products. One index gives details of every supplier active in the relevant market, and another lists every product type. All three sections are cross-indexed.

The problem of gathering and disseminating a complex body of information is essentially mathematical. So is the solution, a computer programme which will digest and dissect information from suppliers, categorise it, cross-index it and, with a small amount of literate assistance from humans, generate a "drive tape" which, by numerical control of suitable

equipment, will automatically photoset all text and headings. The result is a continuous phototypeset print-out of text, set in position with tabulated matter. This is made up by the printer with the combined page headings/folios and illustrations according to a page grid without any specification other than the computer programme. The same programme is used

87

in subsequent editions with further changes and additions.

Because the information will be rendered in book form, the computer system also executes graphic decisions – type size and weight, the width of setting, fitting of different languages into equal columns.

"Unjustified" typesetting allows blocks of information, built up in uneven fragments, to appear "uniform". By altering the "weight" of the typeface, headings and sub-headings are made clear in one type. All these considerations involved the designers in the planning of a computer programme. Not something they normally get close to.

A grid is necessary so that the printer can assemble type and illustrations accurately and consistently on some 500 pages. It also enables the editors to assess the amount of text which can be accommodated.

Two page grids were developed, one for product entries and one for the cross-referenced index and directory pages. The basis for the product entries is three columns for the A4 English edition, and four columns for the wider "extended A4" dual language editions, maintaining a standard full two-column width for colour illustrations. The index pages are similarly based on five columns for A4 and six for the

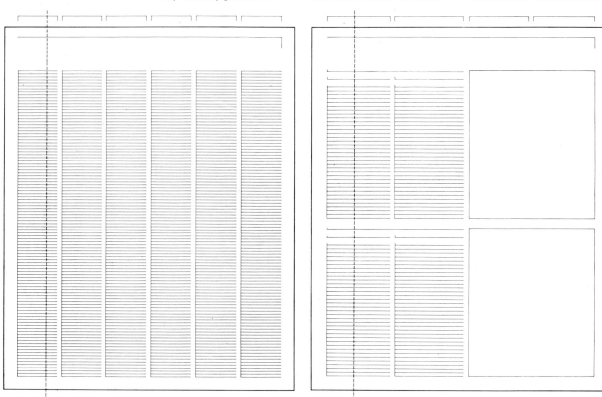

Information design: Systems

larger version. The column width was determined by the optimum line length and type size for this type of information.

To the browser, the functionally large size of running page headings with their sub classifications, simplifies and shortens the information search.

The product pages are set out according to a rigid format so that the Compendium offers comparable product data.

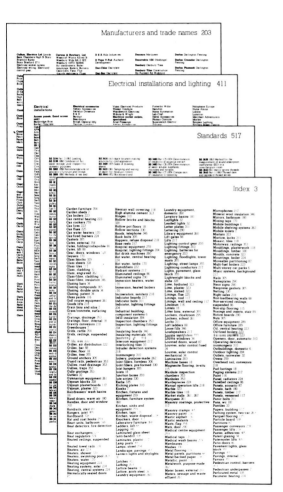

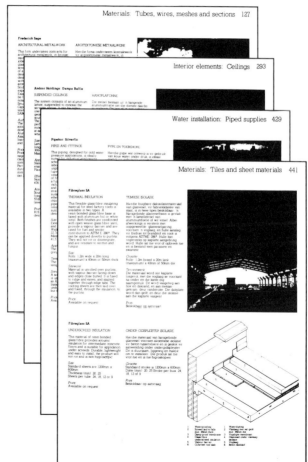

89

Kodak

The *Kodak* corporate programme included the design of the overall system of company print, and its application to stationery, forms, documents and a book of rules called the *Stationery Design Guide*.

A series of publications on corporate style were also produced to ensure correct use and handling of all printed items; for example this *Office Guide to Typing*. A carefully designed letterhead can be ruined by a typist's bad layout.

The corporate design policy for *Kodak's* international operations is of course determined by the parent company in Rochester, New York. However, the UK company has a permanent corporate design committee, with the power to authorise design policy within certain international limitations.

When the company decided to make changes in their stationery it was decided to rationalise the entire range of stationery and printed matter. *Kodak* were at one time producing some 10,000 separate items of printed paper.

This quantity was reduced to less than a third.

The two documents on this page illustrate a before and after treatment, and the miscellaneous collection opposite shows the application of the new style.

Each item had to fulfill a different function. It was essential to avoid a rigid set of layout rules, yet at the same time it was necessary to maintain a cohesive appearance. In fact to create a housestyle and not a strait-jacket.

Office guide: typing

APPLICATION FOR AN ACCOUNT WITH KODAK LIMITED

Application for an account Photographic dealer

Information design: Systems

The *Stationery Design Guide* included all the essential technical information necessary to maintain the corporate style.

This information included sections on the application of the logotype, typefaces, paper, layout, rules for typesetting, proof correction symbols and a glossary of printing terms.

In addition each section had illustrated examples, and proofs of the major pieces of stationery and documentation, with measurements and print instructions surprinted.

The purpose behind producing the *Stationery Design Guide* was not only to establish the style and layout, but also to enable future adaptations to be made by

Kodak staff, not necessarily trained in typography and layout. The guide even indicates how staff can decide whether a newly proposed item of stationery is in fact needed.

The stationery system and the applied designs received an unexpected accolade when *Kodak* in America introduced a new trade mark; and the

transition was accomplished with consummate ease.

The company letterhead won first prize in the *British Stationery Council Awards*.

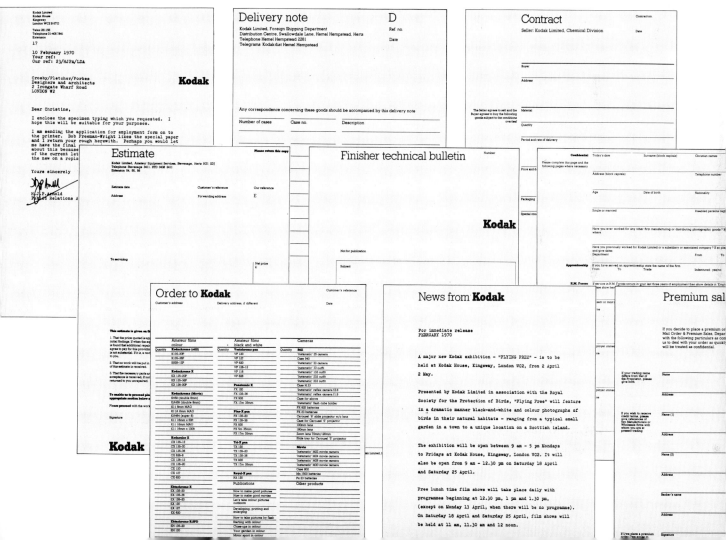

The book *A Sign Systems Manual*, published by *Studio Vista*, was based on the method of implementing signage on the *QE2* liner.

Many organisations, hospitals for example, often design their own signs, and this do-it-yourself publication explained and demonstrated how a complex system could be designed, assembled and applied, even by someone lacking typographic experience or professional design training.

Complex sign systems demand planning and their implementation is as important in achieving clarity as the graphics themselves. A misplaced sign will actually have an effect that is precisely opposite to its intention. Similarly it is the designer's business to ensure that signs are easy to maintain or replace.

Without organisational and administrative structures, the design will inevitably fall short of expectation.

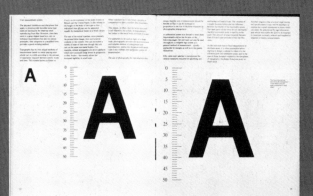

Information design: Systems

A selection of pages from this manual show the process and sequential staging of the design, construction and display of a sign system. They demonstrate how the instructions are illustrated pictorially. The complete sequence is best indicated by reproducing the listing on the contents page.

Type alphabets:
Terminology
Letter styles
Letterforms
Letter proportions

Sign alphabets:
Display and sign letters
Airport letters
Airport alphabets

Measurement:
Unit measurement system
Letter, word and line spacing
Margin spacing

Scale:
Panel sizes
Letter sizes
Message sizes

Layout:
The arrow

Typographic layout
Panel layout
Panel combinations
Symbols

Organisation:
Sign classification
Colour coding
Sign locations and fixings

Production:
Unit spacing chart
Specification, reproduction
Sign schedules
Type style rules

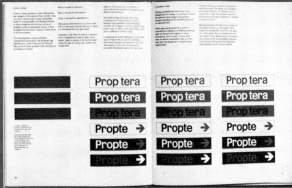

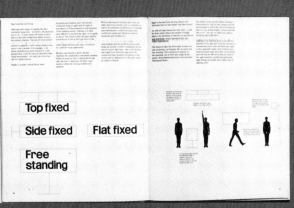

94

24 Ore is the Italian equivalent of the *Financial Times*. The new publisher inherited a forbidding and pedantic visual style. His brief was explicit, he wished to improve the graphic presentation to emphasise a new editorial policy. The problem was twofold, the design of a graphic style, and the need to explain this through a design system in the form of a manual.

The design of a newspaper is a difficult undertaking. Compromise on the niceties of typography is inevitable, control of layout minimal and perfection unobtainable. Practically therefore, the graphic style had to be forceful and distinctive to be visible, as well as be easy to achieve despite the pressures of a daily production schedule.

The existing title piece arose from an amalgamation of two daily journals, *Il Sole* (the sun) and *24 Ore* (24 hours). It was a cumbersome logotype and a staged programme was implemented to convert the design emphasis to *24 Ore*. These designs illustrate two of the steps, the original form and the final proposal.

comparison between a front
age in the old format of the
ewspaper and one in the new
yle, made the point in our
resentation that a
rpographic discipline will
reate a positive personality.
he reality under the
mitations of production
onditions is another matter,
evertheless in terms of
ewspapers the improvement
as considerable.

The manual comprised
modular permutations for all
the major design ingredients.
Each typographic element
was thus interrelated to ease
the assembly and layout in a
situation of constantly
changing editorial needs. The
cake, so to speak, might vary
in taste according to the cook
and the mix of ingredients, but
the appearance was always
substantially the same.

These illustrations show six
pages from the 48 page
design manual: the basic nine
column grid system with
variations on that theme, a set
of instructions relating text
columns to bold headings,
subheadings and so on. The
manual demonstrated
virtually all the basic
typographic elements
individually, and in various
combinations.

The grid of nine columns had
the advantage of providing a
framework which readily
allowed for subdividing into
six and three columns as
indicated by the diagram.
These widths were in turn
keyed to sizes of type,
headings and photographs,
and provided a similar
modular structure to which all
the design elements could be
related.

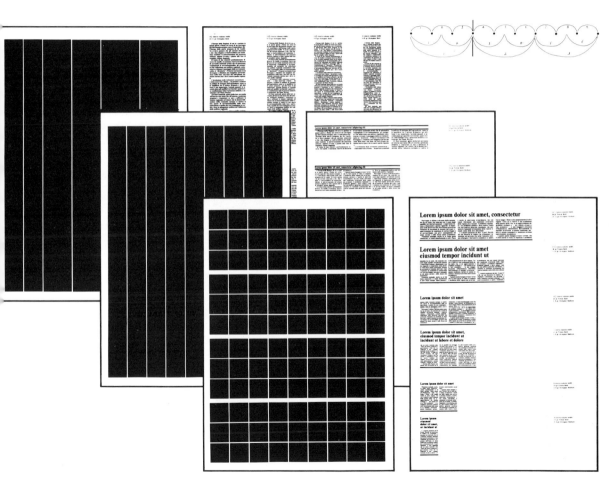

95

Bill Board and others

Bill Board was a fellow art student in London during the early fifties who aspired to be a "poster artist", and along with the rest of us, hoped that *London Transport* would accept his class project designs and he would thereby acquire instant fame. After many rejections he became disillusioned – changed his name to *Marcus Cornelius* and disappeared. Maybe he was right, because by the sixties the consumer society had arrived and the increasing sophistication of marketing and advertising techniques put paid to the "poster artist".

The earliest printed public notice is attributed to *William Caxton* in 1477 and carried the byeline *"Supplico stet cedula"*, which was translated by an eighteenth century hand as "Pray, do not pull down the advertisement". However it was not until the early nineteenth century that the technological advances of the invention of lithography by *Senefelder,* machine made paper and the high speed press, extended the creative and commercial potential of the flysheet beyond the verbal message into the colourful world of pictorial imagery.

At the same time artists and designers were exploring new techniques, flouting established conventions and seeking new media and styles. Indeed the tenets of one of these movements, *"art nouveau",* was the removal of the distinction between the fine and applied arts, and the most visible and immediately successful accomplishment of this purpose was the poster.

At last art was brought out of the studio into the street, and a French art critic was to declare that he found a thousand times more talent in a poster by *Cheret* than on the walls of the *Paris Salon.* At the same time the medium was given an ideological impetus by the socialist movement. *William Morris* stated "I don't want art for a few, any more than education for a few, or freedom for a few", and the

American *Louis Rhead,* who was attempting to communicate his notions of the ethical function of the arts in society through his poster art, was even moved to deliver a lecture in the 1890's on *The Moral Aspect of the Poster.* Anyone with even a modest interest has heard of those first painters who brought art via graphics into the popular domain, *Cheret, Toulouse-Lautrec,* the *Beggarstaff Brothers, Beardsley* and *Mucha.*

Although figurative art entered this new communicative medium with a panache borne out of the tradition of illustrative and narrative painting, the emerging abstract painters were less successful in doing so. In 1919 *Malevitch* designed a poster consisting of a collection of abstract shapes titled "What have you done for the Front" and although a dynamic design, it was undoubtedly ineffective as propaganda. More appropriately his disciple *El Lissitzky,* the constructivist painter, produced the famous "Beat the whites with the red wedge", another civil war poster. Indeed this was such a precise graphic interpretation of the slogan with a red triangle spearing into a white circle that he must have also written the copy

The realisation that the use of pure abstract form and colour was not enough to get a message across to an undiscerning audience, led to increasing use of photo montage and recognisable graphic images, and instead of the painter occasionally turning his hand to this new commercial enterprise there soon appeared the first professional "poster artists".

In truth they were also concerned with illustration and the other paraphernalia of the designer's craft but the title, like that of "graphic designer" today, placed them above the dross associated with the label "commercial artist". In America *Edward Penfield, Will Bradley, Louis Rhead* and *Maxfield Parrish* produced posters for the emerging ational magazines, in England *Dudley Hardy* helped popularise *Gilbert and Sullivan* at the *Savoy Theatre, John lassall* promoted *Skegness* and *Coleman's* mustard, and n the continent *Hohlwein, Cappiello, Metlicoviz, Dudovich* and a host of others produced posters which re now avidly sought by collectors.

his new cultural involvement with mass communication ed to a fusion of ideas between fine and commercial art, nd brought new energies and vigour to both. In the 930's *Cassandre* communicated through cubist echniques and designed his famous poster the *Etoile du Nord,* and others for *Dubonnet* and the *Normandie. Herbert Matter* and *Herbert Bayer* combined cut out photographs and bold Swiss typefaces in *Bauhaus* style, nd *McKnight Kauffer* converted the landscapes passed ry *London Transport* into elegant but recognisable bstractions, well tailored to the mood of the modern urties. Conversely, in painting, the simple techniques ssential to instant and mass communication are reflected n the work of *Delaunay, Léger, Matisse* and *Picasso,* all of vhom also designed memorable posters, and eventually roduced the total poster paintings of *Stuart Davis, Andy Warhol* and *Tom Wesselman.*

Dwing less to painting than lampooning, visual humour nd wit can always transcend the barriers of aesthetics. n England the pungent social caricatures and visual bservations of *Hogarth* and *Rowlandson* were, in their vay, the forerunners of the famous *Guinness* posters of ue thirties and forties. These were the unlikely joint roduct of the thriller writer *Dorothy L Sayers* and *John Gilroy,* doyen of *The Society of British Portrait Painters,* vhose own portrait, by the way, regularly appeared in ue form of the ubiquitous zoo keeper. The stature and ersonal vision of *Savignac* and *André Francois* brought umour to France, and *Herbert Leupin* to Switzerland. Vhile in America, land of the ethnic joke and wisecrack, ue photographic posters for *Levy's Bread* and *Volkswagen* will undoubtedly be milestones for a future istorian of visual humour.

he enlarged and abridged advertisement that occupies oday's hoardings is usually a visual echo of the press ampaign and television commercial. Although at first ight it seems to have little in common with a poster by a ugene Grasset or even a *Peter Max,* the truth is that all re part and parcel of the art tradition. The visual realism, ue unlikely proportions, the juxtapositions of improbable

images – all are the dreamland props of commercial surrealism, a surrogate reality. A bottle of whisky twenty feet high, an egg as big as a house, a glass seemingly containing enough beer to satisfy a docker for a year.

The reasons for the demise of the poster as a popular artform in western society are well expressed by that eminent designer and creator of some of the most innovative posters of our decade, *Milton Glaser.* He has written, "Because the communication of a specific body of information to a mass audience is central to the poster's intention, its capacity to be completely innovative in terms of its audience's perception is limited. The new, by definition, is never really understood". There are however always a few who can analyse and resolve visual problems without compromise to idea or ability. The occasional poster work of our immediate peers such as *Paul Rand, Pintori, Müller-Brockman* and *Saul Bass,* clearly communicate concepts without recourse to stereotyped imagery.

The function of the poster (as opposed to enlarged advertisement) is not however dead, and as an inexpensive means of communicating ideas it has achieved a new vigour in the hands of committed groups. The crude but colourful sheets published in *The Art of Revolution* provide a welcome vigorous visual language; the blunt aggressive images produced by the rebellious students of the *Ecole des Beaux Arts* in Paris, a reminder that economic solutions can produce extremely effective results. The psychedelic announcements for *Fillmore* and *Avalon* in San Francisco and the anarchistic flysheets of the London pop scene in the sixties, outflanked our jaded preconceptions. All put to shame the disproportionate number of bland and boring hoardings advertising commercial products.

The poster, an immediate message and distillation of form and idea, has always been an indicator of culture – images of its era. Often, in addition to its intended purpose, it tells us something of the social, political, and aesthetic climate. The poster can for example determine the popular image of an individual for posterity. *Alfred Leete's* famous illustration of *Lord Kitchener* and his accusatory finger in "Your country needs YOU", gave *Lloyd George* the opportunity for one of his famous quips: "Kitchener", he observed "is a great poster".

Alan Fletcher

Information design: Posters

Often the poster is only one element of a campaign, and although done some years ago, this do-it-yourself bus side for *Pirelli* slippers still seems to evoke amusement.

Shops were provided with slotted cards so that in this case the dogs did the work. *Bob Gill* thought of the idea and drew the dogs.

As one of the elements of an advertising campaign announcing reduced fares for *Pan Am*, the design of the poster speaks for itself.

Although the idea seemed simple enough to execute, we found after much trial and error that the letters could not merely be scaled down from a type, but needed to be hand-drawn to cope with problems caused by overlapping faces and shadows.

To accompany the poster display, a multifold plexiglass dispenser was designed to hold cards bearing details of flights and prices.

99

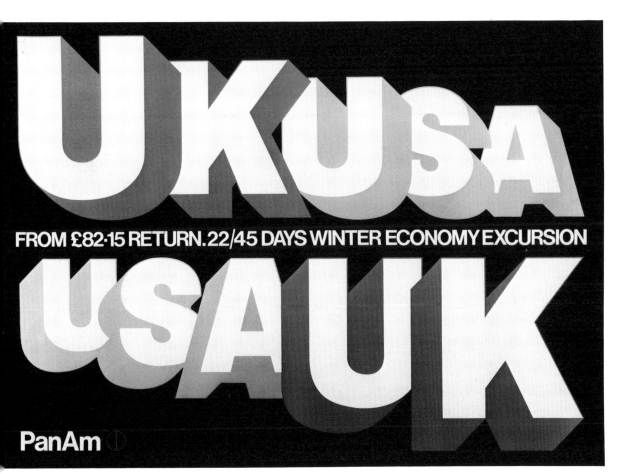

Letters, alphabets and typefaces have an intrinsic appeal for designers, and typographic games have been played since the invention of the ideogram. These posters show a few of the ploys.

BANG, designed in very early days for the *Committee for Nuclear Disarmament* of *Ban the Bomb* fame.

Colour can often express a concept more immediately than a word, the two can be doubly effective: printed in vivid red and green, *BANG* made an optical explosion.

A minimal change to the wording on a petition against museum charges, and the substitution of famous signatures made a poster. This kind of exercise should never be seen to be extravagant! In anticipation of further irritating correspondence, the illegible signature is *Isambard Kingdom Brunel.*

100

We, the undersigned, deplore and oppose the Government's intention to introduce admission charges to national museums and galleries

Write in protest to your MP
and send for the petition forms to
Campaign Against Museum Admission Charges
221 Camden High Street
London NW1 7BU

In most showbiz posters, sizes and orders of names are regulated by contractual agreements. In a moment of frustration, a good shake of the artwork injected the poster with some visual interest, and outflanked the stultified layout imposed by legal strictures.

By applying stars bought from the stationer's, to Helvetica, a new alphabet was created in keeping with the setting of the musical, a fire cracker factory.

The notion for the poster on *British Painting '74* was to redraw conventional letter forms and take them to the boundaries of illegibility; to convert them into abstract symbols, to interpret typography as painting. It was not considered to be disadvantageous that the title was not readable, as it was in the spirit of the exhibition.

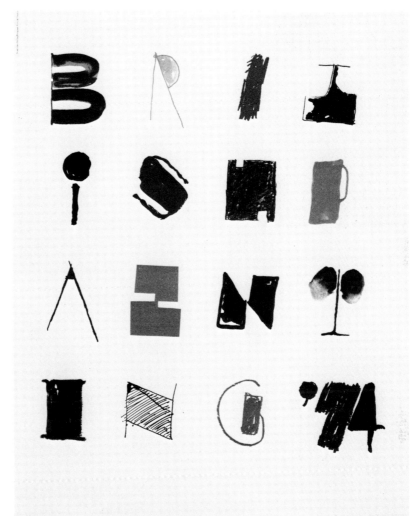

British Painting '74 Hayward Gallery
Arts Council of Great Britain 26 September to 17 November 1974
Monday to Friday 10 to 8/Saturdays 10 to 6/Sundays 12 to 6
Admission 30p/Children, students and pensioners 15p
10p all day Monday and between 6 to 8 Tuesdays to Fridays

101

The technique, style, or character of lettering can be transposed from one context to another to heighten the typographic associations.

Location of this Hampstead art show provided a clue for a pictorial image. A map rendered on a canvas in the painters' vernacular conveyed two levels of information, what it was and where it would be.

This lettering was cut in slate by *Harry Meadows*. Despite reservations about cost, it came to less than a typesetting charge. The exhibition covered a range of crafts, and the image interpreted this spectrum from rugged to delicate, by the contrast of two objects. The image, photographed by *Enzo Ragazzini*, provided a graphic theme for the exhibition, catalogues and invitations.

102

THE KINGS HEAD THEATRE CLUB
THE OTHER SIDE OF THE SWAMP
BY ROYCE RYTON · DIRECTED BY
JOAN KEMP-WELCH · WITH
ROYCE RYTON · PAUL JERRICHO
OPENS 30 MARCH · MONDAY-SATURDAY 8PM · DINNER OPTIONAL 7PM
KINGS HEAD THEATRE CLUB 115 UPPER STREET ISLINGTON N1 · TELEPHONE 226 1916

A mix, or juxtaposition of unrelated imagery can provoke our visual responses through seemingly irrational combinations. A combination of two unrelated images often creates a third, which carries other associations.

This poster for a play revolving around the bickering to two homosexuals, was instantly portrayed by an ink blot, or in other words a *Rorschach* test!

A visual play on the biblical description of *Joseph's* coloured coat, by substitution of contemporary sartorial graphics, enabled the poster and record sleeve, to reflect the youthful spirit of this rock music show.

Information design: Posters

Although born of more humble traditions than painting, the poster can also provide an aesthetic keynote on the wall, as well as inform or proclaim.

26 alphabet posters, using a six colour palette, were designed to promote new typefaces introduced by *Conways' Photosetting*. The idea stemmed from the brief for a promotion to be issued every two weeks over a year. By trimming off the commercial message one could make initials or spell words, and then hang them on the wall.

A chain of dreary *Lyons* teashops needed an immediate, inexpensive decorative idea to cheer up the interiors. A series of brightly coloured typographic posters *(opposite page)* on an *à la carte* theme were able to brighten the environment, stimulate the appetite, and provide some culinary suggestions.

Z is for Zephyr from Conways' Photosetting Telephone 01-402 6141

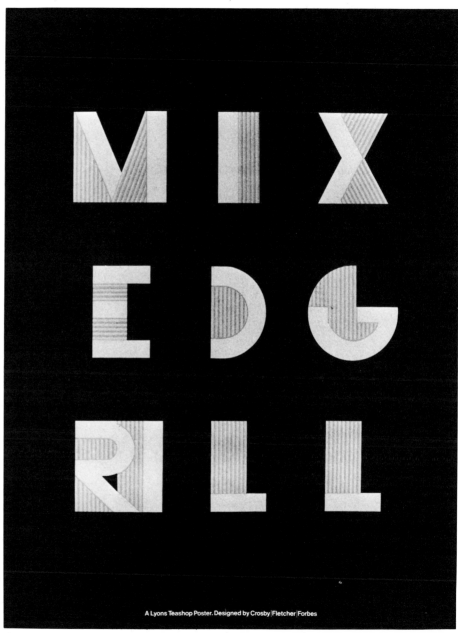

A Lyons Teashop Poster. Designed by Crosby|Fletcher|Forbes

Information design: Posters

Produced for *Conways' Photosetting* company this poster was designed to remind the art departments of advertising agencies that the client had some new typefaces. The theory is held that typefaces need to be seen in use in order to obtain a response.

These jokes, although not original, were neatly adapted by *David Bernstein* to some well known London advertising agencies. The concept of a laugh at the potential customer's expense, although undertaken with some trepidation by the client, proved highly effective and he was inundated by counter jokes. These provided free copywriting for a subsequent poster.

Remember... the consumer isn't a moron— she's David Ogilvy's wife.

"Tell me," said the prospective client "Is this a Jewish organisation?" French looked at Gold. Gold looked at Abbott. Abbott looked back at Gold, shrugged his shoulders and said, "Not necessarily."

"Do you think Ronnie Kirkwood is his real name?"

"Whose real name?".

Client: "What's the time?"
Lintas: "What time would you like it to be sir?"
Client: "What's the time?"
Saatchi & Saatchi: "Are you buying or selling?"

If all the secretaries
at J. Walter Thompson
were laid end to end –
I wouldn't be surprised!

Colman Prentis & Varley installed
a computer to write copy.
They programmed the strategy.
A minute later the card fell into the
tray at the other end.
It read,
"I am leaving to start my own agency."

Wrapping it all up

Packaging is defined in the *Concise Oxford Dictionary* as "the making of a wrapper or container for goods" and it is in this narrow context that we examine its development as opposed to the broader context that brings it within the compass of product design. After all it could be argued that a sewing machine or a cigarette lighter is packaging, the outer casing being a wrapper to the real product, the mechanism. And what is an astronaut's suit if not protective wrapping?

Originally, packaging was born out of the need to protect and transport food, water, belongings and weapons. Traditionally it was executed by the skilled craftsmen in the tribe and reflected the way of life of their people; their harmonious existence with nature, their reverence for everything they experienced, their sense of unity with all things animate and inanimate. And so the skilled among them observed nature's packaging; eggs, seeds, fruits and woven forms such as spiders' webs. They used the same natural materials to form protective structures, bridges, boats, nets, baskets, bowls and jugs, and in so doing went beyond the simple demands of functionalism by expending high artistic skill and love on the thing itself. Witness traditional Japanese packaging, one of the many traditional craft skills now giving way to modern machine methods. The book *How to wrap five eggs* by *Hideyuki Oka* is an outstanding collection of the most ingenious, beautiful and simple examples of that dying tradition.

As technologies changed we observe a succession of new materials and alternative forms. From wood, clay and straw, to tin, copper, bronze, glass and iron, to paper and board and finally on to the modern synthetic materials. So packaging entered the mass production era and the staple foods such as flour, sugar and oil, which in former times had been transported to stores in sacks or barrels, could now be sold to the individual in small quantities in paper bags or flasks.

The invention of the hand-made paper bag in England in the mid-nineteenth century was a great leap forward for space saving containers. But one of the most important contributions to the consumer society was a design by a Scotsman in 1879. It was a machine that could cut and fold card to any size, producing boxes that folded flat when not in use. Mass-produced containers could be tailor-made for goods which could be packaged at manufacturing source and, what is more, branded. As an American businessman remarked, "no boxes, no brand names, no business".

The new mobility brought about by the motor car, the spread of urban populations into the suburbs and the consequent advent of the supermarket was to have a profound effect on the nature of packaging. From simply a means of containing goods that might otherwise spill or break, there was now a requirement, not only to explain content and use, but also to persuade a purchaser to buy. Ultimately the package became the promise and the promise was sought more than the product.

The sophisticated development of advertising techniques to aid sales of goods and the resultant creation of dreams to which the consumer society aspires, has influenced our concept of ourselves, the houses we live in, the clothes we wear, the products we buy and the packaging we choose.

Crammed tightly together on supermarket shelves, packages vie with one another for attention. A new science, consumer research, has been mobilised to ensure successful sales of the product. It sets out to establish the gap in the market and the sector of the public which is to be courted; it tests consumer attitudes towards the product and the images that will be used to communicate that product. A total concept is thereby created and the package, designed to express this concept, is in turn tested for acceptability, readability, desirability and above all, shelf impact.

The inevitable result has been that much of today's mainstream packaging has become slick propaganda, subject to ever-increasing consumer research that threatens to produce ever-increasing mediocrity. Obviously research has a very real and important role to play but if not kept in perspective, its committee-like approach will engulf us in banality. If we wish to establish standards for packaging that will make a worthwhile contribution to the quality of our lives we must not let ourselves be bound by the taste of the lowest common denominator. In the final analysis, there is no substitute for the intuitive inventiveness of the individual.

A story; some years ago, *Salvador Dali* was approached to design a pack for a new perfume for one of the largest American cosmetic companies. *Dali* agreed to accept the commission on the condition that he was given a completely free hand. A nervous board accepted the inevitable consequences of dealing with *Dali*.

Months later, the day for the planned presentation and lunch reception arrived. A reception committee met *Dali* at the airport and he was driven to the hotel. On the way he was pressed on the subject of his design but would give nothing away and it was noticed as they entered the reception hall that *Dali* was not carrying anything that could conceivably represent his design presentation. The tension mounted as *Dali* took his place at the top table. Before he could sit down the photographers surged forward and flashlights popped at a rapid rate. When the activity had ceased *Salvador* stretched out his hand to the nearest photographer and asked for the flash bulb that had just gone off. With all eyes on him *Dali* took the bulb and tapped it sharply down onto the table flattening the hot bulbous end so that it sat upright without toppling.

Ladies and gentlemen", he shouted into the microphones, I give to the world a new perfume – *Electric*".

There is no doubt that in many areas of packaging design the highest standards of creativity have been maintained and a succession of innovations have made our lives a great deal more convenient. We take for granted the toothpaste tube, canned goods, vacuum packed foods, flip-top cigarette boxes, ring-pull cans, screw-on bottle tops, plastic bottles, bubble packs, shrink wraps, expanded polystyrene packing and a host of technical developments such as blow and injection moulding, vacuum forming, extruding and more recently the coextrusion of multimaterials all of which have opened up new possibilities in packaging.

However, the direction that packaging has been taking has also created an increasingly difficult disposal problem. The 1976 statistics are alarming; 6,500 million tons of glass, 500 million tons of tin cans, 1000 million tons of disposable cups and 7,300 million tons of paper bags are thrown away each year in Britain. Of all household waste in the United Kingdom, of which 60% is caused by packaging, only 10% is processed, incinerated or composted, whilst the remaining 90% is simply deposited directly onto rubbish tips. The figures for consumption of raw materials and energy in the production of packaging are no less disconcerting; glass packaging uses 80% of the total UK glass production, plastics 43%, aluminium 10% and paper and board 61%.

We live in a throw away age and the extreme view, as described by *Victor Papanek* in his book *Design for the Real World,* is that if we can throw away packaging and products, why not houses, marriages and other personal relationships . . ."so that on a global scale countries, and indeed entire sub-continents are disposable like Kleenex". *Papanek* admits, however, that the concept of obsolescence can be a sound one. It has tremendous potential for example in medicine where disposable syringes, surgical instruments, protective clothing, and linen substitutes have made an invaluable contribution to standards of hygiene. Furthermore there is every reason to believe that the problems of recycling can be solved. As far as packaging is concerned, significant work has already been done on bio-degradable plastics and disposable self-destructive bottles.

There is of course still the belief that packaging is somehow an intrinsically "bad thing". Yet without it we would be at constant risk of disease from unwrapped food; our mobility would be curtailed to an intolerable level as we tried to transport unwrapped goods from store to home; information about those goods, which we have a statutory right to see printed on packaging, would be denied to us; food that is preserved by packaging at present, would rot and waste in a world where insufficient food exists anyway; self service simply would not exist and although some people might see this as a benefit, shopping that now takes minutes, would take hours. In fact the list of wholly practical benefits that packaging brings, is endless.

So the question of dispensing with it simply doesn't arise. What we are left with is the problem of ensuring that our new awareness of its implications is directed towards providing packaging in more socially acceptable and even more beneficial forms.

Mervyn Kurlansky

Information design: Packaging

The competitive nature of packaging means that of all the designer's activities, this is probably the most measurable. Once when we redesigned a range of *Heinz* baked beans, the client pointed out that as over one million cans of baked beans are sold daily, a drop in sales of one per cent through an unfamiliar design could be enormous.

A new brand *Red Fox* had to convey an impression of a traditional established brand of *Bourbon*. The bottle and label were deliberately designed to meet this requirement. Labels evolved through time acquire additional information, win seals of approval, include new legal descriptions and are in a state of gradual alteration. This label was designed to conform to those probabilities.

St Ivel, a brand name in supermarket dairy products, instituted a marketing policy to project traditional country fare to counter the image of impersonal convenience foods. The logotype was inherited with the client. Whenever possible we used well known illustrators to invest designs with the quality associated with early packaging.

Gibson was the brand name for a new classy cigarette to be launched by *Reemtsma.* The clue for a design came from *Charles Dana Gibson,* famous Edwardian illustrator, now remembered for his creation of the *Gibson Girl.* The pack was white, textured like drawing paper, the signature scrawled across the surface with a soft pencil.

Opposite are two ranges of *St Ivel* cheeses. The cheddars were intended to be similar in visual format and were drawn by *John Gorham,* the regional cheeses had more individual personalities, and archive prints were adapted as images. The pictorial concepts allowed for extension into illustrative promotions such as tea towels and table mats.

CHEDDAR CHEESE
New Zealand

St Ivel

CHEDDAR CHEESE
New Zealand

St Ivel

St Ivel

CHESHIRE CHEESE

CHESHIRE CHEESE

St Ivel

St Ivel

CHEDDAR CHEESE Mature Canadian

CHEDDAR CHEESE
Mature Canadian

St Ivel

MELLOW
DERBY
CHEESE

St Ivel

MELLOW
DERBY
CHEESE

St Ivel

CHEDDAR CHEESE

St Ivel

Mild Scottish

CHEDDAR CHEESE

St Ivel

St Ivel

crumbly
Lancashire
cheese

St Ivel

Information design: Packaging

This was the first air freshener product on the Swiss market which uses a simple pump in place of the controversial aerosol gas.

The container is a standard white bottle, the typography printed in "sky" blue, the design in the vernacular of ethical products. *Super Fresh* is solely retailed through chemists.

The retail cost was a genuine marketing problem as the container, though small, held five times as much fluid as comparable aerosol products.

The small size and apparently high price required clear justification and the paper sleeve carried information and explained the value of the product by diagrams and text. The wing-like shape was intended to convey a light airy effect, and visually increase the size of display.

Multiple display, repetitive patterns and continuous images, are a graphic feature in the supermarket. These examples show simple ideas which exploit this potential, but still allow designs to be effective when viewed individually.

Information design: Packaging

A group of cows surrounds each carton of milk, and can form a herd on the supermarket shelf. The waxy card of the container precluded accurate colour registration or delicate drawings, so the illustrator, *Anna Pugh*, produced these charming linocuts.

Unicliffe commissioned the redesign of *Trimetts* slimming biscuits, to counteract declining sales.

All twelve packs had a pictorial presentation of the biscuits shown against different coloured tablecloths and surfaces to identify different flavours. A tape measure points out the slimming advantages and provides a visual relationship in multiple display.

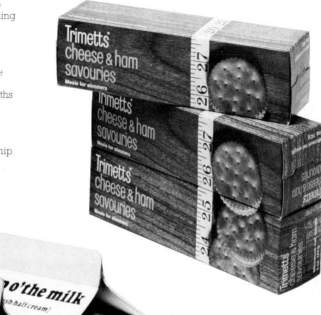

A traditional Italian cake, made by *Motta* in Milan, is consumed in vast quantities at Easter. *Colomba* is the Italian for dove. An important consideration was mass display of boxes, and as there are five different sizes of box, the intention was to conjure up flocks of white doves against the blue background, for shop windows over the festive period.

Information design: Packaging

The pictorial ingredient of packaging can do more than decorate. It can perform a practical function by way of instruction, can evoke associations, can make a product masculine or feminine, cheap or expensive.

These packs for *BP* were the first application of the *Alpha BP* alphabet introduced in the new corporate identity.

Wash and Wax was an impulse purchase product, known in the trade as a

boutique pack, and sold in petrol station retail outlets. Requiring to sell themselves, the packs were without advertising or promotional support, they therefore were printed in full colour to obtain maximum shelf appeal. The design amalgamated both type and photograph.

Paper tissues are paper tissues, but the pack design can infer that they are exclusively for the bathroom, the kitchen or bedroom. The graphic racing device firmly

indicated that they were for automobiles. The explanatory drawings suggested possible usage and also transcended the language barriers.

This anti-freeze gallon can reproduced a bear which had been introduced as a presenter and also appeared on other promotional and advertising materials.

Information design: Packaging

Topsy Turvy was a *blancmange* with a strawberry sauce marketed by *St. Ivel.* The sauce sank to the bottom of the pots, so the name of this pudding was an indication that it had to be turned upside down to be correctly served.

Adapted from "Happy Families", a Victorian card game, *Mrs Topsy Turvy* pictorially demonstrated the complex service instructions. She was drawn by *Arthur Robbins.*

The brief for this range of blended coffees indicated the need for a simple decorative label, which would enable the company to introduce new blends and sizes without recourse to new designs.

Different coffees are easily distinguished by colour coding. They all carry the same illustration which is taken from a nineteenth century steel engraving.

Information design: Packaging

Marketing considerations, sales policies, or more functional limitations often require an informative graphic system rather than an evocative or decorative idea. These two solutions contrast a typographic and pictographic method.

Clear information was the primary requirement of these *Rank Xerox* packs. The form of the bottles dictated the need for an ultra condensed alphabet, which was produced in collaboration with *Armin Hoffman*. The style was therefore established by the design function, rather than by sales appeal.

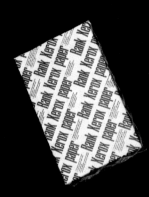

A help-yourself and do-it-yourself curtain rail system manufactured by *Swish*. In contrast to the use of the letters or figures of the *Xerox* alphabet, it was more appropriate to use shapes and colour codes to distinguish the multiplicity of bits and pieces.

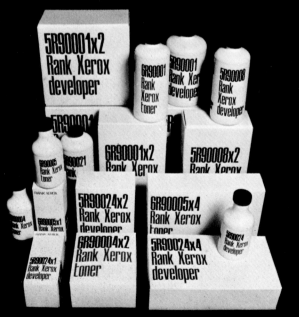

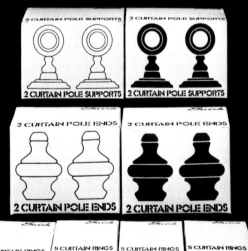

Information design: Packaging

Our cook acting on the daily comments that the studio lunch was excellent decided to leave and set up with a friend. The symbol was designed to be friendly and evoke the flavour of good home cooking. The simple do-it-yourself labelling system not only saved money but allowed for flexibility and created a recognisable style.

Information design: Packaging

These inexpensive cosmetics were designed for *Marks and Spencer* to appeal to a young market, to be sold self service, to be packaged to minimise pilferage, to be effective in display, to be economic in cost. The concept was founded on the notion of creating an abstract painting at the point of sale, a splash of brilliant colour among the sweaters, knickers and socks.

The packs were modular in shape and colour to allow for infinite variations on the counters and for assembly into multipack gifts.

Michèle containers were ready made items, as special forms and shapes are only obtainable if ordered in extremely large quantities. The scheme of applying different colours to lids, containers and to the logotype, managed to disguise the rather pedestrian tubes, bottles and boxes.

118

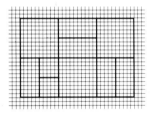

Special counters were made to hold the packs and facilitate purchase and replacement. Evocative illustrations by *Helen Majera* were used for counter placards.

Like many designers' jobs it eventually suffered a decline in verve and quality through the aesthetic modifications implemented by a nervous client.

Powder Eyeshadows · Bold Lash Mascara · Fine Lash Mascara · Cream Tint · Complete Compact Refill · Pearl Lipstick · Complete Compact · Cream Varnish · Cream Eyeshadow · Pearl Varnish · Cream Blush · Cream Lipstick · Powder Eyeshadow

Information design: Packaging

Pack construction techniques, known in the trade as cardboard engineering, can save money, obtain maximum benefit from the materials and provide tactile and visual satisfaction. Whereas buying cosmetics needs reassurance, appeal and the reinforcement of a dream, the purchaser of a simple tool would resent paying for fancy packaging.

The reason for *Stanley* introducing a new packaging scheme, was based on the belief that a better product presentation would produce an increase in sales.

Customers want to see the actual tools. This packaging holds and protects the products in individual packs constructed from corrugated board and held within a printed paper sleeve. These are displayed in a case, made of the same material, which folds up for travelling.

Working in association with the box manufacturer the eventual solution exploited the character of the material, and enabled the packs to be produced without recourse to additional materials such as staples or glue.

Graphics are basic and confined to the salient characteristics offered by the product. Plain colours help distinguish similar tools from each other.

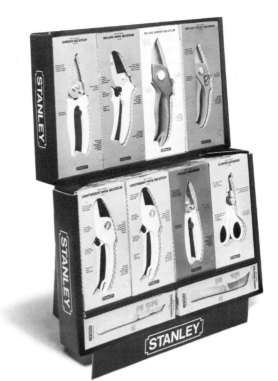

120

These wines, imported by *Cock Russell Spedding,* were required to sell by display on the shelf, there was no budget for advertising. The scheme was based on cheerfully plagiarising old prints, posters and paintings, which illustrate wine. A manipulation of the image produced a label which became a pictorial signal – a tiny poster.

The Bulgarians showed little enthusiasm for the *Boyar* label. The name, chosen by us in ignorance, apparently meant *Bourgeoisie* which with the aristocratic illustration (by way of *Newbould's* menu), was perhaps not altogether appropriate.

For *La Bacanale,* an Italian wine, we reproduced part of a *Titian* painting and named the wine after the title of the picture. The client was so enthusiastic for the label that he felt the wine would not fulfill the expectation, and so substituted a superior French vintage in its place.

Packaging trade descriptions are subject to legal requirements. This not only covers descriptions and ingredients, but also specific pictorial references. For example a picture of a real *château* on a wine label, even if intended solely as decoration, is not permissible unless the wine actually comes from there.

In any event the budget for an extensive range of branded wines retailed by *Marks & Spencer* was extremely modest, and even precluded lettering calligraphy – let alone drawing pictures. Deadlines were tight, and since the range was likely to be continuously changed and expanded, flexibility was of the essence.

We thought this solution for a method of design production rather neat . . . set the text in standard typefaces, and then in artwork stage add the arabesques, swirls and curlicues.

Vin Superieur Rouge

Vin Superieur Rouge

Although this scheme was put on the market it proved a difficult style to sustain as it was subjected to criticism on grounds of legibility by the client who had always followed a policy of plain informative labelling.

The final solution adopted by *Marks & Spencer* was simpler although the basic layout style remained the same. The small type remained constant but the typographic rendering of the description varied according to the quality of wine. Sparkling wines were rendered in italic, chateau wines in classical typefaces, table wines in handwriting and vermouths in gold shadow display letters. This scheme was applied to over one hundred labels and although individually they lack much of the visual charm associated with the traditional wine label, they did project a brand image and a simple visual classification of qualities.

Information design: Packaging

Book jackets can be considered as packaging since, as wrappers, they fulfill the same criteria. Some jackets are one-off solutions, others are individual graphic interpretations of a particular book within a series. One may also be asked to design a format and style for a series.

Do You Sincerely Want to be Rich? This dimensional solution converted the book into a wad of notes which matched the unequivocal directness of the title. For the launch period the book was actually wrapped with the band, but subsequent editions for economic reasons, had the wrapper simulated by printing.

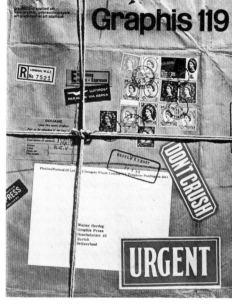

This edition of *Graphis* magazine, a graphic designer's journal, carried an article on our work. The cover was designed around a simple packaging idea. We wrapped the work and sent it to Switzerland with instructions that it be unopened and returned to London. We then photographed the package, and the transparency (in effect the artwork) made the return journey.

The book jackets on the right are for serious academic subjects and the design emphasis is on identifying the series, rather than on promoting the individual titles. Since readers are likely to be perceptive and intelligent, it was felt that the images could be sophisticated visual interpretations of the scholarly subject matter.

Henri Lefebvre
The Sociology of Marx

J.R.Ravetz
Scientific Knowledge
and its
Social Problems

Erving Goffman
Interaction Ritual

Erving Goffman
Encounters

Claude Lévi-Strauss
Structural Anthropology

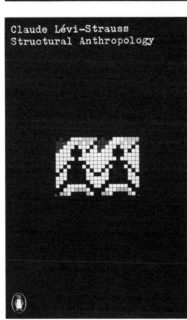

Robert Langbaum
The Poetry of Experience
The Dramatic Monologue
in Modern Literary
Tradition

Information design: Packaging

The designer's preoccupation is to make attractive, meaningful images. Existing imagery can, by subtle change, often produce a pungent visual comment – making the familiar unfamiliar and provoking a second glance.

These images were used for an author who writes lighthearted criminal fiction. The engraving of *Shakespeare* was minimally altered with a wink – the novel being concerned with a literary fraud. The amalgamation of two suits within one card – a graphic interpretation of a dual roguish personality, and the puzzle of linking dots seemed apposite for the unlikely story of a horse which could count.

Two covers from an extensive series issued on business and aspects of management and administration. The solution was deliberately restricted to creating relevant images from the paraphernalia one might find on a businessman's desk.

The trick so as to speak, being to create a pictorial message from the juxtaposition of mundane objects. It's a game we all play in moments of concentration or idleness.

It seemed suitable to illustrate an author's writing of an evocative period, by engravings of the time. Extracted from Edwardian compositions, or montaged using figures from different sources, the engravings were treated as a pictorial pallette.

125

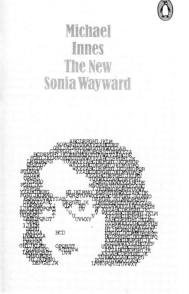

Originally this *Penguin* series was based on illustrative ideas such as the cover on the far left, but apparently the prospective readers of mystery novels are more responsive to photographic realism. The covers were required to be redesigned.

The complexity of this author's plots are impossible to convey in one image, so we decided to make the covers photo-compositions of the clues and let the readers figure it out for themselves.

Design, layout, and typography, like clothes, can reflect the fashion of the period. A famous and very well known publisher of classical sheet music had a quite distinctive and recognisable style, exclusively typographic and distinctly old fashioned. We felt a modern phenomenon such as the *Beatles*, placed in this graphic context was a fitting visual solution for this particular job.

Recreational mathematics are not solely concerned with numbers but also with colours, shapes and forms. The cover for this book of riddles was intended to convey this as well as be reminiscent of the schoolroom and blackboard, an association familiar to the designer who barely mastered long division.

The title of a publication on punctuation provided the same number of spaces as the marks of punctuation on a standard printers type sheet. A typographic combination made the title a design.

XYZ.,:;'"-"!?()*

The vernacular of the traditional wine label is difficult to define, it often has little typographic merit, no discernable style, but nevertheless a wine label looks like a wine label. The label which makes the book jacket for this publication on wines of the world, uses this visual association to identify the contents.

126

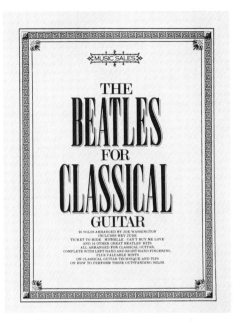

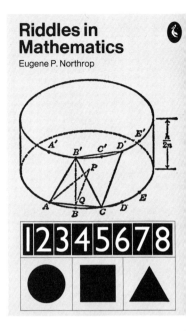

Information design: Packaging

"Letters are signs for sounds" to quote *Eric Gill*, the famous typographic designer. Indeed we are all so familiar with shapes and forms of letters that we can recognise them even when they are redrawn as "signs for pictures."

These compositions for covers of sheet music catalogues issued by *Boosey & Hawkes*, show how by investing the abstract letter with a pictorial device, the message can communicate content more effectively.

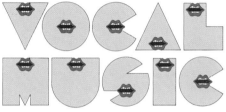

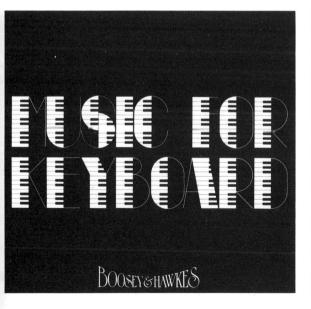

crea

THE ILLUSTRATED
HISTORY OF POP

Brings alive the fascinating period which started in the early 50s and ended in the 60s.
Packed with 'stars-then' photographs.
Tells you all about the stars of the time and the hits that made them famous.

A Music Sales magazine Special

GILBERT
O'SULLIVAN

In Words and Music
Perry
Com

THE
WORLD ATLAS OF WINE

Hugh Johnson

KURT GUGGENHEIM

ALLES IN ALLEM

GUGGENHEIM

Dieser Roman, der vom Aus-
bruch unseres Jahrhunderts
bis zum Ausgang des zweiten
Weltkrieges führt, ist die Biographie einer Stadt, wiedergegeben am
Schicksal des Aaron Reiss. Kein ist es die Auto-
biographie, aber um sein Leben gruppieren sich die
Geschichten und das Geschehen. Aus Erinnerung
Dreams schildert er diese Stadt, die es mit Fünf
Jahren lewohnt und beobachtet. Man in der
mit künstlerischer Leichtigkeit Provinz auf die
Welt hin geöffnet, und alle Entscheidungen der
das Ort Bezogene nehmen auch für das, was dem
all in diesen halben Jahrhunderts geschehen ist.

VERLAG HUBER

Identity Kits: a pictorial survey of visual
signals by Germano Facetti and Alan Fletcher

THE
PENGUIN
WORLD ATLAS

Jobbing graphics

Students leaving art schools usually have very little grounding in the history of their craft, albeit a short history, to sustain them through what will inevitably be a very brutal adjustment between the academic world and the harsh reality of their first job.

The first problem is the practical affair of earning a living and paying rent, so the young designer inevitably needs to accept bread and butter work to earn his living and to build his portfolio.

Although expectations on leaving art school might be focussed on ambitious projects, the design of corporate identities or graphic programmes, the reality is that most of us started by designing letterheads and leaflets on a table at home, or on the floor of our rented rooms. With little help and less money, minimum facilities and lots of hard grind, it nevertheless is the work on which most of us cut our design teeth, acquired experience, gained satisfaction, and on occasions success.

Another problem most students encounter is how to reconcile their concept of aesthetic quality with commercial pressures, and many like myself found that the only guidance lay in looking to the work of those designers who were both successful and innovative. Inhibited by art school principles of "good" and "bad" taste, and without the confidence of knowledge and experience, one desperately clung to whatever one felt was right.

Müller-Brockmann was one of the most influential graphic designers of my early days and like many others I looked to him for inspiration. In his book *The Graphic Artist and his Design Problems* he stressed the functional nature of graphics; that information had to be conveyed clearly and concisely; and that there were certain rules which could

be applied to ensure that information was communicated with maximum effect.

These rules, on inspection, turn out to be a collection of obvious general points which every graphic designer has to master in order to develop a degree of proficiency. Their mastery is not however sufficient to achieve excellence, although many of his disciples believed that simply by closely following his rules they could become just as good. *Müller-Brockmann* also talked of the need for "mental grasp, intuition, and an eye for form and colour", things which cannot be encapsulated by rules or be learnt by rote. They are those magic ingredients which not only put art into craft, but also enable embryo designers to develop their own personalities.

Milton Glaser another graphic "master", instead of stressing the acquisition of basic techniques, concentrates on intuition. "Technical skills", he says, "emerge almost magically as a result of self interest and practice". He advises young graphic designers not to ally themselves with any particular style but rather "to the whole vocabulary of graphic art and of visual phenomena in general". This seems to me to be sound advice.

Obviously the chief function of any graphic design is to convey information, and in consequence, the way it looks must be inseparable from the function it has to perform. A keen awareness of previous and current styles is therefore advantageous, as the point can be made more effectively if the subject is flattered by a style which is both pertinent and attractive.

Fashion is an essential part of style; much maligned by purists it is nevertheless a key to instant response. Difficult to describe, it was eloquently defined by *Coco Chanel,* who once stated that "Fashion is only that which

130

can become unfashionable". Although fashion in graphics can be a useful device, for example to invest a product with a feeling of modernity, it can also render it rapidly out of date. One's sense of timing needs to be accurate.

Even more paradoxically, graphic clichés can also enable a designer to produce really effective and original solutions. By modifying an existing form or cliché, the design can often grab attention more easily than something that looks new or unfamiliar. *Milton Glaser* again: "Clichés are symbols or devices that have lost their power and magic, yet they persist because of some kind of essential truth. Clichés are fundamental sources of information, debase sources waiting to receive new energy". This new energy is provided by wit and invention, and graphics like any language, only communicates if the audience not only understands but also responds to what is being said.

Conversely of course, a style at variance with the product can be disastrous. This was elegantly illustrated in an anecdote related by *Jeremy Bullmore (J. Walter Thompson)*. "Walking down a country lane you see a sign saying 'Fresh Eggs'. A simple enough message, but the fact that it is hand-written on a broken piece of board actually makes the freshness of the eggs more believable, even though you do not consciously acknowledge it. But if you then walk further along the road and see a similarly hand-written sign saying 'Flying lessons' the effect is exactly the opposite."

Graphics need to reflect the nature and purpose of the proposition. Design is not merely a matter of "taste", it is an understanding of the problem. Does it fulfill the function? Will it capture attention? Can it sustain interest? If the solution doesn't incorporate these criteria then it probably doesn't work – it's really as simple as that!

All considerations of style, fashion or taste relate back to this problem of communication, and particularly to selling. It is often the case that a restrained interpretation can be more effective than a brash and aggressive rendering. As any salesman knows, the stronger the proposition or the better the product, then the easier will be the sale. If a product does not have an obvious selling strength then it is necessary to seek out exactly what is special or unique . . . and having found it, to emphasise it!

Appropriate graphic solutions mean popularity and acceptance, while ill-conceived graphics mean anonymity and rejection. In a crowded or competitive market, acceptance or rejection is often a split second decision, there is not time to let something grow on you and whatever the reaction, it is just as likely to be an emotional response as a rational judgement. Although graphic design is not necessarily an art, it is even less a science. In the end there is only one universal test, "Does it work?" and only one universal principle, "Could it have been better?"

John McConnell

Information design: Promotion

The leaflet and brochure, catalogue and Annual Report, the calendar or piece of direct mail are those bread and butter items which often keep the designer in business.

Although perhaps of little consequence in themselves, they flex the designer's imagination and often provide him with the most satisfaction.

The implication of promotion is that it is of little long term value and essentially ephemeral. This may often be the case but not necessarily so, for example many contemporary posters are in museum collections, a few items such as the *Olivetti Labyrinth* are still hung on walls, and the *Nobrium* perspex paperweight has been seen on sale in an antique market.

The secret one hopes, lies in the quality of the design and in the value of an original idea. Such ideas often are mistakenly called, "gimmicks", which more accurately is a term to describe ideas which have little relation to the problem, and therefore no significance.

Olivetti commissioned a limited edition of this labyrinth design as a gift for important personages to commemorate an *Olivetti* exhibition in London. The maze is made doubly difficult by the graphic dimensional rendering of the walls. Thirty centimetres square, the image was reproduced photographically on an aluminium plate.

Pirelli posed a problem to think of a new idea for the ubiquitous car sticker, in this case to promote *Cinturato* tyres. By utilising the vehicle of national identification plates, the scheme was able to be promoted across the world.

The silk scarf and package was adapted from the August page of a calendar printed in fluorescent colours, designed for *Olivetti*. It was used as a business gift for wives of important visitors, and dropped on bathers from a plane flying up and down the Italian Riviera during August. Well, anyway, it makes a good story!

Christmas is open season for promotional opportunities. The Christmas card in the form of a licorace record not only brought a commercial greeting from *A & M Records*, but also provided some Christmas fare. The label was

illustrated, in the genre of the nursery rhyme, by *Tony Meeuwissen*.

De Little of York have been making wood type for a hundred years and are the only company left in England engaged in this craft. They will cut the letters on the original machine and are very particular about the quality of the wood, Canadian Maple for type over twelve lines and French Hornbeam for anything smaller. The *Face Photosetting* company through acquiring the rights to reproduce *De Little* typefaces, also had to purchase a few tons of wooden type.

132

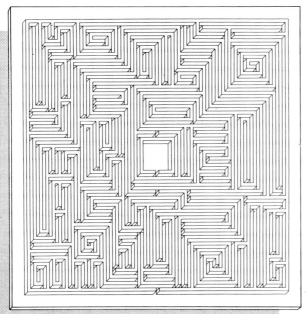

Information design: Promotion

The trade expression, direct mail", conjures up visions of boring and unwanted promotional literature, which if lucky, receives a cursory glance before being thrown away. Such ephemera however, can hopefully be a pleasure to receive.

An *ICI* prestige mailing campaign for plastic reflective foil was aimed at graphic designers. The design solution we proposed was to invite seven designers to interpret a poem on "Reflections", commissioned from the *Poet Laureate*.

These four illustrations were by *Norman Ives, Jean-Michel Folon, Enzo Mari* and *Alan Fletcher*. Designs were mailed monthly in a clear perspex frame with a booklet explaining techniques of foil stamping. To complete the package, die cut labels were designed on the theme of numbers, so the recipient was made aware that he was receiving each edition.

Reflections

Horse at a pool's edge drinking its own reflection.
Aircraft sledging its shadow across the desert miles.
Young girl begging a mirror to tell her fortune.
Lost man's cooee echoed from aquiline mountain walls.
Here are duelling-grounds of reality and illusion –
Endless shimmer of foils and counterfoils.

C. Day Lewis

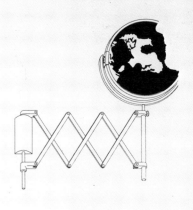

Information design: Promotion

Christmas is a traditional time celebrated by direct mail, and for once the designer can become his own client. To avoid the Christmas card syndrome, *Pentagram* has made a practice of designing and sending out a small book, preferably of lasting interest, each year.

The first was aptly titled *A Primer for Commercial Children* and played the traditional alphabet game of letters and objects with logotypes and symbols, a few of which are shown here. The idea was also adapted and printed by the *Financial Times* as a Christmas divertissement.

Other Christmas publications have included a hundredth anniversary of *Mrs Beeton,* celebrated by reprinting her puddings, including of course the festive plum pudding. The typographic solution as one can see, was virtually provided by that lady herself through a facsimile reproduction of her recipes.

The match puzzles were produced with the charitable thought of helping parents entertain their children over Christmas, when the festivities begin to flag.

Information design: Promotion

The *Pirelli Calendar,* initiated in the sixties and annually produced by distinguished designers and photographers became a landmark in graphics until its demise in the early seventies. The calendar shown right was art directed by *Pentagram* partner *Colin Forbes* and photographed by *Peter Knapp* (1964). Many similar calendars have been produced since then and this one for *Pentax,* photographed by *Sam Haskins,* is in the tradition. Unfortunately our role was confined to the layout and typography without the benefit of the location – Seychelles – and the models.

Designed for *Kodak,* this date box contained a set of 52 tabulated cards with dates and photograph The reverse sides giving technical information, speed, time and film etc. The black polystyrene container was designed to stand on a desk, or by using the key hole device, to hang on a wall. The intention was to distribute a new set of cards each year. Unfortunately it didn't prove successful, being no substitute for pictures of spaniels, and in consequence was only produced once.

136

Information design: Promotion

This set of calendars is produced by *Mears Caldwell Hacker,* printers. The design is intended to convey dates and not titillate the senses. It is made in three sizes, the largest version is clearly readable from a distance of fifteen metres. Each page carries one month in black and white, the typographic nicety being the carry over of the end of the previous month and the commencement of the following, in pale grey. In designing the logotype we accepted that the company was colloquially known as *MCH,* and so we cut off the remainder of the names.

The intention of this calendar, published in a limited edition by *Olivetti,* was to regularly change an environment by twelve number paintings. It was not intended to be legible, but evocative, stimulating and colourful. Hand printed in fluorescent inks, mismatched to produce sensational optical sensations... even the printer had to wear sunglasses. The ink company thought it the most vulgar calendar they had ever seen. It is in the collection of the *Museum of Modern Art* in New York and the *Stedelijk Museum* in Amsterdam.

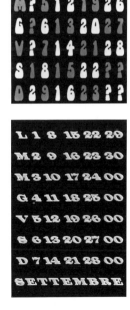

Information design: Promotion

Trade and technical literature is often prosaic in content, and the designer may need all his imagination, techniques and skills to communicate the message with flavour and interest. The examples on this double page show that photography can be an effective means to tell a commercial story.

Conways' Photosetting issued this booklet to promote a new machine which could bend, stretch, condense and distort black and white images. The graphic answer lay within the technology. The spreads had a running line of provocative but relevant text, and the matching illustrated distortions proved the points made by the copy.

Before there were machines which could distort instantly to specification, such tricks of the trade were laboriously drawn by hand. This lettering for a *Pirelli* poster (1961) took us several days of hard labour.

We do our best to follow your specifications

The world of Modigraphics.

Condense logos...

and stretch marks.

We can condense condensed soup

make 'The Times' more square...

Make the dollar equal the pound...

and make justification easy.

Make Laurel, Hardy...

...and Hardy, Laurel.

...bend the rules

or make French curves.

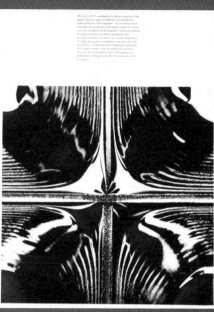

EUROHAUS

A prestige publication for *ICI*, a major producer of plastics. Companies are notoriously fond of their products, an affection not necessarily shared by others. Milk bottle crates, plastic taps, light fitments and the like, offered scant opportunity for prestigious photography.

A change of scale can however, create new worlds, and by microphotography the visual banality of the commercial products was transformed into abstract art. These images evolved from a light diffuser and roll of plastic.

A brochure to pre-sell space in an office complex titled *Eurohaus*, gave us the problem of conveying a realistic presentation of a building which was nothing more than a hole in the ground.

The solution for one of the pages involved building a scale model, consecutively projecting six transparencies of skies, and photographing the effect. The final result is shown here, and we venture to guess it will prove to look better than the real thing. The symbol was an axonometric drawing of the central tower.

139

Information design: Promotion

The ethics of heavy promotion aimed at the medical profession have always been a matter of controversy, and the effectiveness of this programme certainly intensified that debate.

Nobrium, at the time, was the latest development in the field of tranquillisers by *Roche*.

A logotype and housestyle was conceived to give an identity to *Nobrium* and relate direct mail pieces, advertisements and sample packs visually.

Prior to launching this new drug, 600 British general practitioners were asked to collaborate on a trial in order to extend and refine published evidence on the value of *Nobrium* in anxiety.

Trial material was presented in a specially designed desk unit in anodised aluminium and leather. It holds clinical data and trial procedure leaflets, capsules and forms for recording data.

The desk unit had an aluminium flap constructed to fold, to contain samples and test cards, to facilitate packaging and postage, and also to give the doctor privacy when writing prescriptions. Naturally he kept the desk unit when the trial was finished!

140

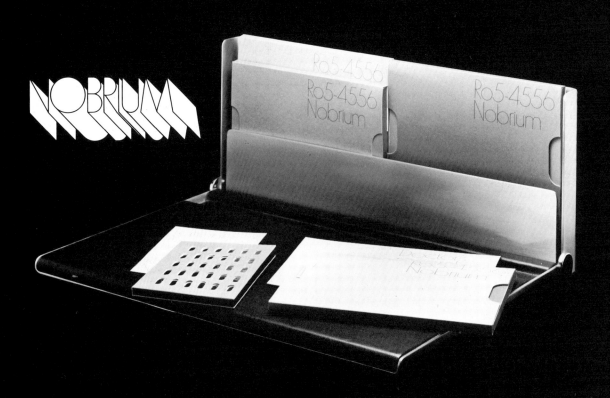

Information design: Promotion

Serious subjects need not necessarily be subjected to dull or boring presentation. A series of "pop-up" mailings colourfully dealt with the various aspects of anxiety. The latest evidence on *Nobrium* effectiveness was more seriously considered, and was printed on a card inserted in the sleeve.

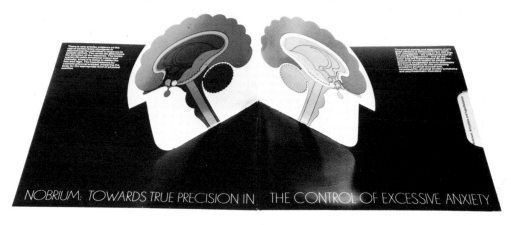

NOBRIUM: TOWARDS TRUE PRECISION IN THE CONTROL OF EXCESSIVE ANXIETY

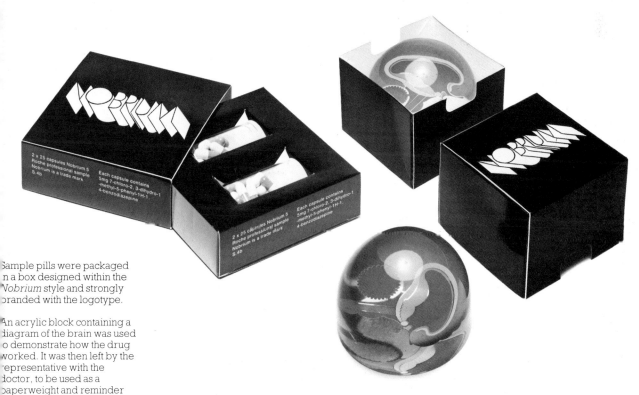

Sample pills were packaged in a box designed within the *Nobrium* style and strongly branded with the logotype.

An acrylic block containing a diagram of the brain was used to demonstrate how the drug worked. It was then left by the representative with the doctor, to be used as a paperweight and reminder of the products.

Information design: Promotion

Communications can extend beyond the verbal message and pictorial image. Colour can provoke emotions, texture can provide sensations, and even simple folds, cuts and tabulations, can highlight information and concentrate the attention on relatively pedestrian information.

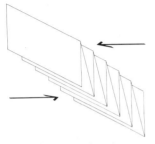

A simple, economic and unusual means of folding provides informative tabulation on both sides of this modest leaflet for *Dictaphone*.

This piece of sales information for *Baco*, a manufacturer of aluminium trim, was aimed at the motor industry. The wrapping of the information served three purposes; a provoking vehicle for text and illustration, a visual pun to emphasise the sales pitch of wrapping cars with practical trim, and the practical means of sending a large, colourful, albeit folded poster.

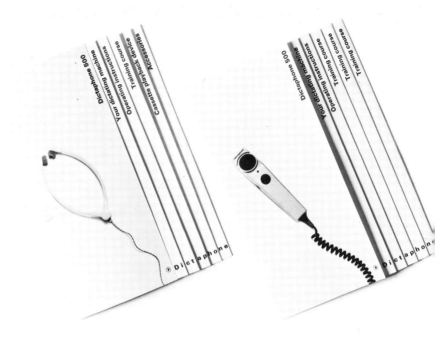

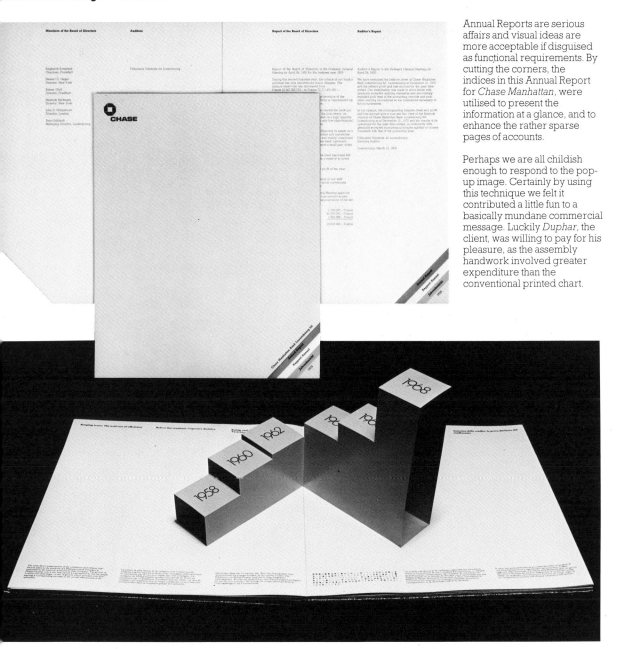

Annual Reports are serious affairs and visual ideas are more acceptable if disguised as functional requirements. By cutting the corners, the indices in this Annual Report for *Chase Manhattan,* were utilised to present the information at a glance, and to enhance the rather sparse pages of accounts.

Perhaps we are all childish enough to respond to the pop-up image. Certainly by using this technique we felt it contributed a little fun to a basically mundane commercial message. Luckily *Duphar,* the client, was willing to pay for his pleasure, as the assembly handwork involved greater expenditure than the conventional printed chart.

143

Information design: Promotion

Diagrammatic pictures can often convey information more rapidly and precisely than verbal instruction. They can also be more imaginative, or at least prettier, than is perhaps altogether necessary for practical purposes.

This demographic map was produced for *World Population Year,* and was drawn to demonstrate the difference of Gross National Products between the first, second and third worlds.

This brochure was designed to express the concept and explain the theory behind the *Herman Miller* "Action office" furniture system. The illustrative method adopted was one of exploded axonometric drawings. These showed the permutations and possibilities of the product and hopefully proved the point that one picture is worth a thousand words.

This particular drawing was to show the flexible modularity of the system's units.

144

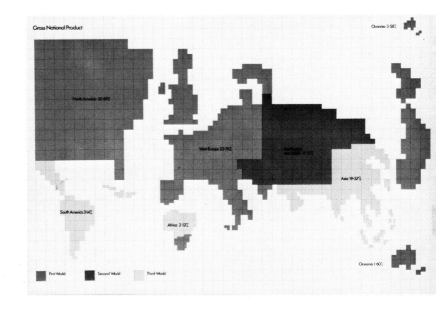

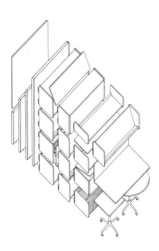

The symbol represents a fire resistant panel against a flame whilst the brochure is one of many we have designed for Cape. This style of drawing provides information, instruction, and also a visual corporate personality. The "builder's friend", rather than a faceless organisation solely concerned with sales.

145

Information design: Promotion

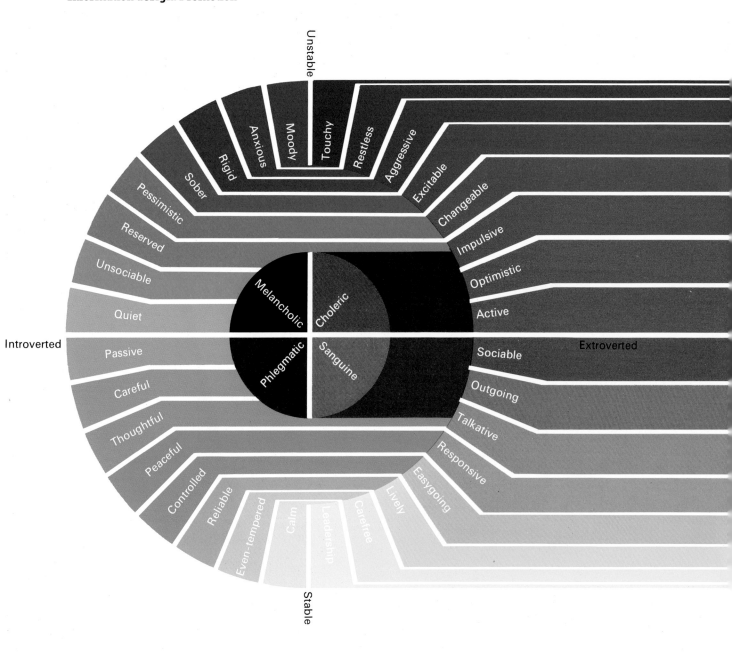

This diagram was designed for *Roche Pharmaceuticals* to show the complex spectrum of human emotions. It was produced in relation to a tranquility drug.

The information carrier

Exhibitions are basically carriers of information, even though the container, historically, is often all that is remembered. The *Great Exhibition* of 1851 in London's Hyde Park is now remembered, by most people, for the structure that contained the exhibits – *Joseph Paxton's Crystal Palace* – but the objective was to bring together the wonders of the world under one roof and to provide information about new inventions, natural phenomena, new art and other people; above all to blow the trumpet of the British Empire, and British commercial and industrial pre-eminence.

Major changes have taken place in internal content and display techniques since the *Great Exhibition* of 1851, and since the *Chicago Colombian Exposition* of 1893, in which *Edison* showed his *Kinetoscope*. The use of techniques borrowed from the film industry and show business has intensified to such an extent that the containers have lost their impact and one now remembers, not the architecture, not the message, but the medium.

The 1951 *Festival of Britain* on the South Bank site, had the *3D Telekinema* by *Welles Coates,* in 1958 Brussels had *Le Corbusier's Poème Electronique* for *Philips,* a stereophonic multi-screen installation, while in 1964 the *Johnson Wax* Pavilion at the *New York World's Fair* – a three screen spectacular – generated huge crowds. The multi-media, electronic environment had arrived.

By 1967 and the *Expo 67* in Montreal, the use of multi-media shows became the predominant means for imparting information and the experimental context of exhibitions, so important to the modern movement, had shifted from architecture to the means of displaying content. The techniques involved in the multi-media display of synchronised images, far outstripped the quality of the information displayed.

One of the most elaborate intermedia environments at *Expo 67* was the spectacular *Labyrinthe* developed by *Roman Kroitor,* where in chamber one, from eight balconies in four levels on either side of the central space the audience could view two 40 foot long screens, one on the floor of the central space and the other perpendicular to it, some 288 speakers surrounded the audience with sound, and for a limited time the audience could experience the wealth and inventiveness that they are not aware of every day. Other complex multi-screen shows were made for the Czechoslovakian Pavilion where 224 slide projectors were used, and for the Canadian *Pacific Cominco* Pavilion, where the six screen installation covered an area of 2,952 square feet – a normal cinema screen averages 450 square feet.

The evolution of audio visual display, from the early, very primitive, shadow shows to the cybernetic fantasies of contemporary world expositions, indicates an increasing capacity for people to assimulate and understand more complex environmental stimuli and information. The moving image used as a means of conveying information via movie and television screens is part of our everyday existence . . . is acceptable and ordinary. The fully wrap around, audio, visual, sensory electronic environment was the next step – where reality is blurred, the screen disappears and the moving image takes over.

At *Expo 70* in Osaka this began to happen. The prima donna architecture of the pavilions still prevailed; countries and industrial complexes vying with each other producing yet more daring inflatibles, larger spanning space frames and amazing structures, but the multi-media and electronic technology making all else irrelevant.

The Fuji Pavilion had a media installation using a new revolutionary "rolling loop" system of film transport, eveloped by *Multiscreen Corp.* of Canada. This allowed much larger frame to be used than is normal, giving a rame size of 70 x 50 mm and enabled a screen of 20 x 15 netres to be used, giving a greater facility for multiple mages and outstanding picture quality. The film itself was kind of composite image of life all over the world and vas shot specially for the exhibition, taking some eight nonths to edit.

he whole of the exhibition site proliferated with multi-creen moving and static images, TV monitors, complex ound systems, circlorama, colour eidophor TV rojection screens and telecommunication gadgetry. In he Telecommunications Pavilion, for example, a set-up of 00 TV receivers closely packed together was continually unning a fifteen minute video tape loop depicting hildren from all over the world crying . . . one way ommunication . . . and adjoining this area was a corridor lled with some 16,000 hanging telephones . . . two way ommunication.

s a carrier of information the electronic medium does ot yet have its own art form; this has still to develop out of s almost chaotic wealth of possibilities, and meanwhile it xists in a previous world exemplified by the written oI d and the static image. New thinking is needed from esigners, and particularly architects, if they are going to arn how to use media technology to create new nvironments where the enclosure and the moving nages are as one.

ı today's economic climate, some argue that if we are ı have great exhibitions we must tailor them to some asonable need; that there is a case for a new attitude to xhibitions. Each country or multi-national industrial omplex could contribute a useful element to the city, a nema, theatre, opera house, piazza, bandstand or

restaurant. The *Olympic Games* are cited as an example, where Munich was left with a vast housing estate and stadium.

Some argue that the days of the great exhibitions are over and that the scene has shifted to complexes such as the *National Exhibition Centre* in Birmingham or the *Hanover Fair* complex, and the changing trade exhibitions that they show all year round.

I believe that a "non-architecture" of controlled environmental conditioning, and an information content that matches the state of the art of the rapidly expanding techniques for multi-media electronic display, could lead to a simulated environment in future exhibitions and might, if history repeats itself, have an effect on "real" architecture. Then maybe the magic of a " new architecture", so beloved by the modern movement, could manifest itself.

Ron Herron

149

BRITISH GENIUS

The *British Genius Exhibition* commemorated the amazing number of British technical inventions and scientific discoveries made over the last hundred years.

The site, on the remains of the old Battersea Fun Fair, was lent on condition that it be handed over as parkland after the show.

150

Consequently the area was paved for car park and events, the rest dug up to make a field for the tent, and an open air laboratory for growing barley and crops.

The excavated material was recycled to form protective mounds which were grassed and planted with trees.

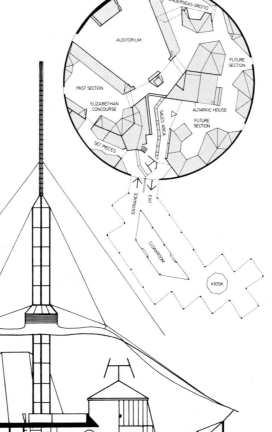

UNDERSEAS GROTTO

AUDITORIUM

FUTURE SECTION

PAST SECTION

AUTARKIC HOUSE

ELIZABETHAN CONCOURSE

FUTURE SECTION

SALES AREA

SET PIECES

ENTRANCE

EXIT

CLOAKROOM

KIOSK

0 5 10
METRE SCALE

Information design: Exhibitions

The entrance pedestrian plaza contained an open sided tent, an experimental structure which covered a refreshment kiosk, tables and chairs, and a depository for coats and parcels.

Around the exhibition were flag poles and banners, colourful signs and sculptures.

The main tent, designed in collaboration with *Buro Happold,* is a circular form suspended from a central mast surmounted by a programmed light sculpture.

Light and ephemeral, the tent provides precisely the right environment and form for a temporary exhibition,

although creating difficulties with internal displays.

The interior was conceived as an analogy – the tent as sky, the structure as mountains sustaining the exhibits and information. One entered a tunnel to emerge into a valley packed with images and objects of the Elizabethan age,

through into a cave for an audio visual revelation of the present and then out into the future on the other side.

The *British Genius Exhibition* was sponsored by the *John Player Foundation* and directed by *Carlton Cleeve* and *Partnerplan.*

Information design: Exhibitions

A cheerful chunky stencil alphabet was designed to co-ordinate the typographics and serve as a logotype.

The original purpose of the stencil was to enable it to be reproduced in inflatable letters, in bas relief as colourfully painted concrete forms, cut out in sheet metal and so on. Rapidly eroding budgets however, eventually confined it to silkscreening on bunting, banners, flags and boards.

Directional signs on the site were systematised. Printed onto individual slatted boards and fixed to simple scaffold structures, they are interchangeable and easily altered.

All exhibition captions were typewritten and enlarged to a readable size.

The information rail not only provided a running commentary on the exhibits but also kept the public off the display. It contained touch buttons for operating various demonstrations, tape recorders, and a voting device for a series of questions.

Pictorial and typographic murals punctuated the divisions between display sections, and the alphabet was deliberately used to give pattern as well as to display information and quotations.

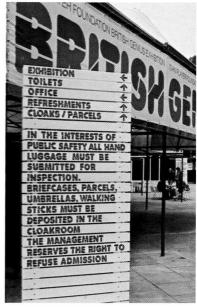

The exhibition contained as much figurative art and as many realistic models as possible.

This helped visitors to understand the technical content of the subject matter and enabled them to relate the information to their own lives.

The *Morecambe and Wise* sculpture by *Nicholas Monro* precisely fills the requirements of a public sculpture for such an occasion – elegant in form and serious in intent, it is witty and amusing – a quality in sculpture lost since the baroque.

The entrance tunnel contained room sets which gave the visitor a cohesive glimpse of life styles over the past hundred years. These were realised by *Peter Darty*, and contained original furniture, pictures and costumes, the latter worn by realistic figures sculptured by *Keith Reeves*.

The Elizabethan concourse contained five groups or tableaux, showing characteristic figures and activities of each of the five year periods of the present reign.

153

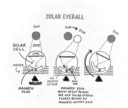

154

The exhibit captions were discs with information in typewriting, and major headings rendered in the stencil alphabet.

Portraits were reproduced in a vertical line screen to compensate for the wide differentiation in the quality of supplied photographs, and also to provide dazzle to the sea of faces.

In addition to verbal messages the caption discs carried simplified hand drawn diagrams to express the essence of the often extremely complex processes.

The three major sections of past-present-future were treated as extensions of each other.

The Past Section is a valley filled with achievements, a maze of models, photographs and captions.

In the Present Section a twelve minute audio visual revelation was housed in the mountain. *Mick Csaky* used the multi-screen projections to recapitulate the industrial revolution, to show how it had changed the cultures of the world, and to indicate the dangers of the present, and the possibilities and fears of the future. It stated a number of choices.

The Future Section is a range of hills and valleys on which current inventions are shown, and analysed in terms of their future potential. They are grouped around an autarkic house, realised in collaboration with *Alex Pike*.

This impression of the Future Section was drawn by *Dennis Bailey*.

How to play
the environment game

How to Play the Environment Game was an exhibition conceived and written by *Theo Crosby,* designed by *Pentagram,* and held in the *Hayward Gallery,* London.

The idea developed from a proposal put to the *Arts Council,* to explore the nature and origins of the forces that act on the environment.

Each was identified – history, finance, technology, resources, rules, art and community involvement – and explained as a strategy in a game where all are players but few win.

To this end it was conceived as an enormous catalogue, an elementary photographic and pictorial display accompanied by captions. The graphics were minimal, a stack of monopoly houses symbolised the message on the poster and catalogue, and typewritten characters were used in place of typefaces.

Designed within an extremely modest budget, the exhibition was also required to be easily travelled, mounted and displayed.

These pictures show the progressive stages in mounting the exhibition.

156

Information design: Exhibitions

The austerity of the interior of the gallery was tempered by a colour space construction; painted walls divided by horizontal lines of contrasting coloured tapes. These established the base lines for laying out the exhibit panels.

The juxtaposition of colours and pictures gave each of the sections an individuality, and large establishing images were made by looping several panels together.

The pictorial matter was photographically printed directly onto panels, which were flexible plastic sheets, coated with an emulsion.

The panels, all a metre square, had brass eyelets and were fixed to the wall line by drawing pins and rubber bands. These kept the plastic in tension. This method of display provided a simple means of mounting and dismantling.

For travelling, sheets were laid in wooden cases, butterfly bolts through the eyelets held them in place and secured the lid. The system is light to transport, can be mounted by unskilled people, and worked well over a year's tour.

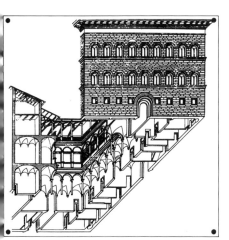

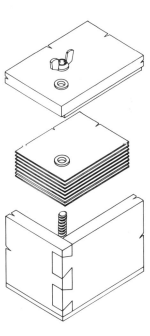

157

Information design: Exhibitions

The pictorial imagery varied enormously and purposefully because of the very nature of the theme, which ranged across many fields of history and theory, and it also kept the visual interest.

Although much of the imagery was obtained from archives, libraries and organisations; slide and film shows, photographs and drawings, were specially commissioned when a particular point needed to be made.

Mel Calman made a series of cartoons lampooning various industries, and on the gallery terraces there were a number of sculptures related to environmental themes, including a four metre high fanciful steel tree designed and made by *Lou Klein*.

Mick Csaky was commissioned to produce a four screen audio visual experience in the "motor" section, which explored the fascination and domination of the car in our culture.

As a finale, *Rod Morrison* and *Ed Berman* produced a five screen slide programme on community action.

In the exit foyer, people were asked to participate in questionnaires, fill in petitions, and local action groups were able to display their posters and distribute leaflets. The intention was to avoid a static exhibit situation, and to try and involve the audience.

158

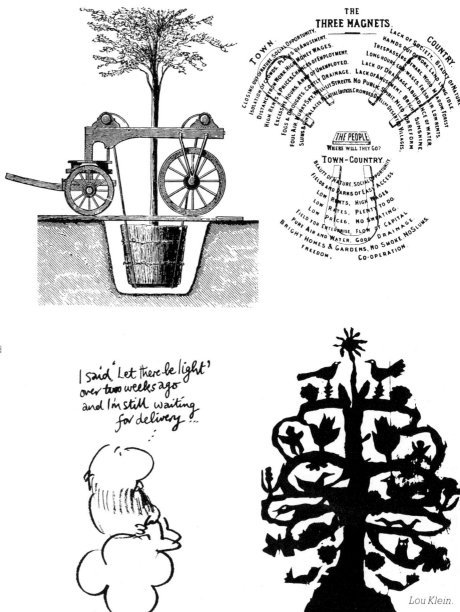

Lou Klein.

The multi-screen slide show of *St Pancras Station*, set to music by *Saint Saens*, emphasised the complexity and richness of the building. Here the conservation argument was presented with details of this great neglected masterpiece.

The photographs by *Jessica Strang* show the involvement and integration of art and craft which gives a building depth, meaning and substance, a lesson architects need to relearn.

It proved to be a prophetic exhibition: the building boom collapsed six months later and there has since been a radical change in attitudes towards environment.

The show was edited to travel around England and Scotland and had its last showing in Stockholm. For each venue a local slide show was made.

159

A catalogue, published by *Penguin Books*, contains all the photographs, text, and introductory essays. It has also been translated into Japanese.

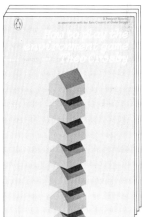

BRITISH INDUSTRY PAVILION EXPO 67

The British Industry Section of the *British Pavilion* at *Expo 67* (Montreal) was a large interior space entered by escalator from the lower floor.

The strategy was to stun the visitor with a three screen six minute film on the "Sources of Power" and then let him wander through a complex curved labyrinthine structure. In practice the film (produced by *Don Levy*) was too good, and often caused a blockage as visitors insisted on seeing it round again.

The interior structure within the envelope of the pavilion building was of reinforcing wire and mesh, formed on site and plastered. It was like a vast inside-out sculpture rising to peaks which housed lights and air extractors.

The floors were carpeted and the walls sprayed a coarse texture. Into this surface, fibreglass elements were housed to contain 16mm film loops, colour slide sequences, randomly switched, back-lit transparencies, and small models.

The overall effect looked like Aladdin's cave. The twinkling lights, colourful projections, and *Tristram Cary's* concrete music – all hopefully conveyed the complexity of modern technology

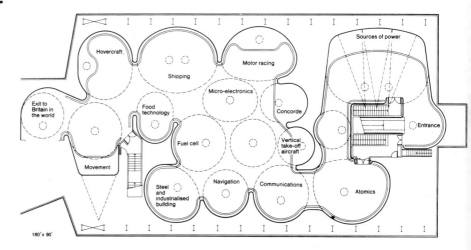

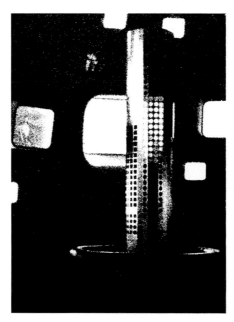

Large models and exhibits were randomly placed in the circulation areas and the public kept at bay by padded leathercloth rails. New inventions or principles, such as the "fuel cell" and "pulse code modulation" were expressed through explanatory models. Both are illustrated here.

Sculptor *Malcolm Carder* designed and made a perspex construction driven by a fuel cell. This exciting exhibit was the result of a close collaboration between artist and manufacturer. The model for "pulse code modulation" was designed by *Alan Fletcher* and explained, through moving lights, a complicated invention which has revolutionised electronic communications.

Complex displays are also likely to engender mistakes. When the film loops were delivered they were back to front. An extensive scouring of Montreal deprived that city of its stock of shaving mirrors – but at least, by reflecting them, the projected images were seen the right way round.

As an exhibit we consider it a qualified success, as in hindsight it was found that much of the available material could not stand up to such an ambitious presentation.

However, in a display which aimed to present industry in a new romantic guise, the presence of static models and miniature hardware would have carried much less excitement than was achieved.

161

162

The British section of the *Milan Triennale* (1964), designed by *Theo Crosby*, was the occasion when three of the future partners of *Pentagram* first worked together. *Alan Fletcher, Colin Forbes* and *Bob Gill* produced an enormous lifesize photo essay which clad a winding corridor. The visitor walked through environments of streets and landscapes.

The main part of the exhibition, illustrated here, was a complex two-centred vault of timber boards decorated with a stencil by *Joe Tilson*. This was on the theme of exports.

Roger Mayne photographed one of the earliest multi-screen slide performances, *Eduardo Paolozzi* and *Peter*

Startup lent sculptures and *Bernard Cohen* designed a marvellous rug which was made in the *Blackfriars Settlement Workshop*. This is now in the *Victoria & Albert Museum*.

The practice of involving painters and sculptors to interpret themes which need to be understood, or at least experienced, is an unpredictable element. One may be saddled with a lead balloon but on the other hand may be endowed with an unlimited and joyful work.

In any event the quality of such exhibitions comes largely from the involvement of artists, and their work takes a central place.

The *Kinetic Exhibition* at the *Hayward Gallery* was an opportunity to explore an art form very closely related to our own work in exhibition design. Apart from selecting and commissioning the work, the main problem was to create a setting for an art obsessed with movement.

The *Arts Council* shows are necessarily economical in presentation, and the *Hayward Gallery* is forbiddingly static. The walls were therefore hung with shiny PVC sheeting, in red, blue and black, to create an illusion of insubstantiality. Against this background, with glints of light reflections, the objects moved and turned.

A slide and movie show introduced the visitor to the

origins of kinetics in nineteenth century toys and inventions, and to the classic experiments of the *Bauhaus* which form the basis of current practice.

The catalogue was a collectio of separate pages in a plastic bag. Each artist had his own separate leaflet and amusing kinetic effects were obtained by the visitors as they sought often unsuccessfully, to contr this flood of paper.

163

nce commercial products
re usually of little interest to
ose outside the business,
ade exhibitions are often a
oring collection of displays.
deas to catch and stimulate
tention are therefore a
ecessary ingredient.

his stand for *Pirelli* scooter
res was aimed at the motor
ycle enthusiast, and the
oncept lay in simulating a
ad on a vertical curvilinear
all, and imposing the
egulations of the Highway
ode in the lanes.

isitors received a multi-
lded chart which was a
csimile of the stand with the
nswers to the "do" and "don't"
les. The shape of the stand
so enclosed the office.

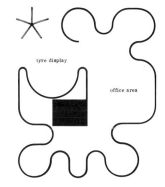

The transfer of new art into a
commercial context can be
rewarding and amusing – if
you find the client.

Building exhibitions are a
maze of competing stands, so
using *Cape Building Products'*
materials, we designed a
sculpture garden; a parody of
minimalist sculptural
tendencies. Behind the
information counter was a
typographic pattern of the
product names.

The materials, corrugated
sheets, pipes and other
products, were juxtaposed,
cut and painted, to form the
brightly coloured sculptures.
These contained hidden
programmed coloured lights
and piped bird song.

...through his work on the environment, the designer exercises a major influence on our way of life. Civilised man first gave expression to a need to usefully perpetuate his purposes through agriculture and architecture. Of those two, it was architecture which was the first declared statement of "improved environment" by which man sought to be judged. Designer or architect; the terminology matters little in the face of the enormous spread of environmental influences in which the designer has a hand.

That spread increased explosively with the development, first of the arts, then of manufacturing processes. By the time of the industrial revolution and mass production, the influence of the designer had increased to a point where his work, good or bad, was influencing and indeed perhaps stereotyping the thinking of a large proportion of mankind. For of course, once we accept that one man's product is the next man's environment, and that fashion, uniformity and cost benefit are the main criteria for products, then the designer as leveller emerges, with the lowest common denominator as his ideal.

No one has protested more strongly against this debased role than the designer himself; *William Morris* and his work stand for this protest. But protest has been difficult in the design fields associated with the environment. The present revaluation of planning and its enormous potential for destruction as well as growth, typifies the size of this problem.

Planning is the first of the four environmental sections with which we are concerned in this book. It is an activity which is often, but wrongly, placed in the lists against *Conservation,* the second of our sections. The two sections are of course, closely interrelated and the examples we show of each need to be seen in a context

which recognises both. Thus the "conservation" work at *Ulster Terrace* in Regents Park has little reality outside the context of the overriding *Nash* plan.

The third of our sections deals with *Interiors.* Here the designer gives close recognition to the influence of the environment on work and living. Designing interiors is designing for intimacy and immediacy, for close physical contact. It is a field in which the designer's sensitivities are fully stretched. Standard solutions are readily exposed in this field; stereotypes and formulae are easy traps. In the design of interiors, the work is tailored to need.

The fourth and final section of *Environment design* covers *Architectural graphics.* This is a field in which design work can be seen as a new popular front; a protest against the uniformity and drabness of the way we have expressed our civilisation in our cities. In this field, above all, the designer can claim the right to be judged as a contributor to the individuality and the life-enhancing qualities we expect from our environment.

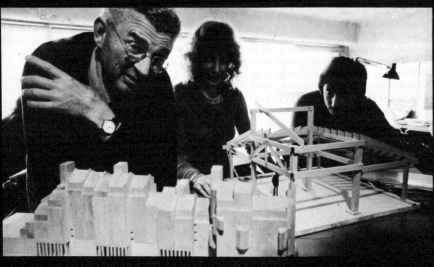

Ground rules

It has long been the intention of the human race to impose its order on an awkward, chaotic and reluctant nature. In all countries the logic and the poetry of the right angle has bitten deep into the landscape, created a geometry within which our senses have found repose; guide lines representing an ill-defined but very real security. The grid subdivisions of Northern Italy established by the Romans can be matched by the mile square chequerboard of the western prairies. From the air, our world is covered by a web of geometry; everyone now becomes a planner with a pilot's overview:

The effect of this new landscape, this new way of seeing the world, begins to work itself out in many ways. *McLuhan* pointed out in the *Gutenburg Galaxy* that the invention of print changed a whole culture in ways entirely unpredictable; so will our new perceptions change our own culture. Once the global view was the private world of the cartographer and the planner, who made his toy models, and looked down at them, and found them good. Now a whole generation has experienced this god-like pleasure, and has accepted the new scale as a norm; the macro world. We have readily combined this idea, this perception of vast spaces with other analogous and characteristic vastnesses of our time: big government, the giant corporation, the big deal. We like to think big.

In the environment we now think and act big, not in houses but in dwelling units by the thousand, not villages, but new towns and cities to cope with our big procreation problem. Perhaps we need this bigness, but each of us remains much the same size as our fathers. Our needs are a little different but our size and the sizes we need to live in, remain fairly constant. In fact, if we look at the rooms of the last century and compare them to those we build now, have we not shrunk a little?

We are so many, and will soon be even more. Yet it is wrong to identify the concept of large numbers with large scale, though there is a close relation. We often fall into the error of simply increasing the size of a single element (a house) into a useful planning element (the apartment house) and then, by an equally simple projection, into a vast skyscraper. The process is geometric and comes easily to our perception mechanisms now that they have been expanded to comprehend the macro-scale. Similarly the idea of repetition of simple elements, useful and necessary up to a certain threshold of numbers, becomes easily inflated into an overpowering methodology, which solves everything by simple multiplication. As *Le Corbusier* said, one dream multiplied by two million becomes a nightmare.

As in many other departments of modern life we are now in a position where we must choose a way of life from several alternatives; choose between technologies; choose to develop some and to discard others. We cannot afford, as we once could, to allow any one technology to run freely through our environment.

In Europe we have sacrificed the wild animals, the marginal lands, the swamps and forests, to intensive food production and industrial sprawl. In the cities a blight of new buildings overwhelms the old centres, and spreads into the countryide. Where once the construction of a house was a long and tedious process, involving the whole community, today the promise of instant mail order habitat is almost a reality. In most great cities there is already an environmental overkill.

To achieve an Apollonian restraint in such a situation (a situation which gets daily more uncontrollable) we need to learn and to exercise numerous cunning stratagems which will regulate our capacities, and thwart our tendencies to megalomania. In the organisation of cities there is a great virtue in inertia, in maintaining the inheritance of centuries. This consists, partly of the actual building fabric, but mostly of the ideas of interval and rhythm which are the result of many generations of experiment and acceptance.

An example is the traditional widths of buildings in various cities. In the grander parts of Paris, the street frontages of the great houses average fifteen metres. In 18th century London the distance varies from ten metres for houses in Belgravia to four metres in working class areas. This insistent planning module relates also to the height of the buildings, and determines too the street widths. Thus a comprehensible system is established, which provides a matrix within which the human scale is in control. Any man can walk within the system in dignity and comfort.

Yet even in the classic city the pressures towards repetition and monotony were strong: endless streets of similar houses in elementary gridiron layouts. Thus the continuous attempts to relieve and to individualise the grouping of houses by means of squares, ovals and circuses. The many examples demonstrate a vast repertoire of urban forms which can be used to contain groups, to create ensembles full of poetry and grace.

It is just these airs and graces that architects and planners have forgotten. It must be recognised that such manipulations of the basic elements work against the economy of simple repetition and economy is the greatest pressure on all environments today. To achieve effects beyond the banal we must spend; learn to be generous or even extravagant.

The choice is between quantity and quality in our habitation; it is a false choice. Dwellings built for economy alone have short lives, and are seldom adequate in an era of changing life styles. Thus these hastily built dwellings turn quickly to slums, and lose their values. More is lost than money, as the environment of the minimum breeds few joys and many troubles.

One answer to this problem, dear to architects, and technologists, is endless and constant change. Dwellings should be treated like telephones, or hotel rooms, hired as a service for a period, changed for a new model when the ashtrays are full. Such a system meshes well with the requirements of technology: a high level of production and consumption and waste, governed by advertising and prompted by a yearly model change. Such a logic has made the car manufacturers and the ten major oil companies among the most powerful economic forces in the world. Each company commands budgets larger than most sovereign states, spends freely and entirely for its own growth and even greater future power. This kind of concentration has already begun in the scattered and obsolete construction industry, and its mad logic becomes daily closer to reality in the provision of dwellings.

In the car industry there is only an apparent plethora of choice. The cars are much the same and the differences are largely in the advertising copy. An expensive education is necessary to tell the difference (and to see the need to pay it) between a *Lincoln* and a *Toronado,* or a *Fiat* 1500 and a *Renault* 1500. If this is to be the promised land to which technology brings us, we will need a great variety of stratagems to keep a humane environment.

Of these, the most obvious is simple obstruction. Let us refuse marginal and dubious benefits. Technology *does* offer marvellous choices, but often that choice favours the cheap and the destructive: cheap paper and polluted water; more and cheaper crops and poisoned streams; cheap transport and poisoned air.

There are alternatives but they require controls, constant supervision and a renunciation of quick profit. In housing we could now provide for each family a tailored individual dwelling, in place of a statistically average apartment. We could go to work in electronically propelled vehicles of great comfort and sophistication. By the intelligent and creative development of existing techniques, we could produce variety in the place of sameness. We could, but in our present socio-economic mode of thinking we are unlikely to abandon economy as a yardstick.

To make alternatives available in such a climate we need more intelligent involvement, and more disinterested involvement. We must devise strategies and tactics which will allow, in the process of creating the environment, the collaboration of alternative disciplines, and above all aim the process at the satisfaction and wellbeing of the user. In the end there is no substitute for the individual client, with his needs, feelings and activities which require unique solutions.

Such a philosophy could produce a variety of forms, of solutions and some possibility of formal experiment, because it is based on no formal doctrine. Each building, each room should ideally be seen as a unique experience, the product of many inputs. Temptations to repetition, to the administratively convenient, have to be avoided by the construction of elaborate games and rules, by the introduction of competing players, and many jokers in the pack.

Theo Crosby

167

CHERRY GARDEN PIER

The offer of a staggering five acre site with 300 metres of London riverside frontage in Bermondsey, less than a mile from Tower Bridge, was an opportunity to explore some convictions and theories about housing.

First, such a site is too big for a single firm of architects, as their solutions are likely to stem from the repetition of a single idea. We felt that this elemental sterility could be avoided by the involvement of several different architects, and were able to persuade our client *Lawdon Construction* to employ three other firms to collaborate on the project.

We set up the ground rules for the whole project. These were designed to relate the

new buildings to the existing romantic but crumbling warehouses.

In *Pentagram's* block on the riverside we set a further series of objectives: to create a variety of accommodation within the block, with every flat and preferably every room being different.

Variations in size and facilities are mandatory if one is hoping to satisfactorily meet needs in accommodating a mix of tenants with different salary scales, ages and families.

The axonometric drawing shows how this was achieved by means of a basic framed structure, which allows for many permutations of accommodation.

By setting the upper floors back, to create balconies, the block form has been destroyed. This block is further broken by adding bow windows, balconies, and a variety of fenestration based on a few primary window sizes.

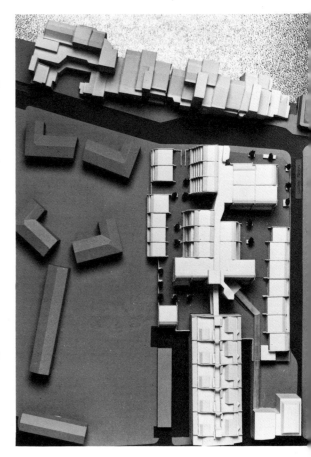

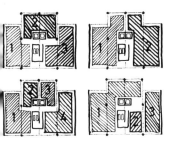

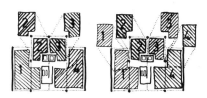

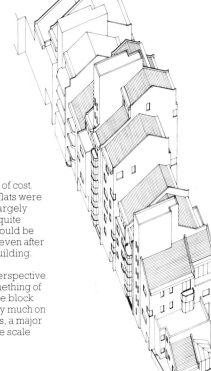

The basic plan mechanism is shown in these sketches above and consists of a central lift and escape stair. The London by-laws require these to be enclosed.

This layout allows for two, three or four flats on each floor, by a simple horizontal permutation, as the group of four sketch diagrams shows.

The other two sketches indicate further possibilities through vertical permutation, flats becoming duplex apartments. But of course an almost infinite variety of accommodation can be obtained, from single bed-sitting rooms to large six room flats.

The site of the *Pentagram* project was a narrow irregular strip between Rotherhithe Street and the River Thames, and as can be seen by the elevation and axonometric drawing, the buildings were to partly overhang the water. This was intended to give a special effect of reflected light in the rooms.

The structure is a very simple and regular frame, with brick infill walls, and the spaces can be easily permutated both horizontally and vertically.

These flats were to be for private sale, and the purchaser was to be offered a wide choice of options, of size, of view, and naturally, of cost. The interiors of the flats were intended to be left largely incomplete, so that quite radical alterations could be made by the tenant even after completion of the building.

The axonometric perspective drawing shows something of the complexity of the block which depends very much on its vertical emphasis, a major factor in keeping the scale humane.

169

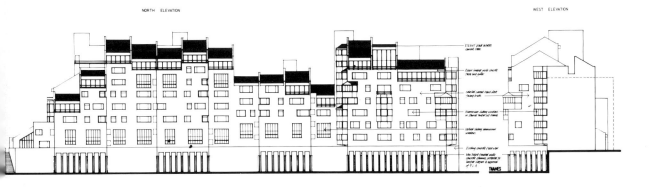

The eighteenth century police station was remodelled and extended by *Richard and Margaret Finch* as offices. The wing with the bay window replaces the old cell block, and under this is the pedestrian entrance to the flat blocks. Cars enter between the bay and the warehouse. Built in 1820 this fine building was to be renovated as studios and flats by *Trevor Dannatt*.

170

A drawing to show the vehicle entrance with a pedestrian ramp on the right and with the warehouse on the left. The flats designed by *Alison and Peter Smithson* can be seen ahead. They were to replace a fairly recent warehouse using the existing foundations.

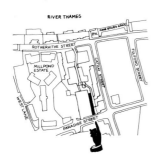

This view shows *Pentagram's* proposal for the riverside block with the famous *Angel* pub at left. The flats face north across the river so windows, except for the ground floor studios, are generally small and concentrated on views to east and west.

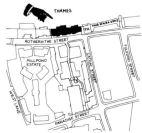

The same block seen from landward with the *Angel* pub at right. The raised terrace over the garage area for all of the flats is on the left and forms part of the *Smithsons'* scheme.

In a year of economic depression, planning and cost considerations killed the project, so these drawings by *Gordon Cullen* were derived from plans and models.

TRYPTIC

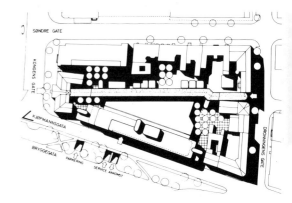

Architectural planning covers a wide spectrum of activities ranging from the design of new towns to the revitalisation of the odd corner of a city block. This project by *Pentagram* partner *Ron Herron* was concerned with the city library complex in Trondheim, Norway.

Our objective was to examine and exploit the potential of "inserting" a shiny new object into an existing old world environment; an attitude in contrast to the current preoccupation with romantic conservation that exemplifies most work in urban areas.

We also felt it was important to retain and reinforce the concept of entering and walking through the internal space of the block, thus maintaining the Trondheim tradition of urban footpaths.

The library is sited on the east side and a second phase development of shops, gallery spaces, restaurants and offices is on the west. Both buildings are sited parallel to the respective street lines.

The structures that bound these two edges of the site are stepped to pick-up existing eaves lines, and are of a scale that reflects and relates to the existing buildings that adjoin them.

The slab buildings develop into flexible two storey spaces on the inside, to meet a route that runs through the centre of the site, in the form of a glass covered arcade. The arcade is centred on the old Town Hall building and can be entered through the southern end, the link occuring at the tower.

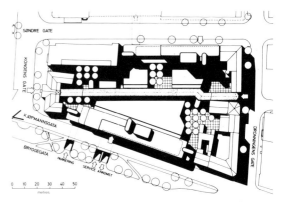

172

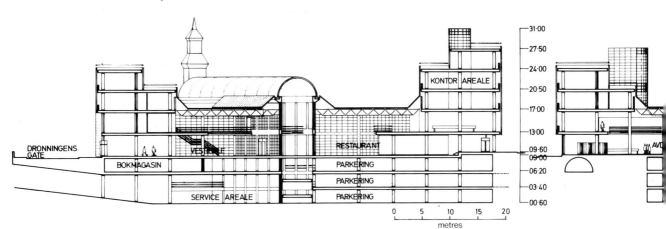

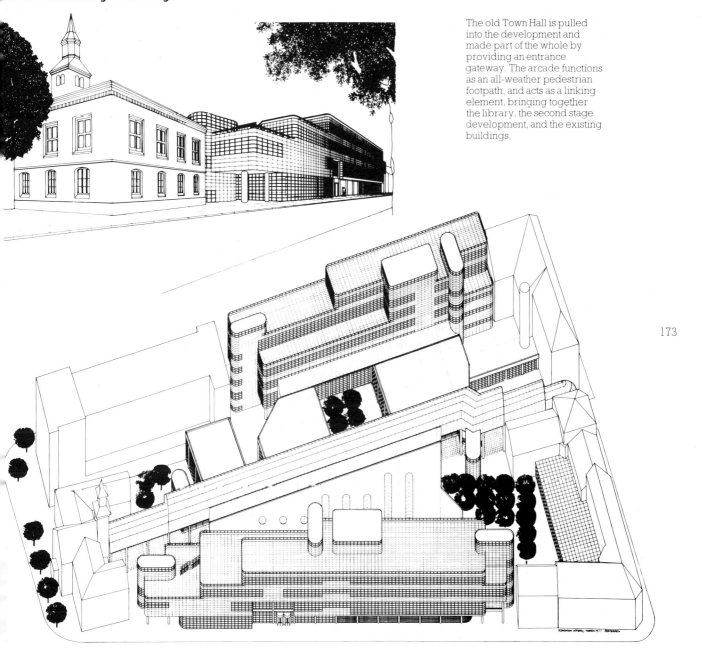

The old Town Hall is pulled into the development and made part of the whole by providing an entrance gateway. The arcade functions as an all-weather pedestrian footpath, and acts as a linking element, bringing together the library, the second stage development, and the existing buildings.

173

Grooming white elephants

The past twenty years has seen the triumph of the modern movement in architecture, and the results are evident in every city in the world. In the past thirty years, we have built more than in the whole of the world's previous history; our cities have vastly grown with a continuous and increasing influx. In this pressure to build, to wipe out the slums, to make a new world for millions of new people, the constructional logic and natural austerity of the modern movement seemed irresistable. It grew from a long historical thread, as the successor to a series of reformist movements in the nineteenth century. These began with *Blake, Pugin* and *Ruskin,* and received a powerful new impetus when *William Morris* linked art and craft to the early Socialist movement. *Morris* stood for honesty of material, the value and joy of handwork, and for the work processes that release an individual's creativity and promote his spiritual maturity. These ideas were always violently in conflict with the industrial system, but they were partially abandoned by his successors, *Ashbee Lethaby* and *Gropius* who came to see the inevitability of machine production. They hoped to control the machine through design, to join the productive capacity of the industrial system to social and aesthetic goals, to produce a radically new kind of civilisation.

It was a wholly honourable impulse and it is perhaps unfortunate that the world should grow and change so violently before a satisfactory and universal aesthetic language had been worked out. The style of our century has too often been established in circumstances governed by commercial greed or administrative expediency, and our cities and landscape have been inevitably, and probably irretrievably, damaged.

We have come, as *Ruskin* predicted, by accepting a machine aesthetic, to accept the imperatives of the production process, and the economic parameters that have always guided industry. Industry is concerned with the organisation of quantity, and its systems of control were developed from the military practice of the 18th century.

In accepting the industrial ethic, we begin to see ourselves, not as individuals, but as mass, and we see our problems as mass production, mass transport, mass housing and mass leisure. The slogans that fit this ideology – economy of scale, bigger is better, history is bunk, less is more, are all deeply ingrained, and they are played out in the environment and made real.

The rapid and worldwide diffusion of such attitudes came at a time when two world wars, and a major depression had made people see the buildings of our cities and villages as grey, dusty, and irrelevant. It was easy to accept the premise that they should be cleared to make a better world, a world sparkling modern, up-to-date and symbolising social justice.

Now, after thirty years of continuous building, our cities look infinitely worse, and we have only recently begun to appreciate the value of what was so carelessly thrown away. Our failure to produce significant, and above all, concordant buildings, has magnified the value of those remaining and undervalued monuments of the 19th century, that like enormous white elephants, still litter our cities.

There has been a radical change, of attitude and of taste, not so much against the principles of modern architecture or to its still unexplored capabilities, but against the illiterate crudity and insensitivity of current commercial and authoritarian building.

Even now in the UK, where legislation and a control system has been in operation for several years, a building listed for preservation is lost every day. Yet the entire list does not amount to half a year's production of new buildings. In spite of much goodwill, and an increasing understanding of the value of old buildings in retaining environmental quality, or as spiritual connections to the past, it is clear that there are enormous pressures for change, for growth and development.

While a building serves its purpose and its value is in balance with its location, it is relatively safe. Once this

174

balance is upset, if the site becomes too valuable (as happens in city centres) or not valuable enough (as happens with country houses), then the pressure for change becomes overwhelming. The resolution of such problems requires a very complex set of judgements, and usually a subsidy.

A building can be made to serve a new purpose, but it requires much care and expertise if its quality is not to evaporate in the process. The judgements to be made will depend on the nature of the building, and the role that it plays in town or country.

In the city, it is nearly always possible for a building to be adapted to a new purpose, and the skill lies in conserving as much of the original as possible whilst effecting the transformation. An important corollary of that skill however, is the ability to distinguish between what is good and bad from the past, and to avoid sentimentality.

In the city, a building can often be saved by a change of use to a higher value use which can bring in the increased return necessary to satisfy the owner. This is the commercial answer, and one very difficult to get around. To bring a new life to a very large old building requires a creative and complicated structure of uses, within which trade-offs of various values can be made which utilises the potential of the building fully – and do not distort its qualities. We have thus seen the adaptation of churches, warehouses and maltings to the extraordinary growth of cultural buildings: art centres, concert halls, theatres, that marks our period, and is its saving grace.

The country house is a problem of quite different dimension. Here the difficulties of maintaining a large structure on an income constantly reduced by inflation, death duties and taxation are probably insuperable. The very grand houses that survive have become lion parks and amusement centres, and their survival depends on a massive throughput of visitors. Such intensive use soon destroys the very quality of the place. That said, it must also be understood that there are only a few of the hundreds of large houses that have much to offer the paying visitor.

These latter houses, mostly of the 18th or 19th century, in their small parks and surrounded by farmland long since alienated from them, represent a way of life which diminishes every year. They become institutions for the old or the handicapped, or training centres for industry. In either case, the quality of the building and its surroundings are usually degraded, and the interior and contents sacrificed to the needs of new, and often uncaring occupants. There seems no way in which such listed buildings can be saved, or protected from change, other than by subsidy or special financial arrangements to relieve their owners from taxation.

There is considerable illogic in a system which lists buildings for preservation on the grounds of aesthetic merit, which controls their use, appearance and even internal fitments with a hair-splitting concern for the letter of the law, yet cannot accept responsibility for their upkeep. Until such responsibility is accepted, it seems inevitable that we will continue to lose these houses, although there are practical measures that can be taken to make them more relevant to the times, on the rare occasion that the opportunity (and money) is available for conservation. The key to such partial solutions can be found in an examination of how they came to be so big in the first place.

In the 19th century, many houses were greatly enlarged, becoming as complex as battleships with a large company of servants to sustain the family in a few grand rooms. They were also largely self-supporting, growing their own vegetables and so on. As these economic conditions no longer apply, they can sometimes be cut down to their more manageable 17th or 18th century size. Conservation may thus require major surgery, and this is as likely to be true in the city as in the country.

But the most urgent problems are not those of particular buildings, but of how we are to bring about the necessary changes in attitude that will guarantee our remaining historic buildings some chance of survival. There is an unwelcome irony in the fact that in seeking to preserve structures which have stood for hundreds of years, we find ourselves with very little time.

Theo Crosby

ULSTER TERRACE

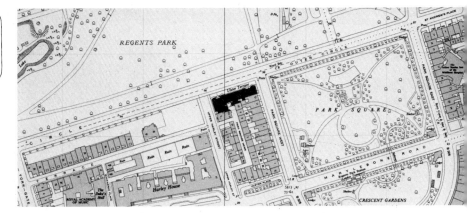

Ulster Terrace is a small terrace of eight houses at the corner of Park Square, facing north across Regents Park. Designed by *John Nash* in about 1818, the individual houses had since been radically altered. During the war the terrace was roughly converted to government offices and a bomb badly damaged the west side.

The intention of the *Crown Estate Commissioners* was to restore the *Nash* facades in Regents Park with accuracy and rigour, so the facade was stripped of accretions, and the balustrades restored.

The conservation and restoration programme, designed in association with *Edward Armitage,* was for a ground floor and part basement of offices, with three floors of flats above.

By manipulating the section, two extra floors were inserted in the rear. These floors, with their half module increments, contain bedrooms and bathrooms, and the small module allows for a variety of plan arrangements.

The rear elevation, visible only from the mews, is a complicated gesture, cantilevering outwards on the upper floors to gain valuable penthouse space. It uses an arcaded treatment to tie in with the *Nash* facades.

Nash's original design, shown opposite in a print of 1820, can be compared with the photograph (bottom left) taken before reconstruction was finished in 1975. The drawing of the new elevation restores the original *Nash* facade, though the dormer windows in the mansard roof behind the balustrades have been enlarged, and two central chimneys removed.

In addition to producing detailed drawings of the facades, a model was made in wood to give a sense of the dimension and volume of the project. The photograph of the completed and finished restoration shows how the terrace appears today, viewed from Regents Park.

Ulster Terrace is an historic stage set, which contains a new building with different uses and activities. However, every care was taken to reproduce the original railings and to reinstate every door case and window.

It represents an attitude to cities, romantic and adaptable which allows the best of the old to be uncompromisingly restored, and where no real precedent exists, as in the rear elevation, to make a romantic invention in much the same spirit.

The building received a *European Architectural Heritage Year Award* in 1975, which was shared by *Pentagram* and *Edward Armitage* of *Green, Lloyd and Adams.*

177

he section shows how the
ew structure has been related
the *Nash* facade. Original
oom heights and depths have
een retained on the north
de giving generous living
ooms overlooking the park.

n the south, two extra floors
ave been inserted to allow a
ariety of flat sizes. The first
nd third floors are
aisonettes. The new south
cade cantilevers outward
give bigger penthouses.

he cornice is in patterned
rickwork, to hold and crown
e complex facade, and to
xploit the south light which
mphasises this.

he precast concrete corbels
ere designed by *Peter Lloyd
nes*, and each level has a
fferent design.

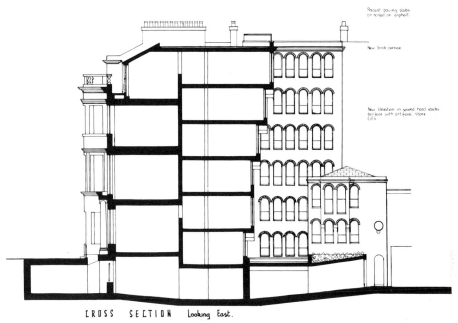

Precast paving slabs
on screed on asphalt.

New brick cornice

New elevation in second hand stocks
fairface with artificial stone
cills.

CROSS SECTION Looking East.

179

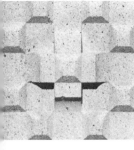

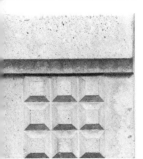

Environment design: Conservation

The restoration of the external appearance and structure of a building also affects the interior spaces. On the east side facing Park Square, the old chimney has been removed and the blind windows opened up, thus restoring the original design, made possible by the benefits of central heating.

Externally, the building is very much controlled by an overriding architecture. Internally, the flats were left as a bare shell to allow tenants as much freedom as possible to create their own interiors from a variety of permutations.

This photograph shows the living room in the first floor flat of *Pentagram* partner *Colin Forbes.*

The four photographs on the opposite page show how the interior was divided with cupboards, drawer units and walls of shelves to create rooms. Within the Georgian shell, modern classic furniture by *Le Corbusier, Rietveld* and *Martin Grierson* finds itself perfectly comfortable, and lively graphics provide a counter point to the vistas over Regents Park.

It is in this contrast between the public face and the private opportunity that architecture might find a clue to a more satisfactory and responsive environment.

Helen Challon together with the *Hille Design Unit* designed one of the large penthouse maisonettes for *Leslie* and *Rosamind Julius*.

The floor levels were altered to get the best view of the park through the dormer windows, and of Central London through the arcaded elevation.

181

In the bathroom an interesting utilization of the round window and hand basin shows a sophisticated handling of fixtures and fittings.

A sensitive manipulation of all the spaces in this penthouse has resulted in a distinguished interior.

Chalcot House

WESTBURY · WILTSHIRE

TELEPHONE CHAPMANSLADE 466

182

Chalcot House is placed on a hill site on the edge of the downs, which has been a settlement for 3,000 years. Several coin hoards from the first century have been discovered, and over 2,000 were found during restoration in 1973.

The house is documented from the twelfth century, when it belonged to the *Lords* of *Warminster* until 1585. By 1680 the structure had been regularised into a Palladian square with a spiralling central stair. The house was refronted also, to a design said to be by *Inigo Jones*.

In 1872 the architect *J.P.St. Aubyn* made radical alterations, moving the entrance to the east side, installing the great stair and the *Adam* style drawing room. A vast three storey wing of bedrooms, staffrooms, and kitchens was added.

The house remained virtually unaltered until 1970 when it had fallen into disrepair.

The new owner decided to concentrate on saving the original house, which contained the best rooms, and to cut away the nineteenth century north wing.

The house had to undergo a great deal of repair. The stone roof was replaced, and the whole central stair and major rooms, infected by dry rot, had to be stripped back to the stonework.

This type of work is always slow and painful, requiring endless supervision and care as the secrets of decay and concealed construction slowly come to light. Restoration was only part of the problem because, at the same time, the house was thoroughly reserviced with new electric and heating systems and many new bathrooms.

The park contains some remarkable specimen trees, mainly American and now at their full size. The garden was cleared and the layout greatly simplified, under the supervision of *Moyra Burnett*.

The house received a grant from the *Historic Building Commission* for the repair work, and a *European Architectural Heritage Year Award* in 1975.

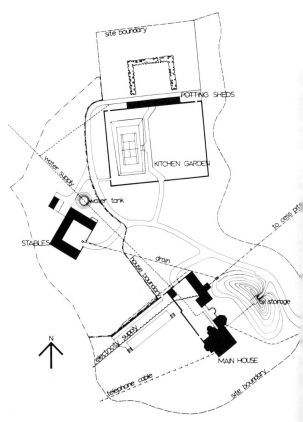

184

The top picture shows the view from the west of the house during the demolition. On the right, the house as it is today, fully restored and completed, seen from the same position. The remains of the demolished wing are buried around the oil tank to form a grassy mound which protects the dining room and kitchen from the access drive.

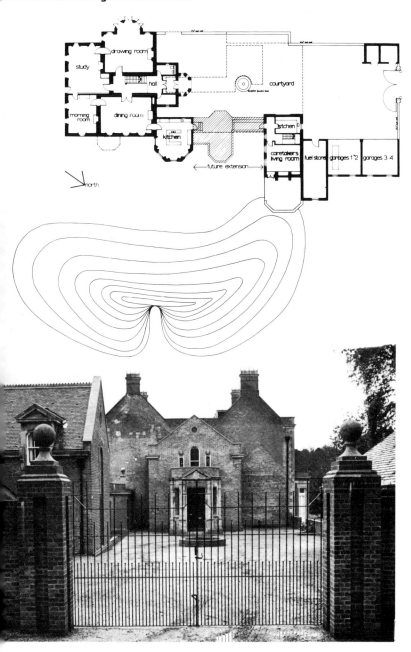

The ground plan shows the extent of the restoration. The original entrance porch, and a new wing, have been built on the north facade where they conceal the scar of the connection to the demolished wings.

The original kitchens have been cut down to form a caretaker's cottage, where the original chimney and dormers have been rebuilt one storey lower. The mound conceals the demolition rubble and oil tank.

Working with an enlightened and adventurous client provided an opportunity for *Theo Crosby* to carve a relief of his head in the keystone of the blind arch of the caretaker's cottage.

The entrance is through the new enclosed courtyard which has specially designed gates.

Environment design: Conservation

Chalcot remains an old house. Internally, there has been no attempt to impose an alien or modern style. The basic principle of the restoration was that we should make it out of what was already there, re-using materials wherever possible, and taking clues for detailing from the existing rooms. All the mouldings were carefully restored by *Mr McGrath*, a local master plasterer.

The *Adam* style drawing room still has the original chandelier. About half of the very complex ivy leaf plaster work had to be restored.

The dining room, once the entrance hall, was originally half panelled and very dark and gloomy. Much of the panelling was lost to dry rot and it was not replaced. The ceiling cornice mouldings were repaired, and the ceiling much simplified.

Where restoration would have become pastiche, new materials and methods were introduced into the architectural grammar. The stairwell, which is substantially new, was softly lit by a new domed skylight. A new screen of uncompromising geometric pattern was designed to conceal the small stair to the new bedroom over the entrance porch.

A decorative motif of *Chalcot* was commissioned from a ceramic designer and has

Environment design: Conservation

been used on crockery, tiles, and door handles.

The *Rudd* family, standing in front of the entrance porch, which is surmounted by the arms of *Henry Phipps* who rebuilt the house in 1870, have decorated the rooms with their family pictures and furniture. The rooms are finished in *Morris* wallpapers

and filled with family furniture and martial obsessions, so creating a level of involvement no decorator can supply.

In addition to the building and interior design, *Pentagram* produced a calligraphic device, which is used for the stationery and a small leaflet outlining the history of the house.

Environment design: Conservation

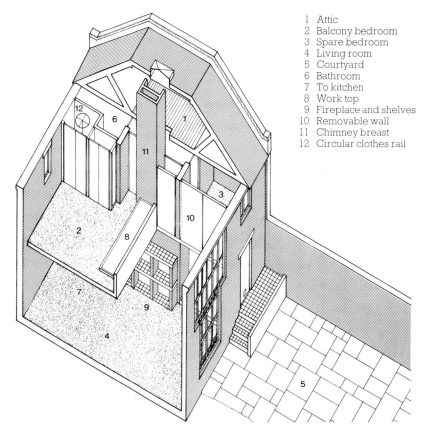

1 Attic
2 Balcony bedroom
3 Spare bedroom
4 Living room
5 Courtyard
6 Bathroom
7 To kitchen
8 Work top
9 Fireplace and shelves
10 Removable wall
11 Chimney breast
12 Circular clothes rail

Jessica Strang, a pillar of *Pentagram* for many years, bought a dilapidated garage in a Victorian terrace near our studio.

This small house was designed for her, a home for a single working girl. Utilising the permitted volume to the maximum, a by-law-busting stair was designed to occupy the minimum possible space. This allows for a symmetrical arrangement – emphasised by the transverse trusses from which the roof is suspended, and also provides a large top-lit attic room.

The photographic sequence shows three views of the transformation.

Environment design: Conservation

The interior is a single space, with skylights and a large window to the courtyard. The structure uses the original bricks with a concrete floor and gallery. Ceilings are in sealed natural pine planking.

Much care was taken in the detailing to produce a maintenance-free home. Features are: aluminium windows in hard-wood surrounds, patent glazing, asbestos cement roofing, under-floor heating, and a gas fire housed in a concrete and brick frame which also holds the stereo and books.

The brick walls are sealed, and covered with an immense collection of art and ephemera.

The photographs show the interior from the balcony, from the stairs, and from the ladder up to the attic; the bedroom cupboard with a shopfitter's rotating hanging rail; and a glass brick on the exterior which allows the meter to be read without entering the house.

The plan allows the house to be converted into a two-floor structure by extending the gallery and removing the plywood wall to the spare room: an acceptance of the facts that conventional houses are better market value, and that single girls often marry and have children.

Identity props

The interior of a new building will generally follow the form, style and detail of the exterior. Indeed it is a tenet of the modern movement that this should be so. But it is a tenet that will be the source of the very first problems to confront a designer who has been asked to re-design an existing interior, whether he is to adapt it to some new purpose or to strengthen its impact in a new commercial context.

The alternatives range from destroying the original work and starting afresh, to adopting any one of an infinite number of stages of adaptation or restoration, but the choice is seldom clear cut. Generalisations are particularly difficult to make with any confidence, simply because of the infinite variety of conditions and requirements that can arise.

However, there is at least one good ground rule: the designer should look to the existing place to find the clue to its regeneration, keeping valuable architectural elements wherever they exist, and whenever it is possible to do so.

In almost every case a main element in the problem is to create an acceptable identity for a client. It is the designer's grasp of this key element that provides a mode for solving most of the practicalities. The place and the user's identity should be fused and mutually reinforcing.

Identity is important to any organisation, for organisations live by style, on their personalities, and their buildings must underpin their working lives: make a life style. An organisation, like a person, must therefore be recognisable and memorable; full of character and if possible, a little beauty. The visitor must carry away an impression loaded with overtones of energy and service, and undertones of expertise and cultural understanding.

It is therefore essential for the designer to acquire a rich vocabulary of style, or he finds himself peddling the same solutions, and thus the same identity to all his clients. In the past, a straight tasteful modern solution, made up of the products of a few top furniture companies, was enough to distinguish a progressive company from the surrounding chaos. Today, as in commercial architecture, the efficient modern interior is the current product of thousands of contract furnishers, the designer has to provide something else.

He finds quite remarkably little fresh material at his disposal, from which to make a new world. He has to make it, much of the time, out of what is already there, because what exists, especially in old buildings, represents a level of craftsmanship and intellectual input he can seldom afford today. He will therefore tend to flinch at the prospect of fitting a client into a standard modern building, which preconditions his solutions to an interchangeable banality. Faced with such a prospect, the thought of the easily earned fee is the only balm. He will be extended by a more complex interpretation at many levels, in an old, complicated and inefficient building. Here, at least, is a challenge with some intellectual respectability.

Problems such as traffic and communications flow, storage and retrieval of information, access to equipment or machinery, control of noise, and endless other practical considerations will appear in a different order or priority, determined by the function and purpose of each successive interior. The solutions will be further qualified by the economics of the situation.

Sometimes, a young company with limited means will need to spend nearly all their money on storage facilities and equipment, and the designer will need to resort to wit, paint and art to create as simple, lively and appropriate a place as he can.

But even where a little more money is available, there are few elements in an interior that can or need to be invented. It is only very rarely possible to choose between a standard product and a unique design. To give individuality to a space, it is therefore essential to isolate those parts, furniture or fitments that will dominate the space, and if possible, design them for their task.

More often than not, it will be a table of one kind or another, in a boardroom, or the receptionist's desk in an entrance hall. Such elements are seldom readily available and the manufacturing processes required for the production of even the most unique table are generally less complex than for most other large items of furniture.

The designer's role is to create situations in which others can find a place, so that as much intelligence as possible can be brought to bear on a space. The creation of an atmosphere and environment that is amenable and conducive to good work is an aid to efficiency that is quite as necessary as filing cabinets or fresh air. That is why the designer should make opportunities, however trivial, to incorporate the skills of sculptors and painters as well as graphic designers, illustrators and product designers.

Even with domestic interiors, or in small private offices, it is possible to pursue these goals by encouraging the client to buy works of art, to form a collection. This allows a scheme of decoration to be subtly changed and kept alive over the years, and above all involves the client (who after all, is the person who will have to live with the results) in the process of design. It also provides a mechanism for a continual upgrading of the interior, that always reflects the taste of the patron.

When larger-scale projects such as airports or shopping centres are undertaken, the rewards of employing artists increase proportionately. The fact that modern art seems so strange to many people, is largely a result of the artist's failure to become involved in the process of building. This in turn has to a great extent, been caused by a misplaced confidence on the part of many designers in their own ability to do everything necessary, themselves. However, we are now rediscovering the truth of an old saying: a building is "many men thick". The artist has the capacity to see a visual problem in a unique and often remarkably acute way: such expertise and intelligence is infinitely valuable. So is the experience of working with different minds and talents, in the process of which the designer's own perceptions are often sharpened and his abilities extended.

The orchestration of these many skills by the designer is as legitimate an expression of creative talent as any work he may personally undertake, and is far more likely to lead to the creation of something truly memorable.

Theo Crosby

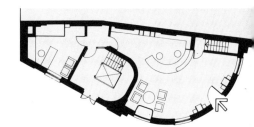

The site, at the junction of the Mall and Trafalgar Square, is tiny but immensely important. We had hoped to build a dome, a marker much more arresting than a commercial sign, but the costs were too high so we installed a splendid flag pole instead.

Malaysia House in Trafalgar Square, in the very centre of London, was transformed into premises for the *Malaysian Trade Commission.*

The building was cleaned, gutted, reserviced and the top storey rebuilt to form a suite for the Trade Commissioner, where he has glass walls giving a staggering view over the square and the Strand.

The interiors have been lined with Malaysian materials as a demonstration of national pride.

192

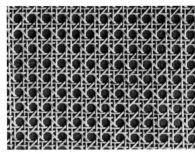

The Trade Commissioner's office has rattan furniture made in Malaysia, and a special table covered with Malaysian marble. The octagonal theme, produced in the pattern of the rattan, is used throughout the building; in the carpets, lighting fittings, door-windows and furniture.

Environment design: Interiors

The entrance hall is in Malaysian woods and pewter. The reception desk was devised to provide privacy, and is a focal point for the space. The ceiling was made with timber slats and randomly arranged multi-coloured balls. The same detail, with a darker timber, is used in the basement auditorium.

Every surface provided an opportunity for craftsmanship and decoration. The basic system, a timber moulding holding panels of various sizes and materials, could be altered without much trouble. This allows for a wide variety of textures. Desks, tables and easy chairs were designed to fit the relatively small rooms.

The Malaysian coat-of-arms is displayed externally on a projecting oval sign, cast in aluminium and painted in bright colours. In the Trade Commissioner's office, it was carved in wood by *John Andrews.*

Environment design: Interiors

The basement, lined in dark timber, contains the cloakroom and a small cinema and lecture room. The screen is revealed by opening panels of pin boards, and speakers are housed below. The air-conditioning outlets are invisible in the ceiling ornamentation.

The lobbies and corridors are fitted with Malaysian timber and glass panels, the latter to protect the *menkuang* matting which acts as a colourful background to cultural posters.

Lighting fittings, were integral in the decorative scheme, and designed to avoid glare. The one in the cinema is a standard glass bowl and a chrome tube giving a downlight.

The octagonal motif derived from the rattan was used to unify the decorations and these photographs show some of the wide variety of applications.

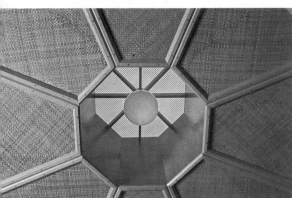

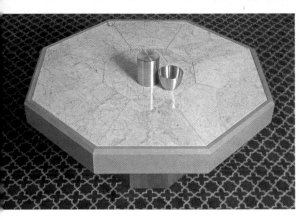

The character of the building is in the details and precision with which everything has been made. Externally, little has been changed. Internally we hope the quality of the facade has been extended.

Door openings echo stair lighting, the skylight in the Commissioner's office echoes the low table, while the rattan cupboard doors and wall panels carry the theme right through the building.

GEERSGROSS

Geers Gross, a young thrusting advertising agency, made a speculative move to a small new building, already fitted with ceilings, lighting and carpets.

The agency had grown to a turning point, handling large complex accounts, and there was a particular pleasure in concentrating on upgrading the remaining surfaces of the interior and making a background of rich traditional materials.

A large polished brass numeral was designed to stand over the entrance while leather, travertine, linen and oak panelling were used internally.

The system of articulating oak louvre panels was devised for the reception, cinema and conference rooms. These give control over light, sound absorption, and privacy. Constructed in two foot square frames for easy assembly into walls, ceilings and screens, they can be varied to create elaborate patterns.

Bob Geers and *Bob Gross* joined to form the agency, and joining their alliterative names formed the logotype.

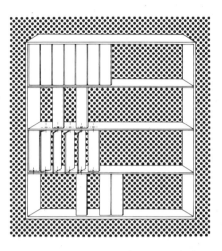

Environment design: Interiors

The entrance hall was altered radically to incorporate a reception and waiting area. A new door was made in bronze and glass while the ceiling is in oak panelling, very complex geometrically, and the floors and walls are in travertine.

The marble was already used in the entrance lobby and its extension into the building brings a unity between the exterior and interior.

The waiting area has a vertical double-sided glass post box, which, in addition to showing mail deliveries, also allows the lobby to be visually controlled from the reception desk.

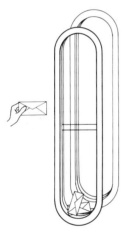

An electronic clock with *Nixy* tube numerals was incorporated into a polished brass case and mounted above the reception desk.

Individual tables were specially designed to a module. They are used as desks, or fitted together to make larger conference tables when so required. Made in oak, with simple leather inlay tops, the drawer units can be added to taste.

The large oval dining table is one of our most ambitious pieces of furniture. It is cantilevered from four massive legs, stoved steel tubes with domed beech feet, and has a framed undercarriage. The table top has a stressed skin construction and is edged in polished beech. There is a smaller coffee table to match.

Contrary to what one might expect it is often much cheaper to design and manufacture special pieces of furniture, than to buy them. The problem of course is to find a contractor who is able to carry the quality into the hidden detailing, as well as the outward aspect of high finish.

199

Boase Massimi Pollitt, the advertising agency, moved to a new very large space, an old railway parcel depot. The deep section allowed the conference rooms to be placed centrally while private offices and open plan areas were disposed around them.

The interior design theme was red stained wood with an impression of great simplicity. Red framing, clear and wire glass, white formica panelling, cork and mirror infills.

The entrance area has a reception desk, again in red stained timber, with leather cloth top. The elbow level surface covers the light fittings for the work top and gives a degree of privacy.

The conference rooms were designed with vast hinged walls able to open and form a great space for big meetings, or remain closed and allow for two private areas.

The plan shows these spaces while the photograph has a view into one half of the area. The conference tables (red, white formica tops) can add together to form a variety of formats for meetings.

The interior is now six years old and has been very heavily used as the agency has grown to remarkable prosperity. The disadvantages of open planning in expanding situations, particularly where space is tight and people are too closely grouped, has resulted in an inevitable demand for separate, private offices.

Large splayed dimensional chromed numerals, fixed to the red stained drum of the revolving doors, announce the entrance, which was originally a shop.

Though the double volume entrance is nearly six metres high, the design arrangement makes the climb not unpalatable, and there is a fat red handrail to cling to.

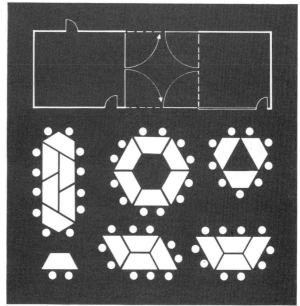

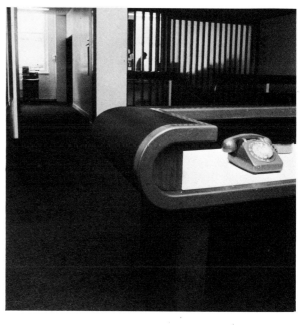

THE MITSUBISHI TRUST AND BANKING CORPORATION

The London branch of the *Mitsubishi Trust and Banking Corporation* is on an upper floor of a modern office building. The space was quite anonymous and unalterable and within this, the design tried to capture some of the quality of a Japanese interior. Pine panelling and sliding doors with shoji screens over the windows.

The entrance hall reception desk and switchboard is backed by a panel of pine veneer with an overlaid grid of timber strips, lacquered vermilion. The raised platform gives the receptionist a good presence in the space and the section shows the structure of the two-level counter with concealed lighting.

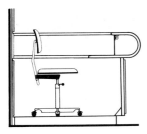

In the Japanese style dining room below, the furniture consists of *Le Corbusier Grand Confort* chairs, a long settee made up of matching leather cushions, and a large low table. This was specially made with a chromed tubular frame and a dark red *Griotte* marble top. It makes for rather formal meals – but it's a wonderful surface.

The dealing table is a series of working desks. The central black polished timber construction, houses a double decker filing system, and incorporates standard *Post Office* and *Reuters* equipment. The leathercloth work top rests on a heavy frame containing the cabling and filing trolleys. The four dealers face each other, with secretaries at each end.

When the stockbroking firm of *Rowe Rudd* acquired a Victorian banking hall in the City of London, they set about a total transformation of the firm.

Every aspect of their activities was studied and the various systems re-thought in detail. All documentation and stationery were redesigned to provide greater efficiency as well as a company look.

The work on the interior, largely in blue stained timber slatting, keeps the scale of the original and complements it. The plan is focused on the electro-mechanical dealing boards; the dealers being backed by their respective research sections on stepped platforms under the domed skylight of the original banking hall. At the rear are information processing and

Environment design: Interiors

meeting rooms and in the basement are the canteen, partners' dining room, and kitchen.

The slatting masks air-conditioning, trunking and pipes, it also screens work areas and obscures acoustic materials and strip lighting.

The logotype, based on a ninteenth-century cheque mark, is used as a watermark on the stationery, embossed on book-matches, reproduced on ash-trays, and even stitched on napkins. Its form allows it to be fitted to any shape.

206

Crocketts was the name selected by the client for this hamburger take away restaurant. By exploiting strip cartoons and comic books on the character, it was possible to achieve the symbol and decor at little expense, but perhaps more importantly as a theme it was attractive to children and families, who were considered to be a major part of the customer market.

Copyright restrictions prevented reproducing pictures directly from existing sources, so the illustrator *Mick Brownfield* drew us pictures in the vocabulary of penny plain and tuppence coloured.

The interior was designed on a shoestring, and the stipulations included simple decorations and robust furnishings. Vandal proof solutions were a major consideration by the client. The ceiling was rough sawn planks stained dark green, the floor earthenware tiles, the seating available orange fibre-glass shells bolted to steel stanchions, and the tables yellow formica. The walls were white with framed coloured photoprints of the illustrations.

The kitchen was open to the self-service counter to reassure customers of hygienic conditions and to encourage staff to maintain standards.

To speed up ordering from queuing customers the original idea was to make a menu over the counter with models of the food and price tags. *Nancy Fouts* and *Malcolm Fowler* were commissioned to make these delectable appetising hot dogs, hamburgers and ice creams, but in the end practicality required spelling out the items and decoratively grouping the models.

As *Crocketts* was essentially a take away operation more money was spent on the packaging than usual. The packs, boxes, bags and wrappers were designed in three colours to be walking advertisements for the restaurant.

Arts Council
SHOP

The *Arts Council Shop* was intended to sell their growing collection of exhibition catalogues and posters, to become a place where the reports and publications of the regions could be seen, where records and books subsidised by the *Arts Council* could be sold, and to be a primary information centre.

The space is quite small and all the display is in green stained modular timber cases, with adjustable shelves and top lighting.

Above head height, the walls and the ceiling are lined with back lit perspex panels which are filled with posters. The floor has green carpet tiles, and an awkward central column was ringed with a postcard display and mirror.

The appearance and quality of such an interior depends on the clear separation and control of the two basic forms of information; the bulk of books and the size of posters.

The changing displays can be kept well under control, although still present a rich collage of material to maintain the curiosity of the browser.

WE♪♪EX

The existing structure of a
Victorian church hall occupied
by *Wessex Sound Studios*, was
too light and too penetrable for
the volume of sound generated
within.

The acoustic treatment of
sound studio walls is
unpredictable, but consists
mainly of alternating boxes of
varying depths, which are
moved around to find a
satisfactory location.

It was clear that an interior
could not be designed on such
variable elements, so the
boxes are concealed behind
a timber frame filled with
pleated hessian (acoustically
transparent), and faced with
metal mesh.

Spotlights on dimmer circuits
play on these surfaces and
produce *moiré* patterns,
dissolving the solidity of the
wall.

A new ceiling of woodwool
slabs and screed was
suspended from double
trusses. The woodwool is
exposed and the new steel is
painted blue.

The new quadrophonic
equipment required a larger
control room, and extra space
was created by a double
glazed bay window, which also
forms a balcony over the studio.

We also did a logotype but it
was not accepted. They felt the
musical pictorial reference to
their trade seemed too
obvious.

209

Urban complexions

"The track of man in space has become of fundamental importance in architecture" said *Theo Van Doesburg* who in 1927 designed the interior of the café *l'Aubette* in Strasbourg. Here he treated the interior surface as he might a painting; it is a work combining architecture and art which has influenced the genre which today we loosely call *Environment graphics.*

The term is currently used to describe that indefinite overlap and interplay between graphics, art and architecture, the visual activation of a structural surface, or the structural visualisation of a graphic idea. It can be expressed in many forms, often serves different functions and generally is large in scale.

The artform has very early origins. The reasons for Peruvian land figures or the carving of the *White Horse* at Uffington are obscure, although it is said that the horse was cut out of the hillside in memory of the battle against the Danes in 871 AD. It measures 335 feet from nose to tail, and 120 feet from ears to hooves. All larger than life, such figures are associated with concepts or ideas beyond their physical characteristics.

The medieval builder and the Renaissance architect well understood the flamboyant graphic gesture within an architectural context. The black and white patterns of *Sienna Cathedral,* the narrative mosaic frescoes of Ravenna, the decorated pavillions of the *Palace of Udaipur,* all enrich our visual senses and stimulate our creative needs.

Even plans may be more graphic than architectural. The labyrinth at *Chartres Cathedral* provides both pattern and purpose, the sick and infirm often crawled through the maze as an alternative to actually undertaking the holy pilgrimage. The chequered piazza at Marostica in Italy

may well have been designed with ritual in mind and to this day is the scene of an annual game of chess played, since the twelfth century, by the town folk in medieval costume.

Sometimes the intent of environment graphics is purely commercial. In England, *Pears* soap, one of the leading Victorian exponents of aggressive and bizarre advertising, proposed to paint an enormous slogan on the white cliffs of Dover. Luckily this scheme was averted by public outcry. One of the largest advertising signs ever erected was the electric *Citroen* sign on the *Eiffel Tower;* it was switched on in 1925 and could be seen 24 miles away, the letter "n" being about 68 feet high. At the *Bauhaus, Herbert Bayer* designed a number of projects which relied extensively on graphics. The most familiar being a structure for newspapers and cigarettes, and his toothpaste pavillion. In these designs he includes the use of projection and sound, and words formed by smoke, a vision which anticipated the visual panoply of the contemporary downtown commercial centre. Shortly afterwards, in 1934, *Bijvoet* and *Duiker* built the Amsterdam movie house *De Handelsblad Cineac* in which a huge three dimensional electric sign became the major element of the design. This cinema still stands today, very much the precursor of Las Vegas neon architecture.

The graphic expression of political propaganda is often larger than life. In 1965 an enormous illustration of Chinese workers was assembled by eight thousand school children each holding colour cards representing a single dot. This created an original and dramatic effect, a background to a gymnastic display held in Peking and probably a graphic experience never attempted on this scale before. More nostalgic and certainly less transient are the American presidents carved out of *Mount Rushmore.*

Environment design: Graphics

The Nuremburg rallies, art-directed by *Albert Speer,* relied as heavily on ambience, theatre and *son et lumière,* as on colour and design or even speech. As an architect, *Speer* was of the same generation, if not of the same political persuasion, as *El Lissitzky*, who designed the *Lenin* speakers platform (Rednertribune, Moscow) with a large screen sign as a backdrop on this amazing cantilevered structure. The *Leningrad Pravda* building project, by the *Vesnin* brothers, also made extensive use of projected images, backlit information boards, loudspeakers and searchlights, so that the architecture was almost entirely created out of these communication systems. Apart from World Fairs, the strictures of a more democratic society generally preclude such characteristic enthusiasms, but the aesthetic impoverishment of many dull and uninspiring cityscapes could be imaginatively transformed by similar techniques.

A more vital use of shape and colour should indeed become, once again, an integral part of what one can term an architectural palette. In the last century Parisian colour merchants painted abstract patterns over their shop facades to denote their trade, while more recently in the same city, the *Colourflage* by *Jean Phillipe Lenclos* on the towers of Crétail, extend the visual impact of the buildings through a pictorial disruption of strutural forms.

Sometimes it is the individual who takes a hand, and the Pakistani immigrants condemned to live in England's grey industrial environments, happily decorate front doors in bright colours which are more evocative of Karachi than of Bradford. In New York, similar frustrations are expressed through the medium of the aerosal can. Though essentially anarchistic, graffiti is perhaps the easiest way for individuals to decorate the environment in which they are resentfully confined.

Art on the city wall is perhaps better served by a more controlled application even of exuberant ideas; and "supergraphics" is now almost a professional occupation. A group of painters called *Fine Art Squad* construct peeling walls in Los Angeles, while *Urban Walls* in Cincinnati have rendered amongst their projects an enormous and unlikely painting of a nut and bolt. Even individual artists join in the fun. *Vasarely* argues the case that "architectonic art should be the fusion of colour and plasticity", *Oldenburg* proposes vast inflatable sculptures floating on the Thames, and *Christo* wraps landscapes and buildings in polythene.

Wall painting can do more than startle or transform, enrich and decorate, it can carry social signals to the initiated. In Rajastan, the elephants and horses framing the entrances to houses, declare celebration and betrothals. Protective abstract designs on the barns of the Pennsylvanian Dutch deter evil influences. Black draped doors on the Italian church declare familial sorrow.

We can still see the remnants of the traditional elements of decorative trade devices, between the new supersites and supermarkets, though they become fewer everyday. The horse's head outside the French butcher's, the boot outside the shoemaker's, the red and white pole symbolising the blood and bandages of surgery, the barber's sidelines in the past. Such pictorial signals and signs, whether social, political or commercial must be kept.

There is even greater need today, as our environments slide into the control of bureaucratic committee blandness, for a massive involvement of artistic energy in the city. Our new buildings are too often determined by economic and technical parameters which benefit only the builder and the speculator. Growing urban populations, condemned to live in a faceless sterile barracks or endless tacky boxes, require a relationship with their environment, a sense of participation and identification. Let us use our environments in a way which enables us to respond to our creative and visual impulses.

Alan Fletcher

212

Environmental graphics can cover a name plate as well as a sky sign. It can also involve a variety of techniques.

On completion of the new civic centre at Harrow, the aldermen asked *Kodak*, a major employer in the town, to contribute a mural to be sited on the entrance.

The solution was based on a *Kodak* process of printing photographs on ceramic tiles. Each of the 1,000 tiles has a different image of Harrow, either culled from archives, reproduced from current printed ephemera, or specially photographed.

The mural has no aesthetic pretensions; it is readily understood and appreciated; it is informative, colourful, bright and it is practical.

Environment design: Graphics

The *Riverdale Shopping Centre* in Lewisham, London is a typical commercial development of large multiple shops.

The stated objective, an intimate pedestrian area with a variety of choices, was clearly in conflict with the reality – a development which comprises large stores with frontages of forty metres or more. The solution is an attempt to humanise the spaces.

The central piazza, containing lift shafts to the parking overhead, was illuminated by predetermined skylights. The space was made coherent by a maze of tilted ceiling louvres, disguising the source but allowing natural and concealed electric lighting to filter through.

The malls are kept fairly dark, the shop fronts emphasised by a rhythm of verticals and the apparent variety created by this complexity of surfaces. Walls and pilasters are of glazed tiles, patterned to reduce scale, and filled at eye level by casual and easy drawings by *Donna Brown*.

The signs are based on a Victorian wood letter alphabet.

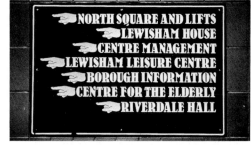

NORTH SQUARE AND LIFTS
LEWISHAM HOUSE
CENTRE MANAGEMENT
LEWISHAM LEISURE CENTRE
BOROUGH INFORMATION
CENTRE FOR THE ELDERLY
RIVERDALE HALL

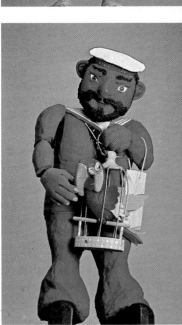

Environment design: Graphics

The lift wells in the piazza are within a steel structure which contains an animated puppet show. There are nine figures which rotate into view from brightly painted capsules every fifteen minutes, they perform to a tune by *John Scott*.

These puppets of London characters were created by artist *Sam Smith*, and are perhaps his largest public work. The brightly painted and decorated structure was the work of *Fowles* the last great painter of funfair roundabouts.

These and other artworks, such as animal rubbish bins by *Derek Howarth*, help to make an environment which is colourful and cheerful without condescension.

The difficulty of achieving even a modest complexity in the normal commercial context, was only made possible by an exceptional client.

Each store needed to be persuaded to renounce standard high street facades for the less competitive reality of quiet pedestrian areas, where people expect to be entertained rather than exhorted.

The results were by no means always successful, but at least we learned that one needs to know a great deal about development controls, leases and small print.

Environment design: Graphics

Illustrator *Donna Brown* worked in *Pentagram* for several months producing a vast number of drawings on every conceivable shopping subject. These are some of the original sketches which were finally translated onto ceramic tiles.

The pictorial concept was for the illustrations to echo the window displays on the pilasters between shops. Several stores, such as *Marks and Spencer*, were encouraged to commission their own special subjects.

The drawings were silk-screened in black line, and colours were added directly to the tiles. In this way a close collaboration was achieved between the illustrator and *Mike Head* who fired the ceramics.

The largest works decorate the entrance to the Old People's Centre and the Riverdale Hall. Here *Donna* had much larger surfaces and a more complex subject matter: dancing, gymnastics, and other sports representing the activities within.

The shopping centre has now been in use for over a year, and to date there has been no vandalism or graffiti. The images fit the place well, without strain, and give much pleasure to all.

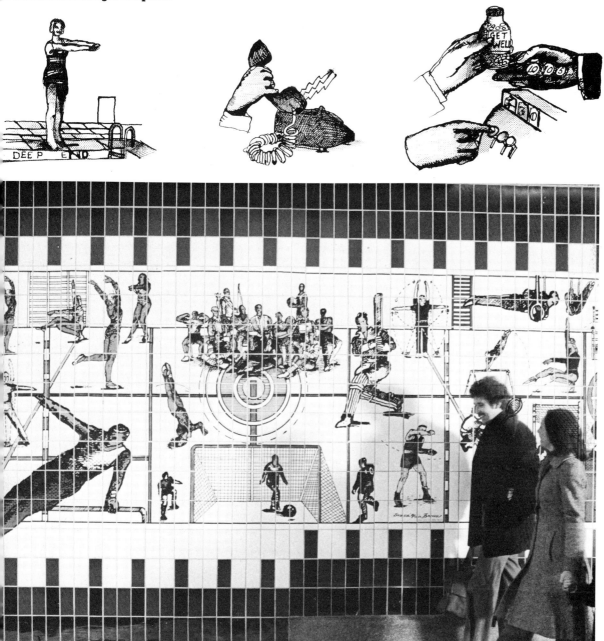

Environment design: Graphics

Signs, like pictorial graphics, can often produce a dominant effect on an environment.

Arrows and pointing fists invariably direct our movements but sometimes an unlikely application can also provide some fun.

These large three dimensional pointing hands were made in silvered fibre glass, and routed the traffic through an exhibition at the *Louvre,* Paris.

Suspended from the ceilings, they were angled, taking people up stairs and down passages, culminating in a flock of hands descending and pointing down over the exit.

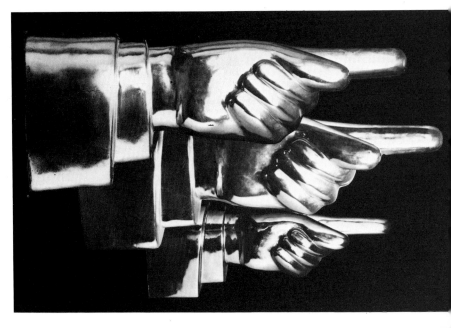

Legislation governing signs is more concerned with public safety and a bureaucratic conception of "good taste", than with graphic quality. Nevertheless ill-considered signs, materials or techniques can degrade the environment.

This advertisement for a sign manufacturer illustrates a variety of sign techniques by using his symbol.

A modest piece of graphics for the *Wallis* dress shop branch in Knightsbridge – one of London's classier shopping streets. This facade sign by *John McConnell* was drawn to stylistically complement the period building, rather than project a trendy image or assault the eye with neon tube.

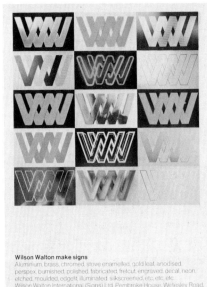

Wilson Walton make signs
Aluminium, brass, chromed, stove enamelled, gold leaf, anodised, perspex, burnished, polished, fabricated, fretcut, engraved, decal, neon, etched, moulded, edgelit, illuminated, silkscreened, etc, etc, etc.
Wilson Walton International (Signs) Ltd. Pembroke House, Wellesley Road, Croydon CR9 1QA. Telephone 01-686 6262.

In contrast to the single sign, complex programmes usually use standard alphabets, which pay little concession to their immediate surroundings. Letters can however be conceived as part of the architectural design, and, even if sacrificing a degree of legibility, can reinforce the ambience in which they appear.

This sign scheme was for *Bush Lane House* in Cannon Street, an unusual building designed by *Arup Associates*.

The curvilinear alphabet was drawn to visually echo the tubular structure. The signs were reproduced by etching letters into steel and filling with vermillion enamel. A guide for letter spacing was also designed.

TE CO LO. KE: LT

ONE UNIT · FIVE UNITS · FOUR UNITS

221

SPRINKLER ISOLATING VALVE

IN CLOSED POSITION WHEN LIT

FIRE TELEPHONE

DRM

FIRE EXIT KEEP CLOSED PRESSURISED STAIR

MEN

222

The *National Exhibition Centre*, beside the London/ Birmingham railway line, considered erecting a vast sign measuring 80m x 80m to inform passengers of present and coming attractions.

The size of the sign, and the windy nature of the site precluded a conventional billboard. A steel space grid suspended between light pylons was proposed, clad on both sides with stainless steel mesh. In the 150mm sq grid thus formed, stove enamelled aluminium plates were suspended on nylon hangers. The wind would ripple the message, but pass freely through the structure.

The various messages on one side are easily changed by simply reversing the plates from white to red, and access is by the mechanical hoists which are already in use at the Centre. The system therefore requires no signwriting, or stock of letters. On the campus side of the sign the plates make up advertising signs, which could be specially signwritten.

This printer's halftone screen reproduction of a *dhow*, made from a colour photograph, was enlarged to 2m by 6m and reproduced on vitreous enamel as a mural for a hotel in Dubai. The image was recognisable at a distance from the reception, but dissolved into a decorative coloured polka dot pattern when viewed close up in the lounge.

Using distance as a technique can sometimes create surprising effects.

Environment design: Graphics

An environment is where one is, and even a conference room can be enlivened by a graphic gesture.

Arthur Andersen & Co wanted to show their world-wide network of offices without recourse to the ubiquitous map with flags or coloured pins.

This large framed design hangs in the boardroom and consists of chromed dog tags, each engraved with an office location, and delicately balanced on pins to shimmer with the slightest vibration.

The mahogany cabinet was designed to hold the business cards of each managing director. Bolted to the wall in the reception it not only dispenses calling cards but is also good to look at.

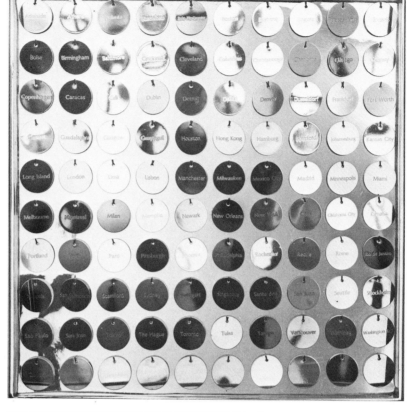

Product design

It is an interesting paradox of the design world, explored in a later essay, that whereas architects and graphic designers in independent practice can be counted in thousands, product designers can be counted in tens. In seeking one practical reason for this, one need go no further than the industrial world which is the main source of work for all designers whether in practice or employed. Most firms build only once a decade, and it is clearly economic for them to go outside for architects, interior designers and planners. As for graphic designers, the industrial client usually recognises his specialist skills as necessary but peripheral to his main products. He usually prefers working with an outsider, and will do so even if he is big enough to employ an in-house resource.

The product design need is different. Most industrialists see product design as an integral part of the manufacturing process, and difficult therefore to buy outside. No product designer in professional practice would deny this proposition, although he might well argue for the importance of overcoming the difficulties, particularly in the present parlous state of the British economy. There can after all be no questioning the central role of manufacturing industries in our efforts towards economic recovery, and those industries depend for their success on the acceptability of their products. Product design therefore is not only an integral part of the manufacturing process, it is a mainspring for management. Whether that mainspring can be wound by the internal design resource, is questionable. Almost certainly the impetus must come from outside, from the product designer or consultant.

The various sections in this part of the book each highlight ways in which the consultant can contribute to the field of *Product design*. The first, *Ashtrays to agriculture* surveys the multiplicity of products with which the product design consultant can be concerned. The second, *Consumer goods* is concerned with the every day mass-produced products through which the manufacturer's corporate image is reinforced. The third, *Working continuity* demonstrates the virtue of a long term relationship between the designer and his industrial client. Finally, the last section *British Rail* is a case history of product design work with one very large customer.

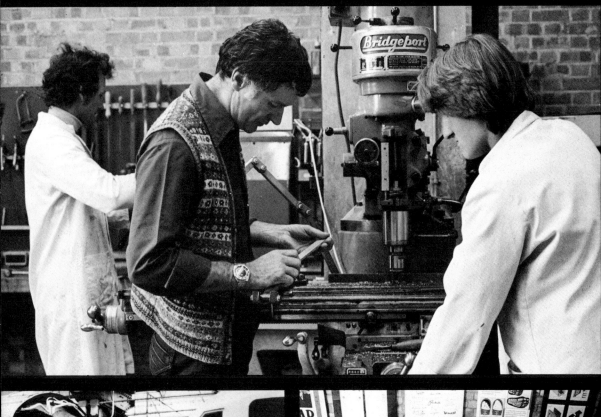

We three

Where in his tripartite obligations does the industrial designer's loyalty properly lie? With his "public" – *the users;* his employer – *the maker;* or *himself* and his own professional and aesthetic integrity?

A stroll down any high street will very quickly reveal the wide gap between sense and nonsense that exists in the products that are sold and bought in our consumer orientated society. It is a variety that is almost as great as that of society itself, and is often indeed a reflection of it. This variety is a reflection, not of social grouping, but of aesthetic alignments – or to put it in more familiar, but undoubtedly more emotive terms – good and bad taste. Simply because it is so emotive, it is more than reasonable to question the role of the industrial designer in influencing such alignments.

The industrial designer is hired above all because he possesses a quality that most people would take to be very subjective, namely aesthetic judgement. But he is not hired by the millions who will eventually use his products (without ever knowing who to praise or blame for their design) but by the maker of those products, who may be either a committee that is wholly unrepresentative of society at large, or an individual with an individual's inevitable prejudices.

There is of course a glib and ready answer to the question posed at the start of this essay. It is often contended that it is only necessary to discover "what the public wants", whether by research or gut feeling, and to proceed to give it to them in order to ensure success. Other considerations, it is said, are mere sophistries – designers talking to themselves.

Designers who espouse this point of view often display an apparently cynical attitude to their work – they may openly disparage it and profess contempt for the users of it. One designer whose designs grace many shops today coined the phrase "a mug's eyeful" so despising was he of the perception of the public. He argued, "glitter is all, make it appeal today" and that this was the prime necessity. The flaw in this argument is that he describes a static world that does not exist.

The tastes, needs and desires of even the most indiscriminate consumers are subject to constant change and it costs almost as much effort to keep up with such changes as it does to keep ahead of them. Indeed if the lack of satisfaction and rewards are taken into consideration, the work of such self-confessed hacks seems much harder, and it becomes clear that their attitudes are more the result of personal short-comings than philosophy.

None of which may be taken to mean that any designer may ignore the consumer, or even research. Such considerations have always had an important influence on "good" design, and an increasingly critical audience – first identified by the evangelist *Which* magazine, and now catered for by national newspapers and prime time TV shows, has certainly not reduced that importance. It would be easy to suppose otherwise, because it is generally the bad design that attracts the most publicity, the designer's response to the phenomenon of consumerism has needed to be essentially positive. On a practical level he has been required to anticipate the higher standards and expectations that consumerism has created.

Indeed at the lower level there is generally quite a long time gap between conception and purchase of a product and no manufacturer can afford to find that his product has become unacceptable before it reaches the shops.

But even beyond the need to anticipate future requirements, consumerism has also caused designers to give a great deal more thought to the user's pleasure and satisfaction, as opposed for example, to problems of marketability and aesthetics.

Today the designer tries to fulfill the initial promise with continuing pleasure. There is an implication here of continuing pleasure. There is an implication here of a reversion to "lasting values" or a slowing down of the pace of change. And even though it would be foolish to exaggerate them, these trends are undeniably an appropriate response to the changed social and economic circumstances that prevail in the UK (and many other countries) in the 1970's. Work in design colleges may be some indication of how these tendencies will develop. Elements which are fashionable and changeable in appearance seem nowadays to have a longer life expectancy; there is a greater concern for stability, which is often exemplified in nostalgia for past styles; socially conscious work is the most respected. The user then is clearly acknowledged in the work of all designers – even bad designers. What's more, the recent increase in concern for the user seems likely to increase still further.

But what does the designer owe to the maker – his immediate employer – and to what extent does allegiance to the maker compromise duty to the user? Most designers will agree that their prime responsibility is to the user, and that in fulfilling it, they also fulfill most, if not all, of their responsibilities to the manufacturer. Indeed, the value of the consultant designer to many manufacturers is derived from his broader contact with consumers (through the variety of his work) and a freedom from localised practices and internal politics.

This independence usually means that there is an ability to present the user's case much better than the production team that is conditioned to view any product from the maker's standpoint. What designers disagree about however, is how far they may play a missionary role in advancing users' tastes and demands.

This brings us to the last of the three major claimants to a designer's loyalty – himself. Designers of any worth must design to please themselves. They must also, and usually do, design to please other designers. Yet many of them prefer to deny these facts, whilst others only admit them apologetically or with reluctance. Why should this be so?

In part, it is caused by a lingering puritanism in our society that deems beauty for its own sake to be somehow decadent. But more often it is a sensitivity to criticisms (almost always justified) of past designs that have sacrificed practicality to appearance. But it would be a mistake to conclude from this that self satisfaction has to be subjugated to other considerations. Products that are hated by their designer, yet meet with approval everywhere else, must be quite rare.

And it is a primary function of the designer to be an innovator: not to impose his fancies on a reluctant market – this popular conception of a designer's role is in fact almost impossible to achieve – but to extend the horizons and enhance the lives of the users. It is palpably true that no innovation worthy of the name ever resulted from market research or indeed any other enquiries into people's needs and wants. The true innovator therefore is always the individual, answerable, in the first place at least, only to himself.

It is also quite legitimate and actually important for a designer to seek the approval and approbation of his peers. Because although users may enjoy and even appreciate design, other designers are the most readily available group which can offer the conscious and informed criticism that is so vital to the maintenance of creative standards.

Loyalties then cannot be apportioned exclusively to user, maker or self. They cannot even be apportioned equally between the three. There is a constant shift in balance between them, and the designer needs to be sure that his allegiance to any one is not overwhelmed by the other two. User, maker, designer – an interdependent trinity.

Kenneth Grange

227

Product design: Ashtrays to agriculture

One pleasure not usually associated with products is wit. If it is functional, beautiful and has some element of the unexpected, then surely that is the product we would most like to own and keep.

This bottle was commissioned by a sherry importer who wanted a distinctive and striking looking bottle – what he did not expect was a design which made a beautiful sound. The air is momentarily trapped in the peculiar neck, when forced out by the sherry it gurgles beautifully – there is the distinction.

Not carried forward into production, this design for a hi-fi amplifier is interesting in that it exemplifies a product group where high style is often the most important factor in the buyer's decision. Invariably our ears cannot detect the difference between one excellence and another, whereas our eyes do not deceive us.

A practical idea to fix a kettle on the wall over the sink, it saves valuable work top space. The best detail however is less obvious: a sight glass which measures in cups, not in pints. The cost saved by not boiling unnecessary water would pay for the product!

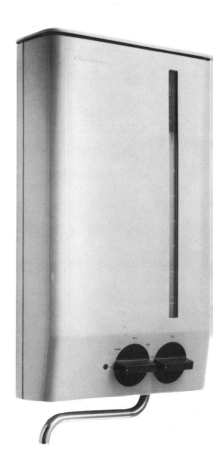

Everyday objects can be elegant. An idea, a function, an economy, an appearance, all qualify for elegance.

The green tree simply made from enamelled steel, casts its own shadow which is naturally coloured black – it is also a bookend.

An ashtray, nicely named the *Clam*, was produced in a range of bright coloured melamine and in an expensive version of chromed brass. The identical halves, made from a single mould, not only provide two ashtrays but also a lid, and teeth to grip the cigarette.

Within two months of its debut it was copied in Italy, Hong Kong, Taiwan and Tokyo.

229

The product designer who has proven commercial success with his designs, will be repeatedly commissioned by a company. If the product is essentially the same, a stimulus is needed around which a new form can be derived. With *Kodak*, over eighteen years the problem has always changed; a new method of manufacture, a new film size – all technological changes.

Unlike photography, time-keeping has evolved minimally until the recent alliance of cheaply made quartz crystals and miniature electronics.

The *Clark Alto* is an electronic clock with a quartz crystal movement, and is accurate to within 60 seconds a year. The digital clock was deliberately aimed at a discriminating buyer. Certainly it could have been made cheaper but the market was already very competitive. We deliberately set up the display on an unlikely cantilever, a visual shock, to justify the shock that would follow the cost!

MINUTES ⠐⠂⠒⠲

A "blind" clock was developed from a prototype made by Dr J M Gill of the *Warwick University Blind Unit*. It tells the time, not surprisingly, by using sound signals which vary in pitch and time.

In the development, refinements have been added which typify the sophistication that is possible through an interaction between product designer and inventor.

Instructions on how to set and use the clock are given on the outside of the casing in both braille and print – a sighted friend may be able to help initially. The front and back are differently shaped to help locate the controls which are all differently contoured and sized, again to ensure tactile recognition.

Finally a "glance" at the time is easy because the switch that starts the time signal is operable by touching any part of the top surface. In all, an essentially tactile product.

For *Taylor Instruments*, two generations of domestic instruments, thermometers, barometers and clocks, primarily show stylistic rather than technological differences.

The first generation of cases used the traditional methods of gravity die casting or wood turned housings for the instruments. The second used the technique of extruding aluminium, enabling any shape of tube to be made with very little tool cost.

This naturally suits any manufacturer who can afford more production time but who wants a low initial commitment. It is well suited to these products which contain mechanisms of extreme accuracy and widely varying size. The same tube can be used to encase a barometer or the thimble-size coil for an hygrometer.

The gold wrist watch designed by *Kenneth Grange* as his *Duke of Edinburgh's Prize for Elegant Design,* uses a conventional movement. What was less so in 1963 was a single mark at noon. As a one-off product it was uneconomical to make a conventional face.

From experiments, the necessity became a pleasure by learning to assess time accurately by the angularity of the hands. The innovative single mark pre-empted a production watch by five years.

Variety is not only the spice, it is the stock in trade of a designer's life. Clearly the consultant designer will rarely become an equal master with those engineers who spend a lifetime in one industry.

His value comes from the variety of commerce and technology in which he moves. He can move across disciplines and practices, pollinating a new project with experience from the old.

In the make-up of every good designer there should be a little of the courtesan. He must find that part in every job where he can give the unexpected pleasure. Every job can be invested with a surprise. In a society as complex as ours, the colour of a face cream, a control layout for a crane or a more shapely parking meter are all grist to the mill of opportunity for the designer. Anything can be done better than the norm, the secret is in finding the opportunity.

Techniques which are common practice in one industry are often nerve wracking in another, and marketing attitudes can be surprisingly applicable in such diverse products as parking meters and potato pickers.

We produced a design for a potato picking machine for *Ransomes*. Dominated by cost conscious steel fabrication, it was still possible to find areas in which design skills to improve performance were not only unexpected but also welcome.

The operator's position and safety were improved, beyond either the norm or the standards established by the industry.

In the fifties, *Venner* licenced from America a well proved parking meter in order to anticipate the demand expected, and subsequently fulfilled, when the government approved the installation of meters on the roads of Britain for the first time.

However the US model failed the approval of the *Council of Industrial Design* although it was used in the interim period while a new model was developed. The model on the streets today is a re-housing of their mechanism. If our society needs such parasites, then even if superficial, any amelioration is worth the effort.

232

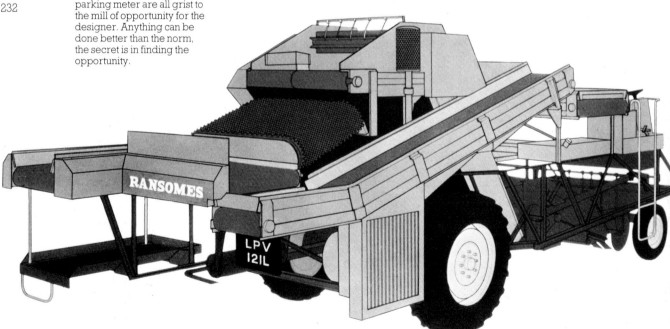

Product design: Ashtrays to agriculture

Confravision is the name of the *Post Office's* long distance conference service. In October 1971 they opened five identical studios in Glasgow, Bristol, London, Manchester and Birmingham.

Conferences are possible via sound and TV. Two large TV screens facing the conferees, give outgoing and incoming pictures and show small objects and fine detail. Anxieties are quickly dispelled and people talk to the screen as comfortably as they do face to face.

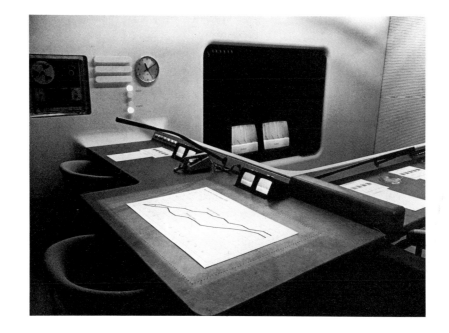

Zygma is a company successfully launching a projected TV system. Three primary colours are simultaneously projected onto a four foot screen, giving an enriched view of any material that goes through the TV screen. The cabinet steers a stylistic course between instrumentation and furniture.

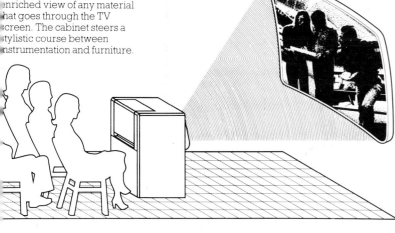

Engineering an image

For all companies, the product is the critical element in the range of design practices which contribute towards its image or its corporate identity. Where that product is manufactured to highly idiosyncratic standards, then the other elements scarcely rate. *Rolls Royce* means a superb motor car and the prime images are the radiator grille, a walnut fascia, leather and engineering. Who remembers the writing paper or even the logotype? Conversely undifferentiated products rely mainly on packaging and related graphics for their corporate style. Discerning breakfast food eaters choose between boxes, and most English kids choose blackcurrant jam from a graphic symbol which makes the hackles of American liberals rise like the hair of the golliwog on the jar.

Similarly, when the product is a service, the peripheral design around the product is very properly the main criterion for image setting. Pillar boxes, menus, cards for massage parlours, they all stand for services which are difficult to present directly.

The manufacturer of a product under use has no such problems. His image stands or falls with the product itself and therefore ultimately with its design. A telling example is the *Kenwood Chef* food mixer. For a variety of reasons this product has established itself as the archetypal food mixer in the UK – it is the image that most British people would connect with the word "food mixer" – it is also the image that most people would connect with the word "Kenwood". Comparatively few would recall the logotype, or even the box in which they bought the product. To have established a strong corporate image through products, as *Kenwood* and *Rolls Royce* have, is clearly of critical importance, even though it may sometimes have occurred almost accidentally. Nevertheless it is often given insufficient attention by both managers and product designers, and their organisations suffer.

Designing a newly conceived product for an established company is essentially how to maintain visual continuity, with previous products, yet announce quite clearly that the product is in fact new. The designer will usually be given every encouragement to make the next product as reminiscent of the last as possible. Success breeds its own kind of caution based upon the dubious premise that what worked once will always work again. Nowadays, when the entrepreneur has mostly been replaced by salaried "management teams", stepping out of line is almost as much of a crime as complete corporate failure; and pussy-footing is given the status of philosophy.

The designer must often learn to judge for himself how much continuity is desirable from the company point of view. Sometimes the company's established image may not be sufficiently strong to merit preservation, although individual products have met with great success. Even so a radically new design would be hard to justify if it served only to attract a temporary attention. But if a company has a reputation for excellence, or high standards of performance then a sensationally innovative appearance is more likely to be found acceptable by consumers.

Most of the purchasers who have been satisfied by the value and reliability of a company's product will allow a high level of indulgence in design and appearance. The prime requirement is that the replacement will function as well as the old favourite and the best of all worlds is a new product which starts as a shock and later becomes a pride and which is still in use ten or even fifteen years later.

The *Citroen DS* was launched nearly twenty years ago and has only just been discontinued. That is the reward for corporate integrity; a design which married product and image, and provided long term capital amortisation and a consequent financial contribution.

Nevertheless, even in the most favourable circumstances giving any product a distinctive company look is far less simple than might at first be supposed. The *Rolls Royce* grille would find little acceptance if it had been designed for the first time today. It is out of keeping with present motor car styles, and it is only long established success which allows it to break the rules, or rather transcend them with rules of its own.

Design creativity is too easily submerged in a world of mass markets and mass production. Consumer needs, expressed through sophisticated market research, are a main determinate of design criteria and one major barrier to originality; the other is mass production.

Henry Ford is credited with imposing the limitations of mass production on the western world – "You can have any colour you like as long as it's black". Certainly the motor industry has studied and applied mass production technology for longer and with more enthusiasm than any other. Today highly complex products are bought for very little money simply because they are made in vast quantities. It would be interesting if more of the general public understood this phenomenon. The camera that costs £5 to buy and which has £5m development behind it, is staggering value for money, and only exists because of the concept of mass production which, irrespective of overall purposes, often seems to have a life of its own. For example, the socio-political platform of the original *Volkswagen* served the ambitions of *Hitler,* promised transport freedom for every man, and ironically finished as a badge of liberal socialism in many parts of the world.

The scale and effect of design decisions on new products in quantities today are frightening. Consider the white goods phenomenon – white goods are all the domestic machines that come in white steel boxes; refrigerators, washing machines, dishwashers etc. How many Dutch or UK purchasers realise the awesome decisions behind the label that modestly says "made in Italy", or made anywhere else? The badge on the front may well be famous and proudly national, *Philips* or *Hotpoint* for example, but the forces of economy have driven the facility for making these steel boxes quite remorselessly into one gargantuan production line in Italy. Because of the quantities, the prices were held incredibly low, and so all the traditional makers joined in what the motor trade has called "Badge Engineering". Every house has the same refrigerator. Only the cosmetics vary.

This will inevitably be the pattern for a variety of products, the scale will be enormous and even if the variety in real specification is reduced, the quality and reliability will be better – at least certainly better in terms of what you get for your money. So painful will be the consequences of design and production errors that more care and time will be spent than ever before. Consider just the space problems if the factory makes a part at the rate of 100 per hour and a fault is found. Then spare space has to be found for 100 parts with each hour that passes

prior to correction. But imagine the rate of 1,000 per hour. No factory could possibly afford to occupy space for that contingency. So quality control procedures figure high in the design decisions, and pressure to adopt a known solution overrides both originality and consumer need.

In a situation of this kind, how do you build in the appearance that will find acceptance in Bangkok, Brussels and Barrow-in-Furness? For many designers the answer is to resort to the kind of inoffensive blandness which has made the *Ford Fiesta* identical with the *Volkswagen Polo.*

It is ironic, looking back, to remember how the Japanese were vilified for plagiarism at the very beginning of their economic recovery after the Second World War. What they apparently knew, and what others have had to learn from them, is that it is a complete waste of time and resources to re-invent the wheel. What must be done is to seek ways to improve it. To make people prefer your wheels to others.

The Japanese have produced great industrial designers of their own, but they have not been in the least reluctant to buy the talents of foreigners. And the reason that they have put so much emphasis on design, is certainly not because "good looks" sell what otherwise are undistinguished products. *Honda* and *Nikon* are world leaders in the sale of motor cycles and cameras – most objective assessments also conclude that technically they are among the best, if not actually *the* best. Both companies' products have a very recognisable style that not only distinguishes them from each other, but also from all the other myriad makes with which they must compete around the world. Furthermore, most of the high design products in Japan and elsewhere are in new technologies.

It is in new artifacts that the interdependence of product and image has the best chance of expression, and the competent product designer will inevitably sense the opportunity to work in these fields. The demands on him will be high but the rewards will be great. If this leaves most products to founder on the rocks of consumer blandness then perhaps in visual terms at least, our future environments will be determined by a few commanding heights. After all, *Rolls Royce* grilles are with us for ever.

Kenneth Grange

235

KENWOOD

The company has developed a large family of related products and these have been unified in a packaging programme, designed by *Pentagram,* aimed at giving the shopkeeper a ready-made, colourful and informative display.

Kenwood, started in 1947, riding the entrepreneurial boom years of the fifties and sixties, headed by an autocratic super salesman, *Kenneth Wood,* rocketed upwards on a range of excellent products.

There were a few bloomers like establishing a massive refrigerator plant in a cold summer, but these were offset – significantly by *Wood's* personality and an unfashionable belief in the need for good after-sales service.

His fleet of small service vans fixed any problem within hours of the phone call, a far cry from the "do-it-yourself" mentality of the seventies.

It's an ill wind though, reflecting on the thirty years of change from flair to corporate sophistication, that the care with which today's products are engineered to erase maintenance also eliminates the personal touch.

Kenwood employed *Pentagram* partner *Kenneth Grange* as their consultant

eighteen years ago. The first commission was to redesign their major appliance, the *Chef* kitchen mixer. With only four days and three nights to present a design, a half model was made and a mirror was taken to simulate the remainder.

It is highly likely that the presentation as much as the design appealed to *Kenneth Wood.* Nevertheless that design in spite of many projected replacements, has been selling successfully for sixteen years. So much so in

fact, that the shape has become archetypal for the type of appliance, and the brief for the latest design specified a clear resemblance to the original – a strangely binding compliment.

Such a product occupies a significant position in the domestic social heirarchy. Like the piano of our parents, it is used more as a symbol of aspiration and security than for its wide functional repertoire.

236

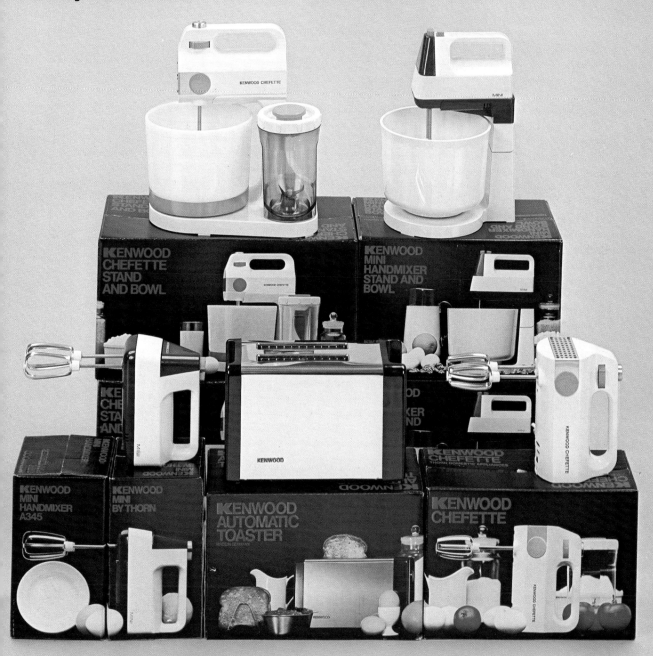

Product design: Domestic chores

The best design in the world is useless if it remains on the shelf. A concern for the eventual sales is seen by comparing the previous and the latest *Chefette*.

When the shopkeeper removed the *Chefette* from the box, he tended not to show the blender which was included as an attachment.

In the second version the blender was included on the stand, and when displayed, looked a richer product. The moral is that product design often needs to be as closely concerned with the point of sale display as it is with the use and function of the item.

For many households the *Chefette* provides for all their mixing, blending and whisking needs. The basic hand mixer can be fixed to the stand and bowl or to a wall bracket. The blender goblet plugs into the rear end of the machine.

These products are sold widely abroad and their design has to take into account bewildering and sometimes unreasonable international standards. Safety in the house is strangely different from one nationality to another.

The design of this blender was evolved for optimum function. The action of liquids on enclosed propellers was closely observed and improved over a number of models.

Product design: Domestic chores

Sharp cutters revolve off centre and asymmetric walls sweep the liquid down and back into their path – the result is uniquely efficient. High impact materials stood up to a punishing test – hard ice cubes dropped onto the revolving cutters.

Even without an awkward thirteen amp plug, the cord on any electrical appliance is a visual sore. Within a wall mounting, a special compartment accommodates the cord and plug. Ease of pushing it in is important. Generous allowance for the impatient user is an essential design criterion. There is no merit in an elegant solution if the user has to work extra hard to use it.

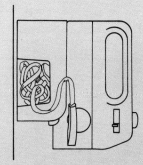

Product design: Domestic chores

There are fifteen attachments for the latest *Chef* machine and they are all powered by various speed outlets from the $\frac{1}{3}$ HP motor, via gearing. The technical specification for these attachments is derived from professional users who prepare food as a business.

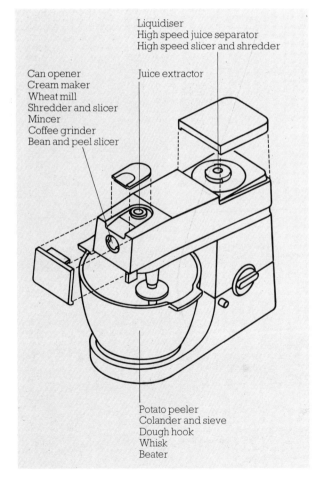

Can opener
Cream maker
Wheat mill
Shredder and slicer
Mincer
Coffee grinder
Bean and peel slicer

Liquidiser
High speed juice separator
High speed slicer and shredder

Juice extractor

Potato peeler
Colander and sieve
Dough hook
Whisk
Beater

Product design: Domestic chores

When the 1961 version was replaced by the 1976 model, the interchangeability of attachments posed, as it did in 1961, a huge logistical conundrum. The result is that Kenwood now have a major business making attachments and their development is an interesting reflection of public tastes and prejudices. Juicers and shredders in the health

fad years, blenders for drinks, and improvements to the coffee mill as, at last, the English took the beverage seriously.

Most recently the wholemeal and homecooking economy of the mid-seventies, produced a mill attachment for grinding your own wheat. Quite probably, if the do-it-yourself

home improvement market develops further, we could even see a small cement mixing attachment. The machine could certainly take it!

Product design: Domestic chores

The *Maruzen Sewing Machine Co* of Osaka, Japan have developed since 1949 to become one of the largest makers of domestic machines. Their major outlet has been the US and their machine designs were aimed specifically at that market. As exports broadened, a more European style of design was sought by commissioning a London studio.

The *804* series, marketed in the UK by *Frister & Rossmann*, reveals the polarities of American and European taste. The American model, to the rear in the photograph, carries essentially the same features and was marketed contemporaneously with the *804* in 1970.

American products of that time owed as much to Detroit as to function, but it is testimony to the global view of many American designers that by 1977 European designs such as this have been a considerable influence on the other side of the Atlantic.

It is from attention to fine detail, allied with sensitive sculptural form, that a distinctive European vocabulary of design has emerged.

丸善ミシン

The Japanese word for sewing machine is *Mishin*. Perhaps the sewing machine, like the needle before it, seemed to be so central to family life that above all other machines it was the only one to take on this universal western word.

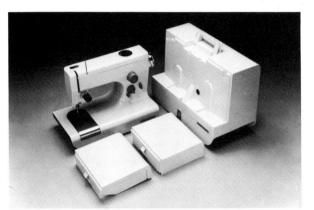

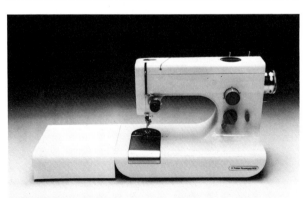

The *804* series is unique in some fundamental details, and pre-empted the now common feature of providing a carrying case, purpose designed to store the multitudinous accessories, in removable boxes. These boxes in turn plug onto the machine base for a further extension of the sewing surface.

Certain distinct details make the machine easier to use. We observed that all sewing machines centre the needle symmetrically in the base, and quite probably this has not changed since the earliest machines, where in engineering symmetry was all.

Today, we realise that the space in front of the needle, where the work is made up, is most valuable. The more fabric that can be assembled allows longer sewing between stops. Accordingly, the needle in the *804* is positioned to the rear.

This change also released space for the inclusion of a drawer to take parts which are frequently needed and changed.

A safety feature is built in by shaping the base, so that the machine can be rolled upright to rest. This is essential for standard maintenance, and avoids the common practice of tilting a machine into a precarious balance.

The range of controls, more complex than those on a motor car, need to be presented as simply as possible, so as not to seem as complicated as they actually are.

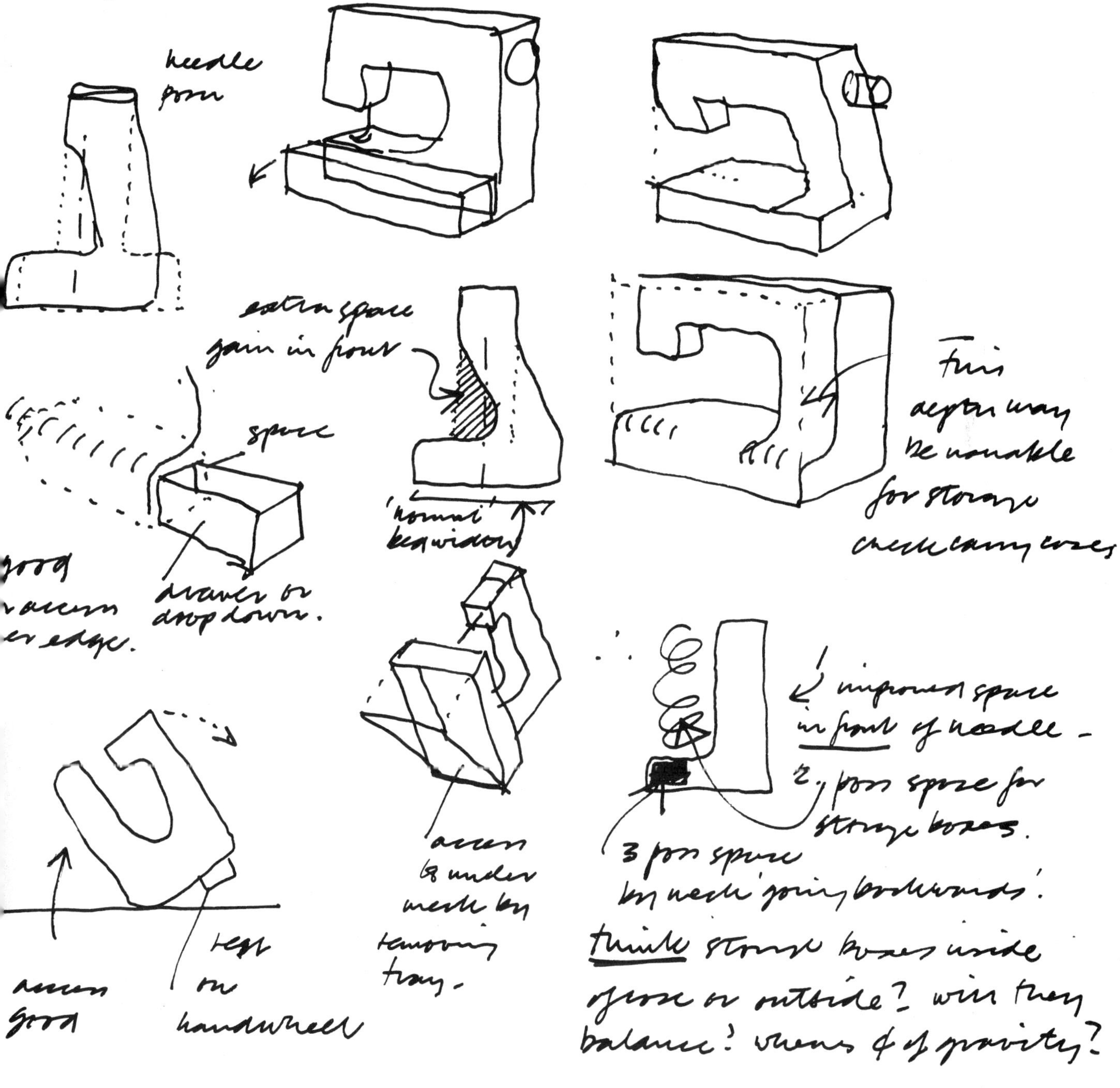

needle
gun

extra space
gain in front

space

good
access
or edge.

drawer or
drop down.

'normal'
leg width

This
design may
be unable
for storage
check carry cases

improved space
in front of needle -
2, poss space for
storage boxes.

3 poss space
by needle going backwards.

think storage boxes inside
gusso or outside? will they
balance? areas & of gravity?

access
is under
needle by
removing
tray.

access
good

rest
on
handwheel

More significant to *Maruzen* in business terms than the *804*, is the *Cub* range of machines.

Following general discussions in Japan about the merits of more light-weight machines, the company engineers evolved a "bread board" design which showed the feasibility of reducing size, while retaining the standard assemblies upon which the industry relies.

The diagram compares the size of the *Cub* with the *804*.

The engineers had concentrated on reducing the length and size of parts

peculiar to *Maruzen*. This proved significant in the subsequent success of the machine, which could be shipped thousands of miles yet still find standard replacements on arrival.

The problem remained to house this full specification works in the minimum enclosure, yet still provide the usual working space. This was achieved by extending the length, like a gate-leg table, and incorporating an ingenious flip-out accessory box for forward extension and an extra work surface.

The *Cub* represents a major step in small portable domestic sewing machines, and provides a good example of leap-frogging alliance with company engineers, even when they are situated at the other side of the world.

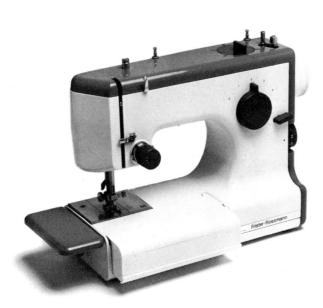

Product design: Consumer goods

These compact, high specification machines are the latest in a number of significant steps which have steadily improved the ease as well as the repertoire of usage. Weight has always been the obstacle to portability. Originally all machines were made from cast iron and a weight of 40 lbs was not uncommon. This was cut by 40% in moving to aluminium and now these compact models are 30% lighter again – a genuine product gain without any cost penalty.

The latest model in the *Cub* series is a free arm machine. "Free arm" denotes the ability to sew inside sleeves etc. because the shuttle mechanism is compacted into a narrow tube. This level of sophistication is traditionally kept for only the most expensive domestic machines and the addition of a free arm model into the *Cub* range is a marketing innovation.

It is interesting that the largest market for sewing machines, the US, has always rejected the free arm concept. A proportion of 90% flat bed to 10% free arm has been the norm until 1975. In two years this trend has now reversed and the larger demand for free arm models will undoubtedly affect the logistics of mass production and *Maruzen's* development of the compact free arm will anticipate a demand in that market sector.

In the free arm *Cub* we have combined the familiar large bed size with the free arm. Merely press a button and the accessory box lifts out.

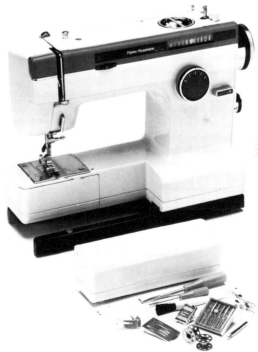

RONSON

Ronson is a name synonymous with cigarette lighters. Exactly fifty years ago in America – coincident with *Gatsby*, *Lindberg*, talking pictures and the Jazz Age, the company started and launched a lighter, appropriately named the *Banjo!*

Today the company is more broadly known. Their electric razors, toothbrushes and hairdryers form a major part of the corporate business. *Ronson* is still an American company and one which has invested very wisely in the UK.

Most lighters have originated in America, and still owe heavily to US influences, except when they profitably ape English gracious living. The electrical products have however been conspicuously successful when developed here. After initially testing the market with an American product, the hairdryers have established a performance reputation leading to a major

share of the UK and export markets.

Technically, a hairdryer is commonplace enough. It is the creative engineering and of course accumulated experience that makes this one or that, more reliable and profitable. As individual tactics within a whole strategy, finite details are resolved then leap-frogged by improvement, and re-resolved, and so gradually a whole product is prepared. The purchaser knows little of the scope of intellect and invention in these mundane products.

Form following function is a glib statement, and invariably compromised. Any simple object with a handle has to suit both left and right, large and small hands. Nevertheless the simplest hairdryer does reflect its working. A fan gives a dominant cylinder onto which an outlet nozzle and handle are fixed; a cost critical product minimising plastic

material. Yet it is still possible to include a minor witticism – the holes trace the spiral of air as it is sucked in, around and out at higher velocity.

The *Rio* handheld hairdryer, the first of a series, has been in production since 1966 and to date 909,400 have been manufactured.

It is of course true that many products are a long way from being essential, and at a cynic glance, the electric toothbrush looks a classic case.

However, that tower of conservatism, the medics, have issued strong support for the efficiency of powered toothbrushes, and on those grounds it is here to stay.

For different reasons the hairdryers hold up very well in that argument. Our parents dried their hair in front of the fire, and that in efficiency and cost is easily eclipsed by *Ronson*.

250

Product design: Domestic chores

Equally in error, whether too soon or too late – wrong timing is the destruction of a good marketing plan. An excellent well-made product, good value for money, will be still born if the time is wrong.

It was logical that *Kenwood*, at first selling small appliances should proceed to larger, and with their dishwasher in 1959 they were soon established in the "white box business". The next step was a refrigerator and in 1962 the time seemed ripe – a hot summer in '61 had shown how few homes had fridges. *Kenwood* bought a nine acre site, borrowed hugely from the bank, and commissioned us to design an unique fridge and freezer combination. These were the

same size and could stand on top or beside each other.

Made on the latest continuous production machinery it pre-empted by ten years that particular design concept. Sadly – almost disastrously – the weather turned cold and unbeknown to one another, every appliance maker in the country had started to make the same product. For the next

five years you could buy fridges at cost price, and in consequence *Kenwood* went out of that market, and very nearly out of business as well.

Cross pollination between different attitudes to the same product can, as in the case of two cookers, spread knowledge and advance a product performance. A luxury cooker and a camping stove were both designed for different clients, at the same time as an awakening public scrutiny of the cost of cooking equipment.

One result was to sophisticate the performance of the cooking stove (shown here) and help take camping out of its rigorous backwoodsman

image. It folds closely flat – or opens to provide wind cheeks which stand up and protect the flame. Meanwhile, paradoxically, the luxury cooker had retreated to simplification and reassessed its priorities – undoubtedly influenced by its camping cousin.

Microwave ovens, similar to that designed for *Dysona* (shown here) have been in production for a decade, but their acceptance has depended on the advent of the deep freeze; an interesting example of the essential missing link.

Advertising can create a demand but other forces in the market place must be in mesh with your own. In the same

252

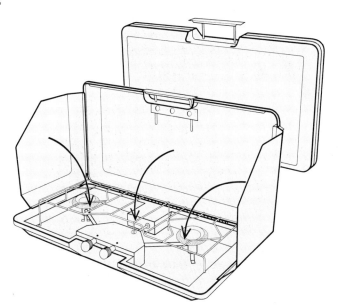

way that you cannot sell watering cans at the beginning of a drought, so more subtly, the microwave oven depended on the domestic use.

This cutlery was originally designed to be sold by *Woolworths* in stainless steel,

and at their prices it would have been a minor revolution. Regrettably the maker had a better business making reproduction Georgian silverware – in stainless steel.

A manufacturer will employ an industrial designer to get the product to look as attractive as possible. Designers can provide more than this.

For *Morphy Richards,* a range of three irons, two shown here and a steam iron, was produced after exhaustive international consumer research had shown the need for more variation than was originally conceived.

For example, in particular parts of Europe, housewives

regard a handle which is open at the front as the normal product because it allows them to iron into sleeves more easily. In other regions the closed handle is the norm, probably because it seems stronger – and anyway, it is what mother always used!

By changing only one part we produced this variety of designs, with the result that more people in more countries were able to benefit by the greater choice of product.

Although easily discounted as a small percentage of total users, a left-handed person is at a real disadvantage when the cable interferes with ironing. We overcame this by

making the lamp lens and rubber cable grommet interchangeable, by enabling the customer to simply open the back and swap them over. This detail cost nothing in production, yet it provided a genuine benefit for the user.

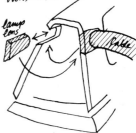

Method of changing cable and lamp lens for left handed housewives

The first fifty years

Designers abound in Britain. This country's design education is perhaps the best and biggest in the world. Architects, industrial and graphic designers have proliferated in the last 25 years, a period in which Britain has gained a world wide reputation for design consultancy, whilst the design reputation of its products has sunk to an all time low. Much effort has been put into correcting this imbalance, notably through the work of the *Design Council,* and although product design improvements are on the way, the imbalance persists. Maybe a clue to resolving this paradox lies in the fact that whereas successful architectural practices and graphic design studios can be counted in their hundreds, the count barely reaches ten for successful industrial design consultancies.

This is not to suggest that the consultant industrial designer monopolises the few good designs. Plenty of good ones are produced without him. What does seem to follow is that product design does not easily flourish through consultancy, but needs an "in house" long term relationship to enable it to work.

The work of the industrial designer, however, is critical to the cost structure. Not only does he commit long term and research and development overheads but his contribution is squarely in the area of prime cost. His alteration to products directly affects raw material and labour costs, the two areas in most manufacturers' businesses where the leverage on profits is greatest; and not only profits. Changes in designs can lead to major re-investment programmes for new machinery. Using plastic rather than wood for toys is a prime example. It can lead to labour redeployment and retraining, to new demands on managers and unions – all major management issues.

The history of industrial design practice is sparse until the industrial revolution. Almost universally, the industrial

designer was bred out of architecture. It started with those rare, long sighted engineers who in the last century accepted production as an inhibition to aesthetic expansion but who saw that expansion as essential to growth in competitive business and looked outside their factories for a skill complimentary to their own.

Architecture provided the skill, and not surprisingly, for it alone possessed a discipline which combines aesthetic talent with a functional need. Cast iron was of course the great constructional material of the Industrial Revolution. This factor, coincident with the Victorian arrogance in fashion and decoration, has led to some assumptions that the aesthetic inventions dominated the great industrial period of the late 19th century. It is only partly true. That period belonged to, and bred, the great engineers. Many of their products were and still are excellent but very few show the broader range of consideration that typifies a designer's work today.

The most important influence came towards the end of the century. *William Morris,* and *Henry Cole* before him, campaigned for "Art in Industry", though they only had to anticipate the need for a place in industry for art, in the process as much as the products. Not until the 1920's was there another formalisation of their objective. It came in Europe in the *Bauhaus,* where a few men produced some sensational ideas for industry; and some industries thought the experiment worthwhile.

The furniture industry moved a tentative toe into this new water of modernism; so did some lighting companies. But we now appreciate how limited was their commitment to the idea of the aesthetic in industry. In furniture it took another forty years before makers started to risk high tooling costs. Investment in tools means a commitment to the longevity of a product, and furniture makers world wide have found plagiarism the safer business method. In England it was not until 1960 that real tooling costs were risked when a small company, *Hille,* laid down a large tool for a polypropylene chair, a huge cost but paid for many times over by their great success.

Even if the first great names of industrial design were usually architects, the art colleges for the last quarter of a century have been determined that the initiative will pass to specifically trained practitioners. This process first started in the USA where the market has always been large enough to generate money to employ specialist skills. Industrial design as a formal skill had a twenty year start in America and the "American style" still not only characterises the products in that country, but also in its post war cultural colonies.

In postwar Europe, colleges of art saw their salvation in the growth of this new commercial art which exploded when the money-rich housewives provided a market potential of a size unknown on this side of the Atlantic. A sudden bonanza fell into the lap of any company that could make a lot of anything which was even half decent. Capital was released for expensive plant and tooling, and that in turn focussed management attention on what these expensive new mass production techniques could make.

For every serious work, there are of course a thousand trivialities, so appliance design produced a mass of mediocrity and a few important examples, notably from Italy and Scandinavia. From a handful of significant influences, *Olivetti, Jensen* and *Braun,* a clear European design vocabulary had developed by the 70's.

Conspicuous in this vocabulary is elegant concealment. It constitutes a discernible trend among designers to gradually strip objects of all ornamentation, and eventually of any distinctive shape. The phenomenon is most apparent in the design of household or domestic appliances, the outstanding example being the refrigerator, which is now universally reduced to a white symmetrical box. The origins of the disappearing object are both interesting and instructive to anybody concerned with the design of domestic appliances. The arguments are concerned with cost-effectiveness, manufacturing processes and their consequent rationalisations.

Another incentive to simplification is what is sometimes described as the "modern movement". Public taste has, over the past twenty years, both demanded and been shaped by tendencies that are essentially encapsulated in phrases like "the new brutalism", "form following function" and so on. In the area of domestic appliance design, this has been a particularly relentless process. The streamlined modern kitchen demanded less and less clutter, until even the suggestion of clutter made by ornamentation became almost totally unacceptable.

Many of the arguments that raged in the 50's and 60's about built-in obsolescence can now be seen as largely academic, because the appetite for newer more refined versions of just about everything frequently outstripped the manufacturer's capacity to produce them. But suddenly in the 70's people have had enough. If one was asked to pinpoint the predominant movement in design in the first half of this decade it would be difficult to avoid defining it as nostalgia. The streamlined kitchen is cluttered again; this time with real old junk, old advertising signs, old bread bins, old bottles.

Revulsion at the extremes that modernism was allowed to reach has itself been expressed in an extreme reaction. Graphic designers, whose ability to adapt quickly is alternatively an asset and a liability, have been quick to respond with nostalgic packs, nostalgic housestyles, nostalgic everything. Architects, alas, are irrevocably lumbered for at least a generation and probably more.

But the industrial designer inevitably occupies a middle ground. The nature of his work prohibits hasty reactions and bestows time to consider, as an unintended bonus. Those considerations include his responsibility as prophet, for the design today must be at a peak of desirability three or five years hence.

His particular skill is to reconcile the benefits of long associations with those of remaining open to new ideas, and in particular the cross pollination of ideas from one field to another. It is a difficult skill embracing problems of confidentiality, a wide knowledge of many engineering and fabricating skills, an awareness of consumer and cultural needs (in the widest sense), plus sympathy with financial evaluation. He extends the normal consulting role into a continuous commitment to his client. It is not an easy role to maintain. Perhaps that is why there are so few of him.

Kenneth Grange

255

44A 1959

Vecta 1964

33 series 1968

55X series 1971

256

Say *"Kodak"* to most people and they think "photographs" whether they visualise family snaps, cassettes, or cameras, is less predictable – but *Kodak* they certainly know. Very few companies can claim their global fame, a few oil companies maybe but whether it's Alaska or Africa, Bangkok or Bradford, *Kodak* will be known.

George Eastman did not invent but pioneered photography.

A man of wit and ambition, he created his company name, a name able to be pronounced world-wide. His first modest factory in England was established in 1891.

Kodak is undoubtedly the largest camera maker in the world. Their staggering volume of products has become a significant part of the business which includes film, paper, chemicals, and the licensing of many inventions.

This was not always the case and it is likely that cameras were made to ensure the sale of film. The simple command printed inside the ubiquitous *Box Brownie* "Use *Kodak 120* film", was believed by many to be the only means by which that camera would function.

Eastman Kodak have employed in the US, industrial design skills both in their own studio and through outside consultants. As the European

55X series 1971

Camera research models

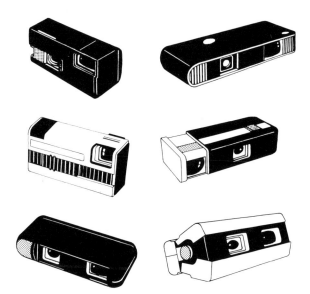

companies developed, their reliance on the parent company for industrial design was reduced. In 1959, the UK company appointed *Kenneth Grange* as consultant.

The cameras which were subsequently launched were the *44A* and *B*. These were followed by the *Vecta Camera* which contained an idea that typifies the contradiction between logic and common practice.

Research showed that most pictures (snap-shots) are of people, and that most cameras held normally, position the single figure in the centre of a landscape shape. In the *Vecta*, the design was planned to use this knowledge so that the film in a camera held vertically would produce a better picture in a portrait shape. Regrettably the life of the *Vecta* was too short to prove this logic because its film size was soon overtaken by the

cassette system of the *Kodak Instamatic Camera*, launched in the sixties.

If numbers count, then more than twenty million cameras vindicate the appointment of a consultant designer. His role in *Kodak* is as one of the contributors to a product which is the amalgam of enormous skills and effort. Few products can claim such value for money and only the large quantities allow such low

prices for technical achievement.

Behind a camera may lie an outlay of ten million pounds, yet if a million cameras are made, then we can "inherit" those millions for only ten pounds.

Although it would seem to be an unnecessary exercise to conduct a market research survey on how hands can cope with hand-sized cameras the results did provide an interesting response.

The prototypes shown here were specifically produced for the presentation of camera design innovations and varieties of handling techniques.

Apart from the shock of the unfamiliar, it was found that smallness is not the optimum criterion. The great need, apparently, is for a camera that can be sturdily held and this implies that a larger, rather than a minimal size, is what people want.

These photographs are of six of the many experimental models that have been made to counter the problems inherent in miniaturisation.

They include different arrangements of the functional parts, different sizes, shapes and different facilities. None are definitive in establishing one particular specification, but they do illustrate some of the variety possible within strict functional parameters.

Even if the great majority of users are satisfied with an approximate likeness, *Kodak* engineers are not, and a major area of work is in combating the camera shake. Quite apart from this and other operational factors there are important emotional judgements in using a camera. "Do I look like a professional?" "Am I embarrassed?" "Do I want to identify with the latest gear?" All these have to be considered in such an experimental programme.

Whilst the cameras have got smaller, the users (admittedly excluding children) have remained the same size. Recently a series of studies has been made to assess in design terms just how small a camera can be, and still remain comfortable and be easily used in our clumsy fingers.

These models show cameras that opened up, that were sleek and smooth, even one larger than it needed to be.

At this stage in the industrial process the designer enjoys his greatest privilege, he flouts tradition, he challenges the nice cosy castle of market research, he is actually paid

to propose nightmares for the engineers. Paradoxically, he ensures his future in the real products, the compromised, "what the people really want".

Cameras, like pens, are the tools of domestic romanticism and they will continue to extend their function and novelty. Experimental programmes such as this provide a ready means of pushing out expected norms of both the practical and the public taste.

Designers often submit design proposals as highly finished, indeed glamorous, drawings. *Pentagram* produce models instead – these prove valuable as three dimensional reference points to the designer, are more meaningful to the engineer, and certainly more understandable for the client.

These models of the *Kodak* experimental series could be handled, and therefore provided a truthful basis for a tactile assessment as well as a statement of function and style.

Photography was created by the capture of an image on a light sensitive emulsion. The camera was the lesser sensation – this pattern has never changed. Of course cameras have become minor miracles of fine engineering, but the development of photographic opportunities has always followed the chemistry and structure of film making.

In the 1960's, the production by *Kodak* of the *Instamatic* cartridge dramatically changed the design of cameras, and the success of that system has been a

profound influence on all the camera makers in the world. Almost universally they have followed the *Kodak* system.

With sophisticated chemistry, the quality of enlargement and colour reproduction has so improved that today we can buy miniature film which is equal to a predecessor four or five times as large.

A few camera makers have persevered in this ambition for many years and the international secrets business has added a touch of glamous to their products.

Those few camera makers became the majority in the 1970's when *Kodak* launched a new system, again a cassette, and a range of cameras to suit, An immediate success, they were appropriately called "pocket cameras", and are small and light enough to make carrying a camera virtually as convenient as a bunch of keys. A long series o steps from the suitcase size of their ancestors, yet these new cameras function infinitely better as picture makers.

Originally glass was used, now high quality lenses are fastidiously moulded in acrylic, flash bulbs no longer need battery power, a piezo crystal fires the bulb, and electronics compute infinitely variable shutter speeds.

Quantities are ten-fold and more important, film technology has dramatically improved. All these factors greatly reduce camera size and therefore affect design and style.

258

The tactile approach, tightly packed mechanisms with padded leather outside treatment.

Shutter release and viewfinder, above lens, follow conventional 35mm format of camera but cassette gives an unusual depth.

The discreet camera, outer case closes to completely hide camera.

Conventional shutter release and viewfinder with strong "protection" to lens.

The ultimate compact, viewfinder retracts and doubles as film transport.

Clear "modernistic" shape with perceived and real size reduced to essential.

Product design: Working continuity

As with *Kodak's* other products, the brief for this camera was originated by the company's marketing department, but modified at the successive stages of initial product development.

The original briefing in the 1960's was based upon the European company's wish to have a distinctive second generation design, which could follow the first US designed *110* cameras.

Sales had shown a substantial market acceptance of the American series, but marketing opinion in England and other European centres had shown some resistance to the lack of identity with European preconceptions about camera imagery. At the same time new techniques of mass production were being studied.

The brief for a re-design came therefore out of change in production technique, a desire for stylistic change to suit European taste, and a new range of functional details.

The specification of these cameras suits the pocket and picture making ambition of a huge market counted in millions. Their scope of technical sophistication is made possible by utilization of major common parts.

A unique feature is included in the far left camera, still a relatively cheap product. By slipping a switch, a change of lenses is made from standard to telephoto, with no need to change or add on pieces. A feature not previously purchaseable unless for hundreds of pounds.

Product design: Working continuity

It is a generally accepted truism that the smaller the product, the greater the refinement. It is fastidious attention to detail that marks out the superlative from the good.

This requires effort which consumes time. The temptation to concede to a quicker, clumsier solution is seductive and sometimes even politic.

Despite such commercial pressures, the giant manufacturer can afford to put the effort into these details.

They add spice to the function of the camera, individually they may give pleasure, collectively they reinforce a distinctive product. They are the components of elusive quality.

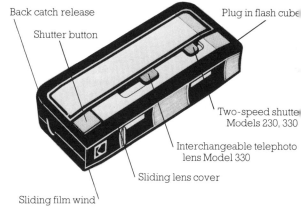

Back catch release
Shutter button
Plug in flash cube
Two-speed shutter Models 230, 330
Interchangeable telephoto lens Model 330
Sliding lens cover
Sliding film wind

Product design: Working continuity

Whereas a camera is produced in millions, a film cutter may only be made in a few hundred. Nevertheless the designer's work is still important as every product affects the image of the company. The work is often completed more economically because sophisticated consumer studies are not required.

In the designer's profession this balance is highly sought, and it is with gratitude that such an esoteric product as a film cutter can be designed with as much care as a camera. The problems are different, the manufacturing methods are not to be compared, but the design is equally fastidious.

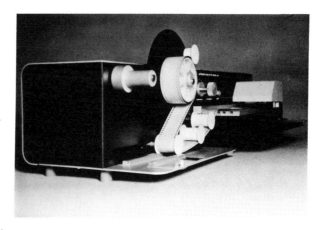

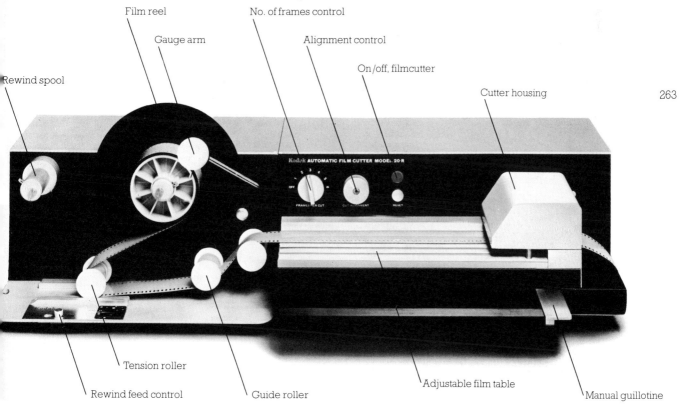

Rewind spool

Film reel

Gauge arm

No. of frames control

Alignment control

On/off, filmcutter

Cutter housing

Tension roller

Rewind feed control

Guide roller

Adjustable film table

Manual guillotine

Binns

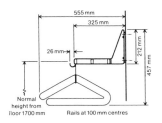

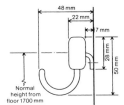

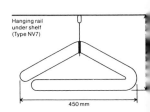

Binns Variset System makes that welcome page in any portfolio where concept, design development and product engineering are all in the tight control of the designer with commercial success completing the pleasure.

The starting point for the design was the recognition that when the builder fixes something, often the painter, who comes along afterwards, spoils it. *Variset* is fixed to the wall by a strong spine so that after the painter has finished, you can slide on the hooks and cover any sloppy paintwork. An interesting exercise in raising the quality of the most mundane product.

The hanger system uses more capital in tooling. Expanded polypropylene hangers on nylon straps in a captive system are well suited to hotel and public installations. All the components are designed for assembly at installation and so minimise space during transport.

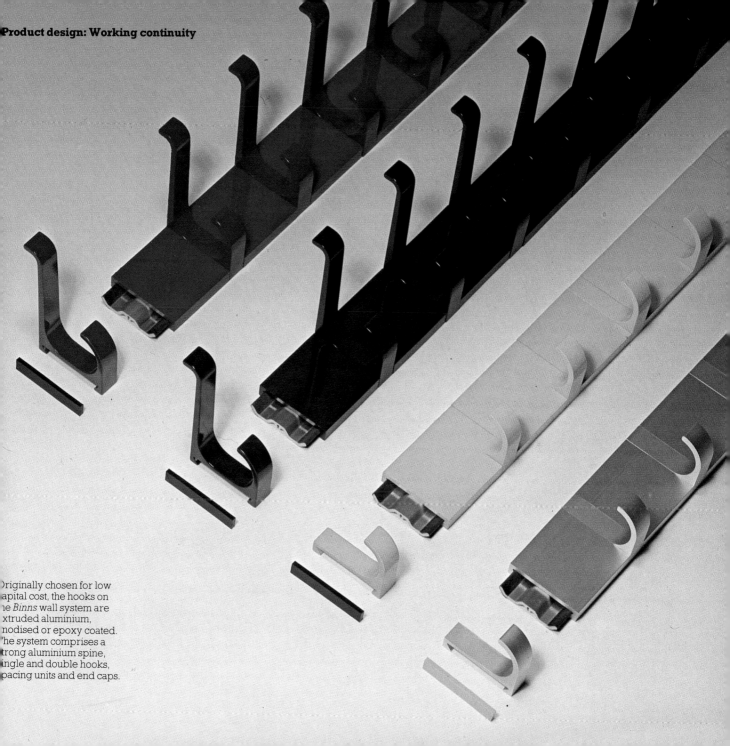

Originally chosen for low capital cost, the hooks on the *Binns* wall system are extruded aluminium, anodised or epoxy coated. The system comprises a strong aluminium spine, single and double hooks, spacing units and end caps.

Parker Pens, like another client *Ronson*, is a famous American company which has established an efficient and profitable production plant in Britain. Until the seventies, the British company had not totally developed any one of the pens they produced; all had been originated in the USA.

In 1939 the company set a new world standard in America, and later Europe, with their famous *Parker 51*, and the name has become synonymous with expensive, high quality pens.

With this background, it is a significant achievement that the market identified for an European product has been so successful. The new pen was required to be low in cost, distinctive, and aimed at a younger market sector (in short, additional business). No matter how sensible their aims were, their realisation was bound to be difficult for *Parker*, whose traditional practices and methods were based upon wealthier and older purchasers.

Happily, the result of collaboration between *Parker* and *Pentagram* is a huge success. The *25 Series* includes a ball point, a felt tip and – for the rebirth of interest in writing for pleasure – a fountain pen. Over 2 million were made last year.

Long discussions raged, as they often do, around the tiniest detail of the design. One elegant detail was evolved to simplify the making of the clip.

Great care has to be taken since the clip must hold the pen in a variety of pockets, from shirts to tweeds, and still not damage the fabric. This was solved by pressing a plastic button into the end of the stainless bar, and in turn this was used for the corporate symbol.

At the time it was an earnest worry as to whether the loss of the famous *Parker* arrow clip would be commercially foolish. Happily sales prove otherwise – it seems that the new generation of *Parker* customers do not venerate the symbols of their fathers, but rather enjoy their own.

Product design: Working continuity

Part of the original brief was the design of a presentation case and, unusually for the industry, this allowed the designers to present a complete integrated product.

Frequently the packaging, often the critical background against which the product is sold, is left until too late – and perhaps even worse, left to supporting suppliers who have not even been party to the product concept.

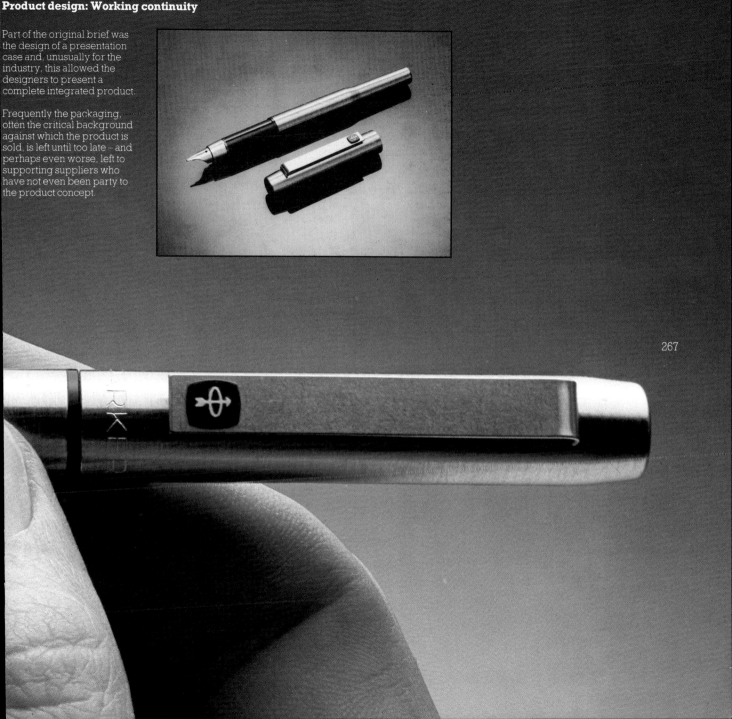

The *Milward shaver* shown on the left is mains/battery powered, and was developed from the award-winning Courier shown in the centre with its carrying case above.

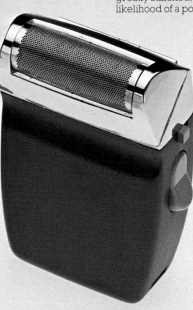

A cynic, probably rejected for the umpteenth time, once called design awards a kiss of death. Certainly a poor product made conspicuous by a misplaced award embarrasses everybody – even those only remotely connected.

Over the years the *Design Council* may have been sometimes naive but always well meaning. It is certainly true that standards for checking products have greatly stiffened, so that the likelihood of a poor product receiving a design blessing is now remote. It remains possible of course that an excellent product, even with an award to help, can be poorly marketed and subsequently fail. Awards alone do not imply a commercial guarantee.

Even if sales are less than sensational, an award can help a designer's career. In 1963 the *Milward battery shaver* won the *Duke of Edinburgh's Prize for Elegant Design*. Apart from the advantage of a client who would settle for nothing but the best, in both toolmaking and material choice, the designer also had a client who wanted the product to be superior to anything comparable.

Tiny switches were built into the head so that the shaver operated as soon as it touched the face, thereby saving precious battery power. It also switched off, the moment the shaver foil was removed. This safety factor was well worthwhile since the circular cutters were hollow-ground and honed to razor sharpness.

From this model, another product was developed to use battery or mains power, and also to give an adjustment for the user by revolving the head to raise or lower the depth of cut – not unlike the roller on a lawn mower.

All this experience proved invaluable when subsequently working for *Ronson*. Their conventional razor product allowed little room for design innovation, but again provided knowledge which was invaluable in developing a more innovative product, an angled head razor.

In his book *Technics and Civilisation*, Lewis Mumford writes of the effect on product design of the human image. Originally steam engines stood up, their funnel like a head, their pistons and cranks like arms. There is a great truth in this. Every product "seems" more natural when there is no doubt which is the face and which is the back. The angle head razor seems more purposeful for having a clear direction.

A reputation as a designer of razors eventually led to two further commissions. *Wilkinson* had decided to control the use of their major product, their razor blades. For years they had been forced to see their blades being daily put into razors of *Gillette*, their greatest competitor – a strange alliance! The first commission was therefore to design a conventional double edge razor.

The design is unremarkable, except perhaps in that it makes the ubiquitous product more elegant, and more easily cleaned. More interesting as a design is the second commission, the single edge razor. This follows a development by *Wilkinson* engineers who knew that by moulding a blade into a plastic support, they could control the critical accuracy of the blade angle. The button on the back rejects the blunt blade, and the holder snaps a new one into place without handling.

269

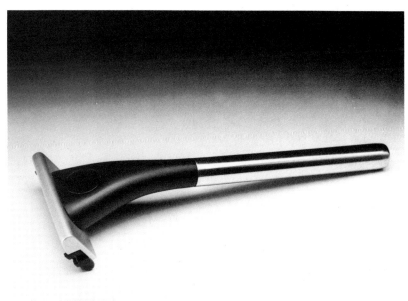

STC

Standard Telephone and Cables is the giant British limb of the gargantuan American corporation *ITT*. Its range of *Star Radiotelephone* equipment is a comprehensive system for radio control, typically installed by police, ambulances, taxis etc.

These are quality products in which ingenuity in the design has enabled the production of a range of items from common parts, and so expensive tooling is restricted.

Today communications is a smart word – and with good reason. Policemen, perhaps in a technological world less ponderously self assured than in the past, are able to be more efficient by their use of radio. Staff at labyrinthine airports find missing aircraft and children, train controllers communicate with platform staff at large stations . . . and the *STC Star Radiotelephone* is the tool they use.

There are many such tools but this one is distinct in its complete freedom from an outside aerial. That helps pocketability and supports the discreet detailing appropriate to its use. Lightness of weight was achieved by the use of an expensive but super tough polycarbonate exterior.

270

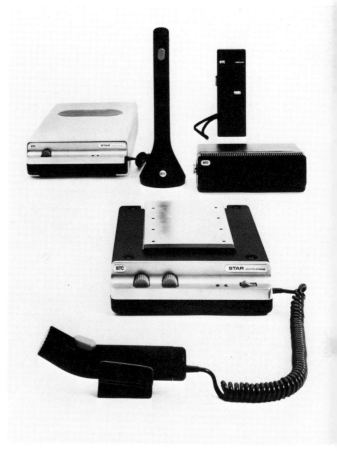

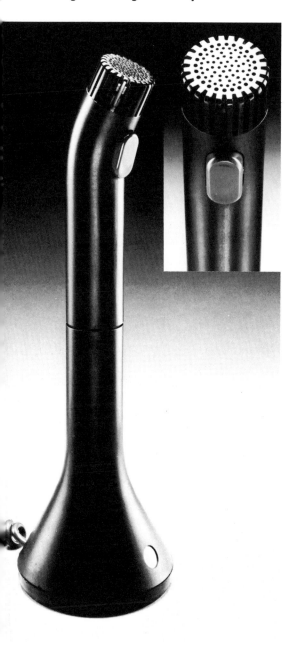

Two products, one in production, one not, one small and simple, one complex and large.

The microphone in production is for "hands free" use, but allows for the top assembly to be sold for hand held application.

The desk console was the result of a lengthy and sophisticated development involving extensive ergonomic study to determine a high efficiency cordless switchboard for telephone operators. This allowed the operator to interrogate her information store and hold a number of queries and answers simultaneously. On the cathode-ray tube the rate at which queries can be processed is significantly improved.

A refinement is in the sloping surface at the right of the machine. This is a result of the ergonomic study which showed a worth-while easing of strain in the hand when using the keypad. At rest, the wrist is in fact not at right angles to the body; a small point, but in such a critical work station an important factor.

271

B&W

B & W represent the efficiency of autocracy. Creative and devoted, *John Bowers* is the catalyst around which this highly successful company revolves. More than 89% of their products are for export,

and the company is one of the world's half a dozen top quality loudspeaker makers.

B & W spend more than some of their mighty rivals on research staff and equipment. All that is determined by the inspiration of *John Bowers*, who directs research not only into refined technology, but also into the quality of musical appreciation.

The *DM6* was the first UK linear phase loudspeaker. The system is calculated to reduce the phase distortion which arises in the traditional practice of mounting speaker units on one common plane front board.

Allowance has to be made for "mechanical response" and "crossover unit phase shift" when positioning the three

loudspeakers in the cabinet. Their respective acoustic centres then produce the sound in phase at the listening centre.

The appearance and design of the cabinet reflect this unique configuration. Acoustically transparent fabric is stretched over a perforated metal frame on the face of the speakers.

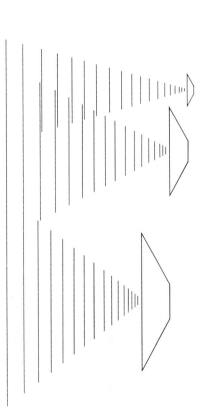

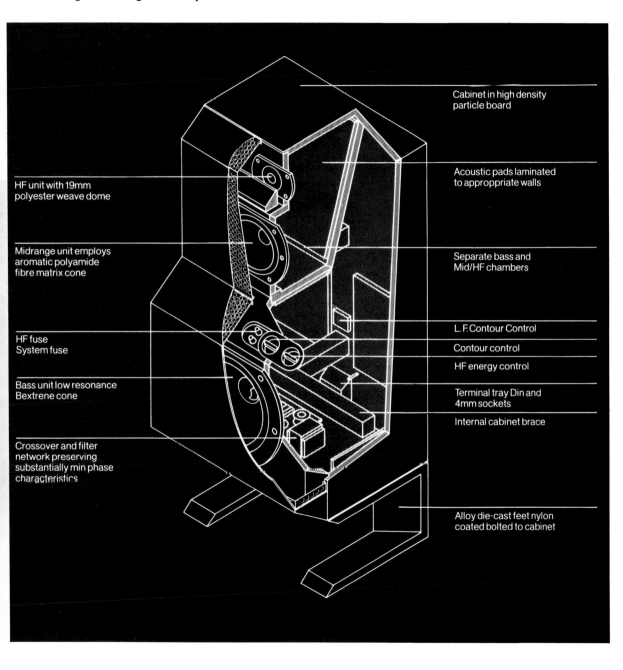

HF unit with 19mm
polyester weave dome

Midrange unit employs
aromatic polyamide
fibre matrix cone

HF fuse
System fuse

Bass unit low resonance
Bextrene cone

Crossover and filter
network preserving
substantially min phase
characteristics

Cabinet in high density
particle board

Acoustic pads laminated
to approppriate walls

Separate bass and
Mid/HF chambers

L. F. Contour Control

Contour control

HF energy control

Terminal tray Din and
4mm sockets

Internal cabinet brace

Alloy die-cast feet nylon
coated bolted to cabinet

273

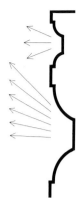

The diagrams compare the smooth radiation of sound waves obtainable with the *DM7*, left, with those given by a conventional angular speaker, right. Below is a photograph of the moulded baffle and fret, and the die cast alloy speaker chassis. These combine to form the smooth edged frontal construction of the *DM7*.

274

B & W were challenging a well-entrenched norm for the industry. It happened with the *DM6* and again with the *DM7*. Their proposition was that music coming from the speaker units sounds smoother and truer when encouraged to roll around the units, and not, as generally assumed, beam solidly forward.

The appearance of a product can more or less visually express its function and it was from this precept that our design work started. The first proposal was exhilarating, inspired, and a severe shock to anybody who knows what loudspeakers look like! We called it the *Bathysphere* and in that form it would have been well received by other designers, some architects, a few acoustical engineers and it may very well have won a design award. But it would undoubtedly have been a resounding commercial failure.

It was a perfect example of a logical result, devoid of the romantic ingredient that is

essential in all products where the purchaser has a choice for which he is prepared to pay. Consequently, design and technology must meet the normal and aspirational needs of the purchaser.

Whilst we accepted the inevitable furniture role of a speaker, so *B & W* found another formula for unit relationship with enclosure. Like the best of anything, their

Product design: Working continuity

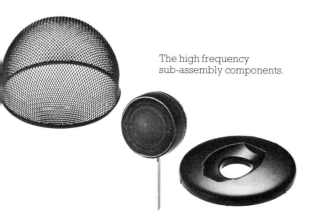

The high frequency
sub-assembly components.

solution was deceptively
simple. They took the units
close to the cabinet edge and
softly profiled their junction.
The sound still eased around
the sides of the whole
enclosure. Consequently the
cabinet is slim, with startling
performance.

A simple woven wire dome
covers the exposed spherical
high frequency unit – the
tweeter. Acoustically
transparent, this is visually
reinforced by a thick
aluminium top plate in which
the frequency weighting
control sits smoothly flush.

Our intention is that the
product will have a distinction
by this new balance between
perceived technology and
furniture, at least until the
world comes around to our
bathysphere!

Sometimes design is like a
maze; from a logic, a romantic
idea, or just for somewhere to
start, you move up one of the
channels, trying all the little
byways *en route*. Sometimes
you can part the hedge wide
enough to get a clue from the
route next door. Sometimes
your first channel leads to a
lovely surprise; most times
you have, admittedly more
wisely, still to return to the
beginning and start again.
But experience shows a very
few blinding *eurekas*.

By the time the speaker was
launched we had spent nearly
1000 hours on its design. Even
so, with a client who believes
in constant improvement, I
know we'll still be modifying
it by the time it's withdrawn,
but we expect that to be a long
time off.

275

How to draw a train

It is custom and the common object which fashions our view of what is or is not beautiful. Beauty may indeed be in the eye of the beholder but that eye will have been conditioned by familiarity. How many times have we been outraged by a fashion in clothing even more ugly than the last? Yet how often, for example, does yesterday's outrageous fashion become today's convention; and later still, of course, incur the contempt that familiarity also eventually breeds. And not only clothing; communications systems in this century have allowed a relatively small number of consumer products to exert a disproportionate influence on our ideas of what is good or beautiful. We have equipment; the calculator at the office, the machine tool at the factory or the vacuum cleaner and TV at home. We have our buildings; and of course above all we have our much beloved car.

It is the motor car, and all the various modes of transport which are the most persuasive representatives of our aesthetic. It is for this reason that designers are so obsessed by things that float, fly or roll along on wheels. A designer who is not fascinated by the world of transport is about as common as a Frenchman with no interest in food. There are many reasons why this is true, but not least of them is the sheer challenge. If you have any idea of how many hours of effort and anxiety may be expended on something as simple as a coat hook for example, then the prospect of designing a car becomes simultaneously irresistible and terrifying. All the more so as the end product may be out of date in a year.

The history of transport offers as many warnings as it does encouragements. What about the *Brabazon* for example – straight from the drawing board to moth balls. Or even more daunting, *Brunel's Great Eastern;* the world's biggest steamship (at the time), but too big to be effectively launched, so it simply flopped onto its side.

If we consider how many makes and models there are for cars, motorbikes, boats, coaches, buses, trains, planes and dinghys, it must be fact that somewhere in the world there are two or three new models being produced every week of every year. There is a mass of aesthetic and engineering decisions contained in every one. With this level of cost and effort we must recognise the transport world as one of the major employers of design.

And so imperceptibly and to a greater extent subconsciously our transport is a moulder of public taste. Inevitably therefore the students of public aesthetic should look around at what moves, and perhaps test its essence against a child's view of the world. For a child's drawing will probably tell us what the archetypal form is for practically anything. A tree, a train, a house, a shoe, a car, all will be reduced, stripped of local detail and shown in a current representation of the essential form. If you draw a box with windows on two levels and wheels at front and back it is clearly a London bus. We interpret the rest immediately: red, a platform on one corner, a driver on the opposite, wheels four feet high and a dozen other details. The vehicle stands strong in our aesthetic memory.

London Transport is justly world famous for pioneering advanced environment design in the public sector; our concept of an underground space is framed by our knowledge of the tunnels and platforms of London's underground. How unnatural it will seem to the Londoner if the next generation of station should have square corners between wall and ceiling.

The strength of the *London Transport* design image is best reflected in the famous tube map that for most of us is the real map of the city. There are thousands of Londoners who see *Green Park* in a straight line between

Piccadilly and *Victoria* or *Paddington* slightly north of *Ladbroke Grove.*

In contrast, *British Rail* has often projected a less cohesive image in recent years; a reflection perhaps of the various forms of indecision that have bedevilled railways in many countries in the past few decades. When railways in the UK were nationalised after World War II, the size of the design opportunity was glaringly obvious. The airlines with their big new offices, shiny vehicles, and smartly uniformed staff, the floating hotels of the *Cunard* line, and *London Transport* surrounded *British Railways* (as it was then) with pitiless examples of how outdated their environmental design had become.

However, after a few false starts, the *Design Research Unit,* the only really qualified design house of the fifties was employed to stir the squalid giant. The architects' department was massively enlarged and the fifties and sixties saw the first benefits in buildings, vehicles and liveries. Now the long-term programmes, the main line terminii, and whole train developments are beginning to come to fruition. We can be sure that the child's train drawing in ten years' time will not be the cylinder with smoke cloud pulling separate boxes on wheels but will be a dart fronted continuous tube.

The world of transport has become such a political arena that we forget how rich it is. From skateboard to supersonic transport our lives are moulded by the impact of moving things. It is in the most popular transport that romanticism, the saving grace of our civilisation, is found most abundantly. The romantic elements in the design of a car or a train seem to lend support to the illogical, uneconomic, even the uncomfortable. In fact there is commendable logic in providing some relief from the wholly practical and what's more, people are prepared to pay for it. Romanticism in design actually helps to make an increasingly impersonal world more bearable, and in that sense has an important contribution to make.

It is easy to ridicule the *Alfa Romeo* family saloon that has a plastic spoiler added to the back – a totally redundant symbol of the *Grand Prix* circuits. But such extreme fantasies are the exception, not the rule.

During the *Concorde* development, the engineers argued that the speed was the selling feature and the massive problems they faced must not be complicated by pandering to emotional factors – they had provided portholes no bigger than a fist instead of windows. Fortunately they were persuaded otherwise. Now with awe the first passengers tell how the sky is not blue but black, and how from 60,000 feet the earth really is round! Clearly there are some other reasons for going in *Concorde* besides going fast.

A few years ago, a design group put up the proposition that the *Jumbo,* with its crew on the first floor, provided an unique chance to give the forward passengers a window in the nose – what a prospect! Anybody who has flown in a bubble nosed helicopter will underwrite a design of that kind.

The romantic is perhaps after all an essential ingredient in transport design and perhaps the child's drawing of a train will on careful inspection provide the important guidelines to future design needs.

Kenneth Grange

277

Inter-City 125

As part of the modernisation programme in the sixties, *British Rail* established a three stage programme. First, widespread electrification; second, a new generation of high speed trains; third a more audacious ultra-high speed train, the *APT* (advanced passenger train). The photographs on this page show the details of a completed HST (high speed train) which is illustrated opposite.

Like the cathedral for the architect, the design of a train comes rarely in the lifetime of an industrial designer. Such products are invariably tightly controlled by the engineering teams who have had years of detailed knowledge and experience.

British Rail, under the guidance of the Director of Industrial Design, *James Cousins,* has a broader view. In the fifties, consultants were widely used on a corporate image programme and on locomotive development.

This train was unique in many ways; improved efficiency of power unit, better braking, lighter weight, unified push and pull from a power car at each end. Probably most important in human terms, it was the first opportunity in many years for the railway engineers to design a complete new train from scratch.

The *British Rail Technical Centre* employ 1,200 engineer in the most modern and comprehensive workshops in the world. The *HST* more than fulfilled their heritage by establishing a new world speed record of 141 mph on 11 June 1973, within weeks of running the first prototype, see below.

278

Product design: British Rail

Four times the power is needed to raise speed from 110 mph to 150 mph and it follows that weight reduction and attention to aerodynamic factors have a special significance at these speeds. Furthermore, at high speeds new problems occur from the shock wave when passing other trains, station canopies, tunnel mouths and so forth.

Consequently, as designers of the cab shape, we needed an unusual freedom in the exterior shaping. Many tests were made with reinforced plastics and in wind tunnels. The results established the preferred forms for the critical front of the power car. This led to the first design which *British Rail* ran on 8 February 1973.

This was based on a seating arrangement which gave the driver a central position where he commanded a good view of the track through the single central window. Unlike previous locos the window was armoured with thick high impact glass, necessary to protect the driver from various missiles. That limited the dimensions to the maximum glass size obtainable, and in turn impinged on the shaping and therefore aerodynamic qualities, and provided the most intransigent problem in the design.

The first layout proved unacceptable for several reasons; one of which was that the unions considered that the two men should sit side by side as driver and co-driver (traditionally the fireman). Design is not solely a matter of solving technical problems, but also has to allow for cultural and social attitudes.

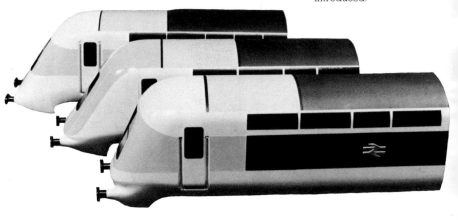

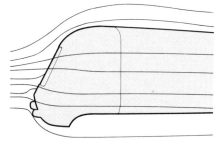

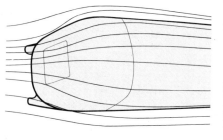

Left, the *British Rail* scheme submitted for restyling. The models below were among the new designs produced for wind tunnel testing.

A prototype resulted and the photo (right) shows the train at the running trials. The layouts compare the alternative seating arrangements and show the driver's angles of vision.

Models at bottom right show the double windows which compensate for the narrow angle of vision and the final version with the large single window. Buffers were eliminated at this stage and concealed couplings introduced.

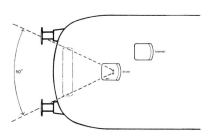

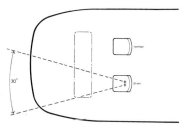

41003

Fortunately this replanning coincided with an increase in available glass size, and the exterior shape underwent a major change. As in many design processes, components in the brief are accepted by traditional practice until they obstruct or contradict. The *HST* provides a good example.

The buffers, although aerodynamically clumsy, were within the acceptable total airflow, largely because the majority of the air was helped to adhere to the body by smooth shaping from window edges at sides and top.

However, when the window was widened, that shape at the left and right was too sharp and the aerodynamics suffered. Wind tunnel tests revealed that this could be compensated if the angle was increased; this allowed more air to be induced over the top, and the performance to be maintained.

281

This problem, being resolved, created yet another, in that the buffer now projected beyond the prescribed forward position. This brought into question the need for buffers, and the realisation that their prime use, erroneously thought by the public to stop the train at the terminals, is in fact for the shunting and changing of locos in conventional train assemblies.

The *HST* differs in that it is constantly assembled in one train – and therefore the use of buffers is hugely reduced. The conventional buffers are no longer essential, as in a collision, the moulded front is easily replaceable. A towing hook is reached via a removable front panel.

Product design: British Rail

The final design problems were concerned with the appearance of the train as a whole. Part of the *British Rail* programme for increasing efficiency is centred on the design of coaches, and since these represent, in traditional form, a weight greater than the passengers, a radical new coach design was evolved which was more in character with aircraft construction.

Designed by *British Rail's* industrial design department, this coach, the *Mark III*, has proved a major breakthrough in passenger/cost/weight ratio. The size of the *Mark III* is the new basic element in train make-up. Seat and interior planning are in development.

One aspect of the coach design anticipates the whole train concept and consequently, a continuous style of surface decoration can be applied.

The yellow on the front derives from safety studies which show yellow and black as high contrast. These are now virtually standard on all road vehicles, on building sites, and on *British Rail* tracks where groups of maintenance workers need maximum warning of oncoming vehicles. On the production train the black is continued around to harmonize the dark window openings, and become the diagonal, reflecting the shape of the train.

Yellow

Light grey

Blue

Dark grey

The final livery

Product design: British Rail

Within the *British Rail* programme for train design, seating forms a major study. Seating design justifies special attention in the context of higher speeds and economy. This prototype chair was developed around a terylene net fabric, a similar technology to that used in hammock design in the US space craft programme.

This fabric is capable of withstanding high forces and under tension provides an unique body support. The net has a further advantage in ventilating the body and this alone has high value, particularly in air-conditioned environments.

A comparison with aircraft seating is appropriate. A greater seating density, with all passengers facing one way, and flip-down trays, has the disadvantage of being less sociable and so was rejected, with preference to the existing arrangement in which passengers face each other.

A less dramatic design, the chair at right has plastic mouldings for lightness and incorporates the option of a tray or magazine rack for one way seating plans. This sculptured model was used as the basis for the present standard *Inter City* seat.

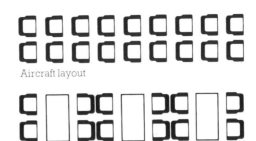

Aircraft layout

Train layout

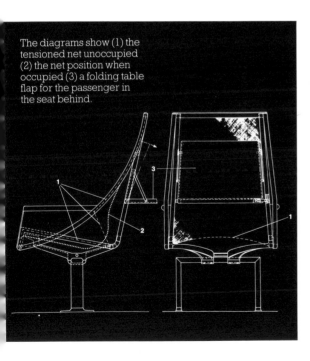

The diagrams show (1) the tensioned net unoccupied (2) the net position when occupied (3) a folding table flap for the passenger in the seat behind.

Living by design

This last part of the book is about three aspects of *Pentagram,* the place, the people and the partners. Unlike the rest of the book, it is not divided into sections but comprises a pictorial description of the partnership, preceded by an essay on how *Pentagram* works and followed by a postscript on the partners. The first essay cannot of course be comprehensive. What it tries to do is to pick out some highlights which are worth emulating and some pitfalls which are worth avoiding in the practice of one design consultancy. It is essential reading for those who want to join the world of the design consultants, and perhaps relevant reading for those who wish to use it. A comment on that world and the current pre-eminence in it of British design consultancies, will perhaps provide a useful context in which to view *Pentagram.*

There have always been designers wherever civilised man has established himself and in some places where uncivilised man has done so. Nevertheless at certain times and in certain places design leadership has existed. The *Bauhaus* in the thirties, New York in the fifties, and Italy in the sixties have all in their turn supplied design leadership. The surprising and relatively unknown fact is that now, in the field of design consultancy, Britain leads Europe and indeed the world.

The British design industry is based on one of the best design education systems in the world and it culminates in a handful of major consulting practices of which *Pentagram* is one. None of these "top ten" is quite like the next. They vary in style, size and their client lists. What they have in common is a London location, a profitable activity, significant overseas business and a style of managing their affairs which is bred out of confidence.

Although these consultancies operate in a competitive world, their growth possibilities place them in the forefront of the British drive to create wealth. As a result, they are beginning to attract the attention of those in Britain whose business it is to influence the direction of the investment of resources, not only money but also people; and not only for profit, but also with a commitment to environmental improvement and to a better way of communicating ideas in nearly every field.

Commitments of this kind lead us to anticipate with some confidence a continued growth in design consultancy in Britain. However, the shapes it takes are likely to be as varied as those of today's design practices. It is a purpose of the two essays in this section to describe that variety, and in particular the unique *Pentagram* variation.

John McConnell

Ron Herron

Mervyn Kurlansky

Kenneth Grange

Theo Crosby

Alan Fletcher

Colin Forbes

How Pentagram works

The people who work at *Pentagram* "live by design" because they believe that they, and their work, are enriched by the environment which they have established for themselves. Their "design for living" embraces the process of design itself and its end product. If this activity sounds presumptuous, compare the many illustrations in the first four parts of this book with the relatively few pictures of people and places in part five.

It is not the purpose of this essay to reiterate in print a description of the end products of *Pentagram*. The preceding pages will hopefully have achieved this. Nor would it be appropriate to delve into the personal lives of the members of the group. It is important however to discuss two areas which have not been touched on elsewhere. The first concerns the organisation of *Pentagram* and how it achieves its tasks; the second, that elusive and qualitative element in all good design work; creativity.

Nearly all small "elitist" groups fall into one of three organisational patterns. These cover most professional partnerships, many small businesses and co-operative organisations. The leading design practices fall into one or other of the three organisational systems. Before describing them it must be remembered that numbers are critical. No elitist group below about six or seven people is worth much organisational study, and above about sixty people wholly different criteria apply. The handful of leading design consultancies fit comfortably within this spectrum. *Pentagram* in fact employ about fifty.

The organisational origins of these systems lie with the founder members. When, as in the first system, one man is the moving spirit, the organisation is a traditional one, akin to the standard authoritarian structure of most group enterprises. There are a number of design consultancies

organised this way, and they work well. Their procedures are familiar, and only different from other organisations in that succession problems are particularly difficult. Without sound leadership, creative organisations crumble or splinter more readily than most

The second organisation framework is a diarchy, run by two people with equal, different but complementary skills. These organisations often disguise their structure by admitting directors or partners into the peer group; or by one of the two assuming a leadership role. But their success nearly always depends on the reaction between opposites. However disguised, the organisation needs them both to survive. Diarchy makes for a dangerous organisation structure, almost certain to collapse if one of the pair goes. However it is particularly suitable to design consultancies and other creative groups, with one of the two, the creative contributor, and the other the manager.

The third and much the most traditional system is the "partnership", which usually comprises three or more equal people at the top of the structure. *Pentagram* falls within this category. It is a partnership which has grown to seven people, and has faced in its time many of the problems and opportunities characteristic of this kind of organisation. It is worth noting that although the "partnership" is generally common among professionals, management consultants and the like; *Pentagram* is the only one of the handful of top design consultancies which has successfully organised itself in this way.

They had the inevitable trouble with names as the partnership evolved. *Fletcher, Forbes and Gill* became *Crosby/Fletcher/Forbes* when *Gill* left and *Crosby* joined. Before working out how to add *Kurlansky's* name, they joined wiith the industrial design practice of *Kenneth Grange* and decided to stop imitating the telephone book. *Pentagram* was adopted as a generic and when *McConnell* and then *Herron* joined, there were no further name problems. Names aside, it has been a carefully considered growth which has avoided some of the more obvious pitfalls of professional partnerships. The organisation now works as follows; seven senior partners are supported by an inner core of financial, technical and management services which are centripetal in effect. Each partner is also supported by a group of designers and architects whose influence is centrifugal. Thus the partners are at the centre of an organisational tug of war which is part of their daily life, and an essential aspect of their client relationship. This system, usual for a law practice or a management consultancy, is unusual for a design group. It leads to a special relationship with clients who come either to the parntership as a group, or to an individual partner.

The international creative reputation of the individual partners is very high. Collectively it is certainly higher than that of any other major design consultancy. For the client, even when the first contact was with *Pentagram* as a group, it means that he interfaces directly with a partner, with no intermediary account executive or project manager. For *Pentagram's* partners it means the kind of direct contact with design work which they find both rewarding and renewing.

But the method has its problems. It implies a special kind of client, one who understands design and who enjoys the tantalising (and perhaps even dangerous) experience of working close to high creativity. As a result *Pentagram* has a reputation as the designer's designers. A reputation of this kind is in danger of attenuation. The committed clients are fewer than the uncommitted, and the world is bigger than design. Closeness to the work also brings its problems, of which the main one is overwork. It is always important to stand back for a rest or an overview. The partners know this, and recognising that their organisation does not allow for it, have built in personal mechanisms to make it happen. But these mechanisms can have sharp edges, the inevitable result of organising creativity.

Both of these problems are a constant preoccupation of the partners. They recognise that they must move beyond designing for the converted, that they have a responsibility to proselytize, as well as a profit opportunity in so doing. They are also very conscious that their partnership extends beyond sharing office facilities, to above all, sharing problem solving. The partners are always explicit to their clients about the referral of problems from the "contact" partner to the group as a whole.

A second layer of complexity in the partnership network is the resolution of specialisation and work area. There are four graphic designers, two architects and one product designer in the partnership, and this spread roughly reflects the staff support and the current nature of the work load. Although all of the partners contribute in all areas, they tend to defer to specialists internally. Indeed they would be unwise not to. The benefits that this brings to the client, and indeed to the designer, are obvious. Less obvious is the personal willingness of the partners to make integrative designing work. The maturity and balance this needs is all too often absent in "elitist" groups.

Perhaps the greatest value of the partnership system is the ease with which it can allow for succession. There is fourteen years difference between the oldest and the youngest *Pentagram* partner but below the partners, the inevitably flat hierarchy means that young designers tend to come and go with little chance of internal promotion. This too is probably good for *Pentagram*. It is after all made quite explicit to everyone, and the renewal it provides is invaluable; particularly the creative renewal. *Pentagram* will be around a decade or so from now, and the decade after that. It will not be quite the same place but its metamorphosis will have been relatively painless, and it will still be recognisable for what it is.

Apart from its organisation difference, *Pentagram* is set apart from its peers by its style. No other design consultancy has quite the commitment to design itself. With this level of commitment at the top and a constant and changing creative input from below, there is simply too much creativity for client needs! The practice seems to hold an overload circuit, a degree of creativity which gets itself manifested as the style of the practice. This can be criticised as a form of self indulgence, but it is enormously valuable when a demand surge occurs. On these occasions *Pentagram* shows its best side; with a speed and quality of response which would be difficult to equal elsewhere. It means too, that *Pentagram* is less likely than most, to be repetitive. It is after all quite respectable for consultancies (even design consultancies) to present repeatable packages. Although design consultancies draw on their experience, and although some repetition would be both cost effective and acceptable, it is the inclination of *Pentagram* to turn away from this route. At the cost of some muddle and much more work, they would prefer to treat each problem anew, and to bring a high creativity load to bear each time. Somewhere within the organisation they know that this is essentially what they are about. They call it living by design.

Peter Gorb

287

Pentagram

288

Pentagram works in one of those speculative buildings in which ugliness dices with anonymity. Built as low cost light industrial premises, *Pentagram* adapted the interior by exploiting the raw features of the structure to the best advantage.

Entering the reception area, the visitor is confronted with a large open space bounded on the far side by a wall of sheet glass yielding one of the most spectacular views in London.

A predominant feature is the spaciousness obtained by a dedication to open plan. This allows for work areas to be adapted at will, responsibilities to be shared and makes participation in the activity almost unavoidable.

Below the window is the *Grand Union Canal,* beyond that is the taxi ramp digging into *Paddington Station* and beyond that, *Brunel's* massive iron arches over the platforms; a panorama of nineteenth century transport.

The view on the other side has unkindly but accurately been described as the best view of East Berlin you can find in London.

Living by design: Pentagram

Although the building doesn't meet the challenge of the view, *Pentagram,* in designing an efficient working area, has tried to compensate for the speculator's lack of imagination.

The lift up to reception on the first floor has so far defeated any long term solution: the interim answer has been to cloak its featureless utility by providing it with plastic grass and imitation brick wallpaper.

The floors are carpeted with dark grey felt squares, a practical solution in an activity concerned with inks and paints. The walls are exposed *Fletton* bricks and the ceiling sprayed with a neutral coloured acoustic material.

Exposed pipes, which are in abundance, are painted bright red and any doors or sliding panels are natural pine.

Furnishings are uniform – same table, same lamp, same storage and, except for the two conference rooms, strictly utilitarian.

Storage space helps control clutter: *Remploy* sliding shelves on rails for work specimens, and shelving for samples and books, large envelope folios for paper layouts.

For personal belongings you won't find desk drawers with their inevitable accumulation of apple cores, pen tops, and hair grips, but open topped containers. These take anything from files to lipsticks, and expose personal detritus to the accusing eye of the beholder.

The building is basically divided into two levels, the first floor coping with reception, meeting and dining areas, and the second with the studio, workshop and darkrooms.

Meetings are held in one of two conference rooms. The larger has several tables butted together to accommodate a group of people, and an area with comfortable low seating to allow for less formal situations. A collection of ethnic masks almost covers one wall and relieves the austerity of the brickwork.

The smaller conference room has a display of current work, and is equipped with slide projectors to give presentations to clients.

291

The remaining space on the reception floor is given over to a dining area. Here, lunch is provided for everyone in the studio, and often caters for clients and passing friends. Apart from saving time and money it is also an opportunity for the whole studio to sit down together.

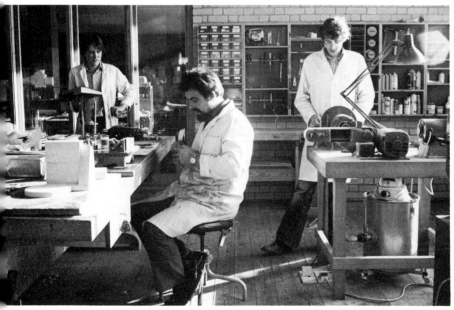

The studio itself is a vast open space bounded on one side by glass which provides plenty of light. The groups each have their own working areas but share plan-chests and equipment such as a *Xerox*, dyeline machine and *Grant* projector.

Living by design: Pentagram

Pentagram is an organisation of young people. The average age is 28 and there are fifty of them.

They function broadly across five areas of activity: design and architecture, modelmaking and photography, secretarial and administration, accounts, and household.

The work in design and architecture is divided between the partners and their respective groups of designers. Partners tend to initiate creative concepts and the designers have the responsibility for projects, working closely and directly with the client, and providing the pivots around which the design activity of the studio operates. The senior designers, highly professional men and women usually in their late twenties, are helped by younger design assistants who are often just out of art or architectural school.

Every design job needs a lot of administration to nurture it from its initial problem-solving stage through to the final realisation. Secretaries, for example, may also find themselves progress chasing and typing specifications.

Similarly, design needs technical services. *Pentagram* has its own workshop and small photographic studio. The three modelmakers make precise models or prototypes of products or architectural schemes. This function is not a cosmetic presentation for clients, but a working method to determine the validity and viability of the design solutions.

The photographic studio has a couple of darkrooms, and the

two technical photographers produce photoprints and product shots. More personal and creative jobs are commissioned from outside.

The overall administration of the studio is the responsibility of a studio manager. Her assistant and the switchboard operator are concerned with the day to day business of phone calls, postage, deliveries and stocks; and all those necessary chores which enable the studio to function efficiently.

One of the less typical features of the administration is the *Pentagram* archive. This holds proofs, samples and slides of work, providing the source for reference, presentations to clients and magazine articles. Indeed without such a system this publication could not have been produced.

Running an organisation without a full time business manager requires an efficient method of keeping track of expenditure and income. This is run by the partnership secretary who has one assistant to do sales and purchases, and another who does book-keeping.

Housekeeping, whether fresh coffee or clean windows, is an essential part of the design lifestyle. The dining room and kitchen is allotted a budget and centres around a cook. This important person comes from the *Cordon Bleu Cookery School* and has two helping hands to make coffee and prepare lunch for up to 75 people a day. The studio is cleaned nightly by a couple, so that all is mysteriously spick and span when everyone turns up for work at 9.30.

293

Living by design: Pentagram

The list of *Pentagram* staff (at time of publication) is divided into the working groups, and the chart explains the structure of the partnership. The axonometric diagram (opposite) shows the layout of the studio.

294

Architecture design

Theo Crosby *Partner*
Marvin Shane *Designer*
Kathy Tilney *Architect*
Rosy Slater *Student*
Elissia Noble *Secretary*

Ron Herron *Partner*
Tom Politowicz *Architect*
Adrian Ciobotaru *Architect*
Peter McCannon *Architect*

Graphic design

Alan Fletcher *Partner*
Jules Alldridge *Designer*
Amanda Tatham *Designer*
Vyvyan Thomas *Designer*
Paul Anthony *Designer*
Lynn Thorogood *Secretary*

Colin Forbes *Partner*
Bruce Nivison *Designer*
Rose-Marie Jones *Co-ordinato*
Rosie Sharpe *Secretary*

Mervyn Kurlansky *Partner*
Lora Starling *Designer*
Sue Horner *Designer*
Julie Depledge *Designer*
Nikki Woods *Secretary*

John McConnell *Partner*
David Pearce *Designer*
Barbara Whitaker *Designer*
Nancy Williams *Designer*
Elizabeth Rees *Secretary*

Georg Staehelin *Associate*
Hans Peter Dubacher *Designe*

Product design

Kenneth Grange *Partner*
Ian Buchanan *Designer*
Johan Santer *Designer*
Veronica Steel *Designer*
Ian Wood *Ergonomist*
Apryl Swift *Secretary*

Technical services

Bruce Watters *Model maker*
Chris Wills *Model maker*
Malcom Norden *Model maker*
John Stone *Photographer*
Peter Mahoney *Photographer*

Administration

Janice Entwistle *Partnership sec.*
Celia Pruen *Accounts*
Jo Garlick *Accounts*
Sue Gasson *Studio Manager*
Julia Greenwood *Archivist*
Arlene Mollison *Girl Friday*
Kim Worthington *Receptionist*
Tamar Fburn *Housekeeper*
Brigid Harpham *Cook*
Alice Smith *Kitchen help*
Don & Maureen Dicks *Cleaners*

Pentagram

Ground floor:
1   Entrance lobby
First floor:
2   Reception
3   Accounts
4   Dining room
5   Large conference room
6   Small conference room
7   Projection room
Second floor:
8   Administration
9   Archives
10   Graphic design
11   Library
12   Product design
13   Workshop
14   Spray room
15   Storage
16   Photo studio
17   Darkrooms
Third floor
18   Architecture design

61 North Wharf Road
London W2 1LA
Telephone 01 402 5511

295

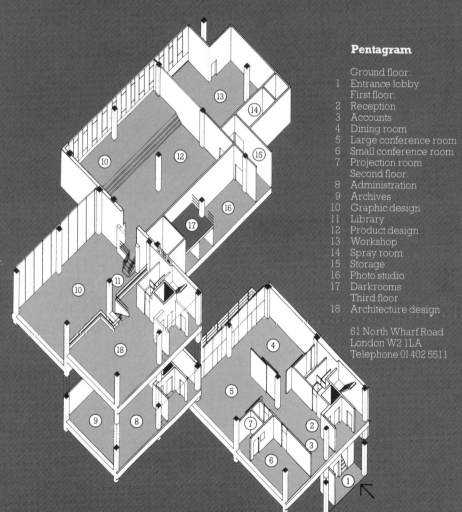

Postcript on the partners

The origins of *Pentagram* lie in the original graphic design partnership of *Fletcher, Forbes and Gill*, the architectural practice of *Theo Crosby* and the industrial design office of *Kenneth Grange*.

In the early sixties *Alan Fletcher, Colin Forbes and Bob Gill* had dimly perceived that big companies would be more interested in dealing with organisations, than with individuals. Two or three years after they got together, they were joined by *Theo Crosby,* who at that time was involved with a project for the town centre of Hereford.

296

This expansion converted a very small intimate office into a rather larger practice with more complex projects, and when *Bob Gill* asked *Theo Crosby* when the first buildings would go up, *Crosby* replied "About 1973". "That's a long time to have to wait for a proof" said *Bob,* and shortly thereafter departed.

Theo Crosby is the most heterogeneous of the partners. His activities vary from being Chairman of a school for mentally handicapped children, to membership of the Board of Trustees for the *Whitechapel Art Gallery.* An architect without a large scale building to his name, an enthusiast for innovation and change – yet also an active preservationist.

Immensely practical as well as entrepreneurial, he is particularly well known for his work in exhibitions; a media which enables him to combine his passions for structure and communication. He designed the British section of the *Milan Triennale* (1964) which won a *Gran Premio,* and the Industry section of the *British Pavilion* at *Expo 67,* Montreal. More recently he wrote and designed *How to Play the Environment Game* shown at the *Hayward Gallery,* and designed the *British Genius* exhibition celebrating Jubilee year.

Alan Fletcher began his professional career working in New York during the late fifties. At that time New York had the greatest concentration of graphic talents in the world and he openly acknowledges the debt to that experience.

As a designer, he is intrigued by visual ambiguities and paradoxes for their own sake, as well as in the practical design problems posed by clients. Like his graphic partners he is also involved with the wider implications of design, and has served on design juries all over the world – from Hong Kong to Toronto, Warsaw to Brussels. He has been President of the British *Designers and Art Directors Association (D&AD),* has won a gold medal at the New York *One Show* and a *D&AD* gold medal. In 1977 he shared the *D&AD President's Award for Outstanding Contribution to Design* with his partner *Colin Forbes.*

For *Colin Forbes,* order and logic are of prime importance and his particular skills are demonstrated in complex informational programmes and corporate identity schemes. Whereas most designers start by trying to equate their ideas with the businessman's needs, *Colin Forbes* has the ability to integrate the two and see the problem as a totality.

A friend once told *Colin* that it was possible to chart a business in advance and drew a graph to prove it; what growth the business would sustain, how many employees would be needed at a given time, and so on. He didn't pay much attention. When he glanced at it three or four years later and saw that the predictions were accurate, he sat up and took notice, and realised that a design practice followed business principles.

The growth and organisation of *Pentagram* are largely due to his energy and financial acumen, and the rest of the partners acknowledge that in addition to his design activities he is also the executive partner.

The tendency over the years has been to take on long-term clients and corporate programmes, rather than a variety of individual jobs. This has been due to outside pressures rather than a rule of the house, but as *Kenneth Grange* the industrial design partner has said, "It doesn't mean that if a client wants us to design their razor, that also means we insist on designing their building."

Kenneth Grange is able to bring a range of skills and technical knowledge from many industries, whether it is to help resolve single problems, or complex production programmes. His work covers the whole field of industrial design, including appliances, products and capital goods, but he is best known for his sophisticated approach to consumer products. These are immediately identifiable by their style and the care in detail that comes from working closely with the client's engineers.

As a designer of products, he considers that the designer represents the interests of the consumer as well as the requirements of the client. It is this uncompromising attitude that has made him one of the few British industrial designers with an international reputation, seven *Council of Industrial Design* awards, and recipient of the *Duke of Edinburgh's Prize for Elegant Design*.

Ron Herron was a leading member of *Archigram* before he joined *Pentagram*, and as an architect, like *Theo Crosby*, he is fascinated by graphic ideas and communication devices as by formal structures. His attitude towards architecture is that it is more than sticks and bricks or even proportions and scale, but rather a heightened and exciting view of how people want to live. This concern with ideas and environments also accounts for his demand as a lecturer, as well as his teaching posts at both the *Architectural Association* and the *University of Southern California*.

He has worked on large projects in Britain and America, London's *South Bank*, a *Pan Am* terminal at *Los Angeles International Airport* and *Ford's* new town in Dearbourne, Michigan.

Mervyn Kurlansky is one of the graphic partners whose talents and concern lie in the quality of detail combined with evocative imagery. His ability to translate complex data into comprehensive diagrammatic form and his obsession with pictorial and typographic precision generally means that those jobs find their way to his desk which require the love and care which is his particular hallmark.

His curiosity about visual imagery extends beyond his graphic skills, and it was his initiative that conceived the book *Watching my name go by*, an historic record of the ephemeral graffiti dominating the environment of New York.

As a graphic partner, one of *John McConnell's* many design abilities is his determination to avoid the superfluous or superficial, and a dedication to communicating on all levels, which is reflected in the freshness of his solutions. To this end he often uses a repertoire of sources, and his capacity for seeking out and commissioning the best available talent is a positive boon to the community of freelance illustrators.

His first major success was when he worked with *Barbara Hulanicki* on the creation of the graphics for *Biba*, in those golden days in its small shop in Kensington.

It is his philosophy, as well as his enthusiasm, which has instigated the *Pentagram Papers*: an inexpensive publication which appears at regular intervals, and is concerned with curious and entertaining aspects of design which have come to *Pentagram's* attention.

The ambitions and talents of the partners are diverse, and it is this spectrum of abilities working together all under one roof, which add up to make *Pentagram* what it is.

Peter Gorb

The Director
Institute of Small Business Management
London Business School

Client index

Acknowledgements

The people who now form *Pentagram*, and those who have worked for *Pentagram* in the past (listed here) are responsible either directly or indirectly for the work shown in this book.

In addition we would also like to acknowledge all those designers, photographers, and illustrators who have been commissioned or co-opted by *Pentagram* on projects.

Credit is due to the following in the production of this book:

Kokon Chung, Michael Douglas, Barney Edwards, Tony Evans, Dennis Hooker, John Maltby, Jon Naar, Philip Sayer, Jessica Strang and *Homer Sykes* who took the photographs, and the *Design Council* who provided many others. *Dennis Bailey, Philip Castle, Gordon Cullen, George Hoy* and *Nick Whitaker* who provided diagrams and illustrations.

We would like to thank all our clients, especially those whose work we have reproduced.

Petra Abrecht
Gus Alexander
Judith Aronson
Karen Baker
David Balding
Linda Banks
Teresa Bantock
Rudolf Barmettler
Garth Bell
Madelaine Bennett
Rosemary Bristow-Jones
Howard Brown
Elizabeth Burney-Jones
Lorraine Caunter
Christine Cope
Russell Cresser
Peter Cumming
Brig Davies
Melanie Davies
Lynda Duncombe
Kati Dürrer
Steve Edmonds
Diane Edwards
Cindy Fleck
Liz Gale
Beth Garrard
Clive Garrard
Ray Gautier
Sally Grover
Peter Higgins
Nicky Higson
Paul Hogan
Kathy Holmes
George Hoy
Liz James
Roger Jones
Mary Komocki
John Langley
John Lawrence
Klaus Lehmann
Mike Leslie

Frank Linden
Mark Littler
Jo Llewelyn
Jane Loeper
Tim Long
Tony Lowe
Ron Major
David Marrs
David Matcham
Helene Michaels
Jon Mindham
Ellen Montgomery
Alex Murray
Jill Newsome
Tim Nutt
Ann Oliphant
Jeremy Parker
Mal Parker
Jane Parnaby
Hermione Paton
Paolo Polledri
Pru Reading
Jean Robert
Emanuel Sandreuter
Simone Schlup-Vittet
Heini Schneebeli
Marion Scott
Terri Simms
Sheila Stedman
Christopher Steggall
Phillipa Stent
Jessica Strang
Sarah Truman
Alice Tse
Rosemary Turner
Ian Waite
Barry Weaver
David Wheatley
Jill Westwood
Sarah Williams
Graham Willmott